Charlotte Brontë:
The Novels

MIKE EDWARDS

First published 1999 by
MACMILLAN PRESS LTD
Houndmills, Basingstoke, Hampshire RG21 6XS
and London
Companies and representatives
throughout the world

ISBN 0–333–74778–X hardcover
ISBN 0–333–74779–8 paperback

A catalogue record for this book is available
from the British Library.

This book is printed on paper suitable for recycling and
made from fully managed and sustained forest sources.

10   9   8   7   6   5   4   3   2   1
08   07   06   05   04   03   02   01   00   99

Printed in Hong Kong

Published in the United States of America 1999 by
ST. MARTIN'S PRESS, INC.,
Scholarly and Reference Division,
175 Fifth Avenue, New York, N.Y. 10010

ISBN 0–312–22364–1 cloth
ISBN 0–312–22366–8 paperback

Contents

General Editor's Preface

This series is dedicated to one clear belief: that we can all enjoy, understand and analyse literature for ourselves, provided we know how to do it. How can we build on close understanding of a short passage, and develop our insight into the whole work? What features do we expect to find in a text? Why do we study style in so much detail? In demystifying the study of literature, these are only some of the questions the *Analysing Texts* series addresses and answers.

The books in this series will not do all the work for you, but will provide you with the tools, and show you how to use them. Here, you will find samples of close, detailed analysis, with an explanation of the analytical techniques utilised. At the end of each chapter there are useful suggestions for further work you can do to practise, develop and hone the skills demonstrated and build confidence in you own analytical ability.

An author's individuality shows in the way they write: every work they produce bears the hallmark of that writer's personal 'style'. In the main part of each book we concentrate therefore on analysing the particular flavour and concerns of one author's work, and explain the features of their writing in connection with major themes. In Part 2 there are chapters about the author's life and work, assessing their contribution to developments in literature; and a sample of critics' views are summarised and discussed in comparison with each other. Some suggestions for further reading provide a bridge towards further critical research.

Analysing Texts is designed to stimulate and encourage your critical and analytic faculty, to develop your personal insight into the author's work and individual style, and to provide you with the skills and techniques to enjoy at first hand the excitement of discovering the richness of the text.

NICHOLAS MARSH

Textual Note

As far as convenient, extracts from the novels are identified by chapter so as to enable them to be found easily in any edition. Page numbers of Charlotte Brontë's novels refer to the latest editions in the Penguin Classics series.

Jane Eyre: first published in 1847; Penguin Classics, 1996
Shirley: first published in 1849; Penguin Classics, 1985
Villette: first published in 1852; Penguin Classics, 1985
The Professor: first published in 1857; Penguin Classics, 1989

Extracts quoted are generally as they appear in the Penguin editions, but I have amended two minor misprints.

Where it is clear which novel, or, in the chapter on critical approaches, which essay, is under discussion, reference is usually by page number alone. Other books are fully identified at the time of reference, and reappear in the recommendations for further reading.

PART 1

ANALYSIS

1

Narrators

We begin our exploration of Charlotte Brontë's writing with the narrators whose voices speak in her novels. The narrators make a good starting point for our analysis because they are crucial to the impact of the novels. We can think about the way they present themselves and tell the story, and the mood they establish. At the same time we will see how they introduce us to other characters and to themes which we will develop later on. In this chapter, we will study three extracts in detail, one from the early pages of each novel, and try to see how they prepare us for what follows. We will be concentrating on what is being expressed, and how. Even at this stage, however, we can begin to think more broadly about what the author is trying to do, and how well she is achieving it.

We will deal with the novels in order of publication, and therefore look first at *Jane Eyre*.

I: *Jane Eyre*

This is the beginning of the brief opening chapter:

> There was no possibility of taking a walk that day. We had been wandering, indeed, in the leafless shrubbery an hour in the morning; but since dinner (Mrs Reed, when there was no company, dined early) the cold winter wind had brought with it clouds so sombre, and a rain so penetrating, that further out-door exercise was now out of the question.

I was glad of it: I never liked long walks, especially on chilly afternoons: dreadful to me was the coming home in the raw twilight, with nipped fingers and toes, and a heart saddened by the chidings of Bessie, the nurse, and humbled by the consciousness of my physical inferiority to Eliza, John, and Georgiana Reed.

The said Eliza, John, and Georgiana were now clustered round their mama in the drawing-room: she lay reclined on a sofa by the fireside, and with her darlings about her (for the time neither quarrelling nor crying) looked perfectly happy. Me, she had dispensed from joining the group; saying, 'She regretted to be under the necessity of keeping me at a distance; but that until she heard from Bessie, and could discover by her own observation, that I was endeavouring in good earnest to acquire a more sociable and childlike disposition, a more attractive and sprightly manner – something lighter, franker, more natural, as it were – she really must exclude me from privileges intended only for contented, happy little children.'

'What does Bessie say I have done?' I asked.

'Jane, I don't like cavillers or questioners: besides, there is something truly forbidding in a child taking up her elders in that manner. Be seated somewhere; and until you can speak pleasantly, remain silent.'

A small breakfast-room adjoined the drawing-room, I slipped in there. It contained a book-case: I soon possessed myself of a volume, taking care that it should be one stored with pictures. I mounted into the window-seat: gathering up my feet, I sat cross-legged, like a Turk; and, having drawn the red moreen curtain nearly close, I was shrined in double retirement.

Folds of scarlet drapery shut in my view to the right hand; to the left were the clear panes of glass, protecting, but not separating me from the drear November day. At intervals, while turning over the leaves of my book, I studied the aspect of that winter afternoon. Afar, it offered a pale blank of mist and cloud; near, a scene of wet lawn and storm-beat shrub, with ceaseless rain sweeping away wildly before a long and lamentable blast.

I returned to my book – Bewick's *History of British Birds*: the letter-press thereof I cared little for, generally speaking; and yet there were certain introductory pages that, child as I was, I could not pass quite as a blank. They were those which treat of the haunts of sea-fowl; of 'the solitary rocks and promontories' by them only inhabited; of the coast of Norway, studded with isles from its southern extremity, the Lindeness, or Naze, to the North Cape.

Where the Northern Ocean, in vast whirls
Boils round the naked, melancholy isles
Of farthest Thule; and the Atlantic surge
Pours in among the stormy Hebrides.

Nor could I pass unnoticed the suggestion of the bleak shores of
Lapland, Siberia, Spitzbergen, Nova Zembla, Iceland, Greenland,
with 'the vast sweep of the Arctic Zone, and those forlorn regions of
dreary space, – that reservoir of frost and snow, where firm fields of
ice, the accumulation of centuries of winters, glazed in Alpine heights
above heights, surround the pole, and concentre the multiplied
rigours of extreme cold.' Of these death-white realms I formed an
idea of my own: shadowy, like all the half-comprehended notions
that float dim through children's brains, but strangely impressive.
The words in these introductory pages connected themselves with the
succeeding vignettes, and gave significance to the rock standing up
alone in a sea of billow and spray; to the broken boat stranded on a
desolate coast; to the cold and ghastly moon glancing through bars of
cloud at a wreck just sinking.

I cannot tell what sentiment haunted the quite solitary churchyard,
with its inscribed headstone; its gate, its two trees, its low horizon,
girdled by a broken wall, and its newly risen crescent, attesting the
hour of even-tide.

The two ships becalmed on a torpid sea, I believed to be marine
phantoms.

The fiend pinning down the thief's pack behind him, I passed over
quickly: it was an object of terror.

So was the black, horned thing seated aloof on a rock, surveying a
distant crowd surrounding a gallows.

Each picture told a story; mysterious often to my undeveloped
understanding and imperfect feelings, yet ever profoundly interesting:
as interesting as the tales Bessie sometimes narrated on winter
evenings, when she chanced to be in good humour; and when, having
brought her ironing-table to the nursery-hearth, she allowed us to sit
about it, and while she got up Mrs Reed's lace frills, and crimped her
night-cap borders, fed our eager attention with passages of love and
adventure taken from old fairy tales and other ballads; or (as at a later
period I discovered) from the pages of *Pamela*, and *Henry, Earl of
Moreland*.

With Bewick on my knee, I was then happy: happy at least in my way. I feared nothing but interruption, and that came too soon. The breakfast-room door opened.

  'Boh! Madam Mope!' cried the voice of John Reed; then he paused: he found the room apparently empty.

(pp. 13–15)

This is a powerful beginning. We are thrust immediately into a half-understood family situation fraught with conflict and controversy, and at the same time we are invited to share the observations and feelings of a narrator of whom, as yet, we know almost nothing. Already, however, we feel the desire to understand more.

Let us begin the analysis by looking at the structure of the extract. We can see at once that the earlier part of the extract contains action and dialogue, while the second is reflective. This is obvious, yet it already points to a basic feature of *Jane Eyre*: the split between an external world of contention and an inner world of peace emerges naturally from the use of the first-person narrator, relating experiences and meditating upon them. This interplay between experience and meditation is a central and essential element in the structure of the whole novel.

Now let us look more closely at each part of the extract. We will begin with the simple – looking at what happens – and move gradually towards more complex considerations.

The earlier part of the extract is vividly dramatised: it is full of emotional violence and menace. The narrator tells us that she is aware of her 'physical inferiority' to the other three children – we already guess that they are children because of the reference to the nurse, Bessie, in paragraph two. Bessie is at once introduced as an enemy of the narrator, who is made unhappy by the nurse's 'chidings'. Then we find that Mrs Reed – and we note that the narrator refers to her by that title, in contrast with the Reed children who think of her as their 'mama' – has excluded the narrator in cold and formal language: 'She regretted to be under the necessity of keeping me at a distance'. The formality arises partly from diction, and partly from syntax: 'regretted' is much more formal than, say, 'was sorry'; 'to be under the necessity of' is periphrastic. Mrs Reed speaks quite

unlike a 'mama', in fact: the distant language reflects a distant relationship; clearly the narrator is not one of 'her darlings'. The narrator presents herself here, then, as a child in conflict with her small
world.

The form of the narrator's response to Mrs Reed's reproaches –
'What does Bessie say I have done?' – is bound to anger Mrs Reed,
who sees it as insolence. We, in contrast, are inclined to take a different view of the implication that Bessie is mistaken or lying: it
looks like sturdy defence; it suggests a tough spirit underlying the
narrator's unhappiness. It is no surprise when these qualities emerge
much more forcefully in the next few pages of the novel. At this
point we have already come to see the narrator – even though
unnamed as yet – as a victim, at the mercy of the Reeds. We notice,
too, if we are sensitive to the descriptive element in these opening
paragraphs, that her vulnerability is stressed by the setting as well as
by the dialogue and narrative. In the second paragraph a physical
and an emotional winter are linked: 'nipped fingers and toes, and a
heart saddened'. Everything supports the narrator's point, stressed by
the inverted syntax, that 'dreadful to me was' returning home, that
she feels 'humbled', physically and spiritually, beside the Reed children.

Let us now look more closely at how the use of the first-person
narrator affects our view of Mrs Reed. Mrs Reed's attitude to Jane –
we know from the fourth paragraph that the narrator is the heroine
of the title – is sharply delineated. She expects the child to be 'more
sociable and childlike . . . more attractive and sprightly . . . lighter,
franker, more natural as it were'. Since we identify, almost inevitably
at this stage, with the narrator, and we know her already as a victim,
we are primed to see the flaws in Mrs Reed's demands. The terms
used by Mrs Reed show that she is demanding of Jane something
impossible, or at least unreasonable. The flood of parallel words she
uses (sociable, childlike, attractive, sprightly, light, frank, natural)
hints that she does not know quite what she wants – a suspicion
supported by her vague 'as it were'. We are in a better position to
judge what she means: when she expects Jane to be 'more childlike',
she actually means that Jane should be less wilful; by 'lighter' she
means less serious; by 'franker' she means that Jane should be less

able to defend herself; 'more sociable' implies that it is Jane's own fault that she fails to get on with Mrs Reed and the other children. In short, Mrs Reed is placing all the blame on Jane. It is only to be expected, therefore, that she dislikes 'cavillers and questioners' and objects to being 'taken up' by a mere child; she describes Jane's behaviour, with laughable exaggeration, as 'truly forbidding'. To us as readers, however, it is clear that Jane is being treated harshly and unreasonably, and by the end of the first page, Jane, surrounded as it seems by her enemies, has won in her readers an army of supporters in her lonely battle against oppression.

These first paragraphs are characteristic of the way Charlotte Brontë presents the novel. Jane narrates the whole story, with her focus chiefly on what she sees going on around her. Later on, as Jane matures, there is more opportunity for self-analysis. However, at this childhood stage, the incidents she narrates are carefully selected to illuminate the personality and attitudes of the narrator herself. Much is left unsaid: we do not have to be told that Jane is a victim, for we see the situation enacted; the details of the characters emerge naturally from the action, without the need for lengthy explanations; we are already beginning to understand the character of Mrs Reed – or at least her unfair distinction between favourites (her own children) and the outcast (Jane); we are projected into a family situation which has clearly existed for some time, and Brontë sees no need to develop its history. This is a highly effective style of writing, economical, vivid and rich. It is not objective, though it is not apparent at this point to what extent the narration is biased. Although we know that our perceptions are determined by the narrator, we have as yet no reason to doubt the narrator's point of view.

There is much in these opening paragraphs which points to the rest of the novel. One of the first ideas to emerge is the central theme of personal freedom. It strikes us forcefully on closer study that the novel begins with a series of negatives: there is no possibility of a walk; outdoor exercise is out of the question. After the personal reflection, 'I was glad of it', Jane tells us that she 'never liked' long walks, and that she feels inferior. Mrs Reed then tells her that she is to be excluded from the family gathering and, later, that she doesn't like children who question her authority. There is a strong contrast between the formal, and to that extent unloving language of Mrs Reed, and the emotional responses of the narrator, whose heart was 'saddened'. The effect is to create an atmosphere of grudge and resentment: we know that Jane feels neglected and trapped; already we are waiting to see how she will manage to escape from her situation. This is a pattern which becomes familiar as the novel proceeds: again and again, Jane commands our sympathy as she struggles to overcome obstacle after obstacle to her happiness and development. Her struggle appears to us as a child's instinctive embrace of a positive principle – the desire for freedom, for self-determination – against a negative oppression and restriction masquerading objectively as authority, and subjectively as duty.

The opening paragraph also introduces, in the way the natural world is used, one of the most striking features of *Jane Eyre*. Throughout the novel, the narrator shows a strong sensitivity to the natural world, particularly at critical moments of the action. Always, there is a significant interplay with events and moods. However, the natural world is not used mechanically: the relationship between human events and nature is used in a creative and flexible manner. The opening is a good example. The wintry weather expresses Jane's feelings, as we have noticed, but also reflects the hostile family environment in which she lives. The words 'cold' and 'sombre', and the reference to 'penetrating' rain, cast their shadow over the scene that follows. The walk in the 'leafless shrubbery' tells us that the action takes place after leaf-fall; but it also encourages us to feel a sense of loss or deprivation or even desolation – a feeling which is appropriate to Jane's loveless situation.

The relationship between human life and setting has moral significance, too. Mrs Reed's demand that Jane behave in a 'more natural' way is evidently ironic, for she is at this moment trying to change Jane's behaviour from natural to something else, only vaguely specified beyond the choice offered in 'speak pleasantly, [or] remain silent'. 'Natural', of course, is something of a Humpty-Dumpty word: it means exactly what you want it to mean, and one of the objects of *Jane Eyre* is to explore its meanings, particularly in relation to human behaviour, and more specifically religious behaviour. These are topics which we will consider more fully in later chapters.

The relationship between Jane and the other characters in these opening paragraphs foreshadows much in her relationships later in the novel, especially her subjection to Mrs Reed: Jane is often being placed in the position of trying to behave in a way that will satisfy other people – Rochester and St John Rivers spring to mind, to name no others! – and being thus driven to discipline and repress her own nature. Her ostracism from the inner circle of the Reed children looks forward to Jane's situation at Lowood, where she is made to stand on a chair in disgrace, and to her feelings when the Ingrams visit Thornfield and she is made aware of her lowly status as governess. Jane's isolation is dramatised in the latter half of the extract. Whereas the first six paragraphs present Jane as a social being, the next few reveal her private nature. This duality, which colours the whole novel, becomes more intensely felt later on as Jane develops greater maturity, and a more sensitive appreciation of the interplay between her personality and the world she inhabits. At this stage, Jane's private world is unsophisticated: it is the older narrator who brings subtlety to her mind.

Let us move on to consider that private world which is revealed when, in flight from the accusations of Bessie and the punishments of Mrs Reed, Jane takes refuge in a favourite hiding-place, the window-seat behind the red curtain in the breakfast-room. Here, protected from a hostile social world on one side, and screened by the window on the other from the 'drear November day', she looks out on the wildness of nature. In this scene, as in many later on, Jane is the outcast, unable to participate, and indeed fearful of doing so. Shut out from life, she retreats within herself; her existence narrows to defending her integrity, which she fears to risk in the cut-and-thrust of everyday living. On this occasion, she has Bewick's *History of British Birds* to turn to, and she spends some time absorbed in the arctic scenes depicted therein.

There is a great deal in this passage which deserves discussion, and readers tend to respond in a very individual way to its content, seeing in it meanings which seem to be hinted at without being fully expressed. The effect is characteristic of Brontë's writing: it is part of her achievement to have written about the minds and hearts of her heroines in a suggestive manner which implies depths not susceptible to clear explanation. There is no need, therefore, to be afraid of interpretation. In thinking about such a passage, where the focus is on the psychology of the narrator, personal response is paramount. You can be confident about your ideas, and allow yourself to explore whatever interpretations come to mind: convergence of opinion is not compulsory; divergence is welcome – it is one of the delights of literature. But remember that your ideas should relate closely to the text.

Jane's position is of interest, to begin with. Supplied with a book, on her window-seat, she is 'shrined in double retirement'. We may take 'double' to mean either that she is in physical, geographical seclusion, and in the spiritual isolation of the pages of her book, or that she is sandwiched between curtain and window. (The word 'shrined' is an interesting choice, and we will return to it later.) The curtain is not quite drawn fully closed, and this we may wish to view as symptomatic of Jane's behaviour later, when she is never able quite to shut herself off from what is around her, even though there are times when she desperately wishes to. Jane's posture is interesting, too, for it draws Brontë to use the simile, 'like a Turk'. She shared the Victorian fascination with the orient, and an important element in her early reading was *The Arabian Nights*. The simile may specifically remind us of the charades at Thornfield, when Rochester appears as 'an Eastern emir', and possibly, too, of St John's eastern mission. Those familiar with Brontë's work are alerted by references such as this: they signal romance, illusion, mystery, the power of imagination. Here, slightly incongruously, the Turk image introduces the flight of fancy which takes wing from Bewick's birds.

Before going on to what Jane sees in the book we should look at the use of colour. The red or scarlet curtains foreshadow the imprisonment Jane suffers in the red room a little later. Here, as there, we do not need to argue that the red symbolises something specific (passion, anger, danger, for example, among other, more outlandish ideas); its impact is emotional, not rational. It surely contrasts pointedly, however, with the 'death-white realms' Jane looks at in Bewick's *History of British Birds* in the next paragraph.

The book of birds is fascinating to mull over. From one point of view, it is for Jane a psychological retreat, as the window-seat is a physical retreat: she loves the pictures which describe a world of ideal, lifeless perfection – the frost, snow and ice are suggestive of a world devoid of passion, free of conflict, and removed from human contact. Jane, we feel, might wish to be refined into non-existence because her actual existence, and therefore her vision of what any other existence might be like, is so painful. A little later, the pictures become remarkably suggestive. Every picture seems to suggest a parallel with what happens to Jane, here or later. Brontë as much as invites us to develop ideas along these lines when she says that 'The words in these introductory pages . . . gave significance to' the rock withstanding the 'billow and spray' (Jane's indomitable spirit), the 'broken boat stranded on a desolate coast' (Jane friendless and alone, as often), the 'wreck just sinking' (as Jane's life almost sinks); the 'ghastly moon' those who wish to do so may interpret as a symbol of womanhood distraught. Such interpretations as these are not to be discounted, though they can easily be disputed. The images used – particularly those of ice, snow, cold, whiteness, the moon – recur frequently during the novel, gathering a range and depth of mysterious significance. It is all the more unwise to try to restrict their meaning to a purely rational explanation, for one of the achievements of the novel is to use imagery to trace subtle psychological states which are not open to simple interpretation.

More straightforward interpretations, however, are easier to accept. The scenes match Jane's retreat in their coldness, and their removal from the unpleasant social world she inhabits. Their whiteness and spaciousness suggest an emotional freedom and independence which attract the young victim. Furthermore, the book illuminates qualities in Jane which have not appeared before, namely, a vivid imagination and artistic sensitivity. These, together with her strong moral sense, provide the foundation for her rich character as it develops in response to the situations she confronts during the course of the novel. Her ability as a painter is important in the development of her relationship with Rochester. During those later scenes she recalls the pictures from Bewick's book. The book must also be the seed from which germinate the bird images – captive or soaring, linnet or eagle – which sprinkle the pages of *Jane Eyre*.

Images used later in the passage are equally resonant. Two ships becalmed on a torpid sea we may relate, if we wish, to Rochester and Jane. Then come more violent images: 'The fiend pinning down the thief's pack behind him' is 'an object of terror', as is 'the black, horned thing', which may have a moral or sexual significance. Specific interpretations are, again, easy to develop – perhaps too easy. Suffice it to say that the images in Bewick are those of endurance, desolation, crime and evil, and as such they have a direct bearing on Jane's state of mind here, and on the way she develops in the course of the novel.

The moral ideas introduced here are inescapable. The reference to the fiend and the 'horned thing' make an interesting link with the use of the word 'shrined' which we noted a little earlier in Jane's description of her hiding-place. The shrine image obviously stresses the notion of sanctuary; in contrast with the way Jane has been presented as a criminal, it also suggests a link with saintliness and spirituality. It looks forward, too, to the growing importance the spiritual, Christian life has for Jane, as the fiend and the horned thing look forward to the temptations to which Jane is later subjected through the medium of Rochester and St John Rivers. Here, as later in the novel, moral extremes are presented forcefully to Jane's mind; images of paradise and hell jar against each other as her experience moves through moral vicissitudes and associated moral choices. The opposition of red and white in this episode we may see as reflecting the conflict of passion and duty which absorb Jane's attention in her relationships with Rochester and St John.

We have by no means exhausted the possibilities of the passage on Bewick. There is a great deal of emblemism in *Jane Eyre*, and that always makes for fun for critic and student alike. But rather than stay rooted to this interesting spot, let us move on to the final phase of the extract, which we will deal with more briefly.

At last, there is a homely image of life in the Reed household – Bessie entrancing the children with her tales 'of love and adventure' which appeal to Jane's romantic nature. The reference to the 'nursery-hearth' here is a precursor of other images of comfort which crop up from time to time during the novel. But this snapshot of familial peace, like Jane's private peace, is dashed aside by the brutal interruption of John Reed, who is hunting for 'Madam Mope'. His alliterative sobriquet points to lack of sympathy with Jane, and after the brief intermission in her pain, serves to underline her sufferings. Jane is victim again; now, however, we understand more fully how her situation damages her integrity. Her sensitivity is crushed by John's brashness; her privacy invaded by his person; her dignity set at nothing by his ignoring her rights. This miniature of the relative status of Victorian men and women is echoed again and again during the novel.

As earlier, we are impressed by the manner in which the events are allowed to make their own point. Brontë does not need to explain the impact of John's interruption to us, for its significance emerges vividly from the context. Equally, she does not need to explain to us that Jane is introverted, sensitive, imaginative, independent, thwarted, victimised, intelligent, rebellious and resolute: we can see these things for ourselves, or at least sense them beneath the pace of the narrative drive.

Let us try now to sum up the impact of the extract.

The presence in these opening paragraphs of so many clues to the mood and themes of the events which follow is remarkable. Images and motifs which colour the rest of the novel here find their origin. Here in miniature are Jane's social difficulties, her troubles with men, and her moral problems. *Shirley* and *Villette* are not like this. Only *Jane Eyre* has that sheer intensity of vision which is the major reason for its perennial fascination.

Brontë's narrator is deeply interesting. She is a complex character, and a complex narrator, but here Brontë uses her primarily as a participant who describes experiences with theatrical vividness. On the first page, there are hints which we find it hard to resolve at this stage. Particularly we note the ambiguity of the tone. It is not yet clear from what point of view Jane is narrating the events. Our first impression is that these early paragraphs are fast-moving, even urgent; the use of parentheses suggests a rough, brusque tone, as if the narrator has no time for niceties of style; events follow thick and fast, with character, action and setting intertwined in a perfectly realised sequence. Yet at the same time we sense an underlying coolness – even in this fast-moving scene, and in later more violent scenes – an almost sedate manner gives the impression of an observer involved physically while intellectually detached. Throughout, Jane maintains a considering, reasoned style. Even in the opening paragraphs there is a feeling that the narrator is looking back, coolly and thoughtfully, on events which have lost some of their sting. There is not excitability here: there is something of the nervousness of the immediate, there is urgency, and some bitterness, too; but the emotion is distilled. The economy and selectivity of the writing are evidence of that.

This element of meditation in the style develops further after the introductory clashing of words, in the paragraphs dealing with the calmer retreat of the window-seat. It is not until later in the book, however, that we become aware why this is so. Gradually we gain a stronger impression of a mature intelligence mulling over the events at the same time as they are told, to produce an odd double vision: a child's view, and an adult's view of the events mingled together. Finally we discover that Jane is looking back on events from a space of a decade after her marriage. Her more strictly narrative stance becomes clearest in the latter part of the extract. The language used is not available to Jane at her age in the narrative; it belongs to an older, more experienced person; sometimes it can sound rather like extracts from one of Brontë's father's sermons. The distance between Jane the object and Jane the subject is suggested in the phrase 'child as I was' with which Jane's precocious interest in the book is suggested, and in the reference to the thoughts that cross a child's brain a little later; and it becomes plainer at the point in the paragraph third from last, where the narrator states that 'Each picture told a story; mysterious often to my undeveloped understanding and imperfect feelings, yet ever profoundly interesting'. Here, evidently, a mature Jane is meditating not only on the events, but also on the state of mind of her younger self. This double vision, which runs throughout the novel, is part of its distinctive quality. Experiential storms and tempests are vividly described, but from a calmer, more seasoned point of view, which seems to suggest a broader moral perspective.

There is always a sense of containment about Jane's tribulations, even at their worst. Moreover, although we are encouraged to sympathise with Jane, we also see her flaws. The description of Jane's responses as 'undeveloped . . . imperfect' introduces an important element in the narrator's qualities: it means that we should not be too ready to trust her, and it is clear later, when she returns to visit Mrs Reed in maturity, how far she has developed in the intervening years. Here, in *Jane Eyre*, is a foretaste of the device of the 'unreliable narrator' which Brontë developed in *Villette*.

II: *Shirley*

Given that the opening paragraphs of *Shirley* come from the same pen, a sharper contrast with *Jane Eyre* is hard to imagine:

> Of late years, an abundant shower of curates has fallen upon the north of England: they lie very thick on the hills; every parish has one or more of them; they are young enough to be very active, and ought to be doing a great deal of good. But not of late years are we about to speak; we are going back to the beginning of this century: late years – present years are dusty, sun-burnt, hot, arid; we will evade the noon, forget it in siesta, pass the mid-day in slumber, and dream of dawn.
>
> If you think, from this prelude, that anything like a romance is preparing for you, reader, you never were more mistaken. Do you anticipate sentiment, and poetry, and reverie? Do you expect passion, and stimulus, and melodrama? Calm your expectations; reduce them to a lowly standard. Something real, cool, and solid, lies before you; something unromantic as Monday morning, when all who have work wake with the consciousness that they must rise and betake themselves thereto. It is not positively affirmed that you shall not have a taste of the exciting, perhaps towards the middle and close of the meal, but it is resolved that the first dish set upon the table shall be one that a Catholic – ay, even an Anglo-Catholic – might eat on Good Friday in Passion Week: it shall be cold lentils and vinegar without oil; it shall be unleavened bread with bitter herbs, and no roast lamb.
>
> Of late years, I say, an abundant shower of curates has fallen upon the north of England: but in eighteen-hundred-eleven-twelve that affluent rain had not descended: curates were scarce then: there was no Pastoral Aid – no Additional Curates' Society to stretch a helping

hand to worn-out old rectors and incumbents, and give them the wherewithal to pay a vigorous young colleague from Oxford or Cambridge. The present successors of the apostles, disciples of Dr Pusey and the tools of the Propaganda, were at that time being hatched under cradle-blankets, or undergoing regeneration by nursery-baptism in wash-hand-basins. You could not have guessed by looking at any of them that the Italian-ironed double frills of its net-cap surrounded the brows of a preordained, specially sanctified successor of St Paul, St Peter, or St John; nor could you have foreseen in the folds of its long night-gown the white surplice in which it was hereafter cruelly to exercise the souls of its parishioners, and strangely to nonplus its old-fashioned vicar by flourishing aloft in a pulpit the shirt-like raiment which had never before waved higher than the reading-desk.

Yet even in those days of scarcity there were curates: the precious plant was rare, but it might be found. A certain favoured district in the West Riding of Yorkshire could boast three rods of Aaron blossoming within a circuit of twenty miles. You shall see them, reader. Step into this neat garden-house on the skirts of Whinbury, walk forward into the little parlour – there they are at dinner. Allow me to introduce them to you: – Mr Donne, curate of Whinbury; Mr Malone, curate of Briarfield; Mr Sweeting, curate of Nunnely. These are Mr Donne's lodgings, being the habitation of one John Gale, a small clothier. Mr Donne has kindly invited his brethren to regale with him. You and I will join the party, see what is to be seen, and hear what is to be heard. At present, however, they are only eating; and while they eat, we will talk aside.

These gentlemen are in the bloom of youth; they possess all the activity of that interesting age – an activity which their moping old vicars would fain turn into the channel of their pastoral duties, often expressing a wish to see it expended in a diligent superintendence of the schools, and in frequent visits to the sick of their respective parishes. But the youthful Levites feel this to be dull work; they prefer lavishing their energies on a course of proceeding, which, though to other eyes it appear more heavy with ennui, more cursed with monotony, than the toil of the weaver at his loom, seems to yield them an unfailing supply of enjoyment and occupation.

I allude to a rushing backwards and forwards, amongst themselves, to and from their respective lodgings: not a round – but a triangle of visits, which they keep up all the year through, in winter, spring, summer, and autumn. Season and weather make no difference; with unintelligible zeal they dare snow and hail, wind and rain, mire and dust, to go and dine, or drink tea, or sup with each other. What attracts them, it would be difficult to say. It is not friendship; for whenever they meet they quarrel. It is not religion; the thing is never named amongst them: theology they may discuss occasionally, but piety – never. It is not the love of eating and drinking; each might have as good a joint and pudding, tea as potent, and toast as succulent, at his own lodgings, as is served to him at his brother's. Mrs Gale, Mrs Hogg, and Mrs Whipp – their respective landladies – affirm that 'it is just for nought else but to give folk trouble.' By 'folk,' the good ladies of course mean themselves; for indeed they are kept in a continual 'fry' by this system of mutual invasion.

(pp. 39–41)

Gone is the first-person narrator; instead we have an omniscient author-narrator in something of the mould of a Thackeray, whose work Brontë so much admired as to dedicate *Jane Eyre* to him. In contrast with the narrator of the earlier novel, the voice speaking here is hard to distinguish from the author. Gone, too, is the urgency of the opening of the earlier novel, replaced by a leisurely discussion of curates, taking time for conversation with the reader by the way. Absent, most evidently, is the sharp bite of personal experience, replaced by a general survey of recent history. We miss, finally, the drama; now satire reigns.

The general structure of the extract is not straightforward. Clearly, the first three paragraphs are a discussion of the curacy: only in the fourth paragraph does Brontë begin to discuss characters. There is, then, a movement from general to particular at the beginning of *Shirley*; but although the focus changes to individuals, they turn out later on not to be central characters. Let us proceed, as we did with *Jane Eyre*, by looking at the components of the extract more closely, beginning with the sequence of ideas, which is a little confusing.

The first, more general section of the extract appears odd in creating a problem of time. It seems to leap into irrelevance, for, having introduced 'late years', the author proceeds to tell us that we are going to ignore them, and revert to an earlier era, to a metaphorical 'dawn' instead of noon. She performs the same historical slide in paragraph three, in largely the same words, except that she begins to enter into detail – giving us exact dates, for example.

However, we note that she is dealing with history, and history is sequential. We are therefore to suppose, perhaps, that there is a link, beyond the existence of curates, and as yet unspoken, between the present and the more or less recent past. We guess – because of the subject-matter – that religious history may be of particular interest to the author; but it is hard to be sure, since the subject of religion, in so far as it is represented by the curacy, is treated so lightly. The first of these dislocations of time occurs at the end of the first paragraph, when we are suddenly twisted away from the discussion of curates in the present to focus instead on an earlier era which at first appears brighter, happier, more optimistic. Her readers, says Brontë, are to 'dream of dawn'. The alliterative phrasing emphasises a kind of idealism, and a kind of innocence – Brontë's word is 'romance' – to be contrasted with the curate-ridden present.

This gesture towards idealism is to some degree misleading, for it is at once negated by an address to the reader, with some rhetorical questions, in the second paragraph. We are not to expect romance, or 'anything like' it; instead we must expect 'Monday morning'. Instead of passion, we will read of work. Instead of 'sentiment, and poetry, and reverie', we must expect something 'real, cool, and solid'. These flat decisions are, oddly enough, then retracted: 'It is not positively affirmed that you shall not have a taste of the exciting'. We are beginning to feel uncertain about the direction the novel is taking.

Indeed, it would not be surprising if questions were already to arise in a reader's mind at this point about exactly what was in store for him in his literary journey. Yet paragraph two again changes its direction by a metaphorical sleight-of-hand, turning on the food imagery to revert to the religious theme, and to religious conflict: the dish that is the novel shall be simple fare suitable for a Catholic on Good Friday.

The third paragraph develops the ideas not of the preceding, but of the first paragraph. The repetition is acknowledged in the 'I say', maintaining an informal, conversational mood. The ironic tone is intensified as the 'abundant shower' modulates into an 'affluent rain', and the curates are contrasted with the 'worn-out old rectors and incumbents' whom they are to assist. Again Brontë disturbs the time sequence by an unexpected reference to the present day, when Pastoral Aid is available to provide a new breed of curates, mere babes-in-arms at the time of the action of the novel.

One of the points which emerges sharply is the narrator's complex attitude to the clergy. There is evidence here of impatience with abstract theological dispute, and of broad sympathy for the exhausted rectors and old-fashioned vicars who carry the burden of work in the parish; certainly, underlying that clash, there is a strong awareness of the plethora of schismatic movements in the late eighteenth and the early nineteenth centuries. The topic is introduced lightly in paragraph two with Brontë's reference to the Good Friday fare of Catholics and Anglo-Catholics. It is developed later in her reference to Dr Pusey, one of the leaders of the Oxford Movement, which advocated closer adherence to Roman Catholic practice; the 'tools of the Propaganda' refers to the organisation responsible for the promulgation of Roman Catholic faith. The narrator's tone is satirical, with the absurd comparison between a baby in double frilled net-cap and the imposing 'brows' of a priest; the reference to the priest as a successor to one of the apostles is theoretically accurate, but none the less incongruous. In the reference to 'baptism in wash-hand-basins' we may read an allusion to the diversity of practice between adult baptism and infant baptism. The choice of the three apostles, Peter, Paul and John invites us to think of three diverse beliefs – Roman Catholic, Anglican and Baptist. And the final reference to the flourishing of the surplice suggests the development of a group in the Oxford Movement which adopted Roman Catholic styles of ceremonial. The paragraph vividly illustrates Brontë's complex attitude to the churches: there is non-partisan questioning of theological divisiveness, and sympathy for the priest dedicated to supporting his flock. Later in the novel, we see Mr Hall as the sole representative of the dedicated priesthood; the other clergy are variously condemned. All this introduces a major theme. Religious dissension is dramatised amusingly in the Whitsuntide procession, and religion in different aspects underlies much that happens in the novel.

The bitterest satire is reserved for the curacy. The satirical tone is apparent in the first paragraph in the use of metaphor; the phrase, 'abundant shower', which is repeated in the third paragraph, is not quite oxymoronic, but has sufficient inherent incongruity to make us suspicious. It suggests, despite the common associations of rain, nothing to do with fertility; on the contrary, these curates 'lie very thick on the hills'; they are, anonymously, 'one or more' per parish. The end of the first sentence is climactic, and sharpest in its negative implication: 'young enough to be very active' may imply inactivity, and, in the context of 'ought to be doing a great deal of good', certainly does. The rather heroic reference to 'dawn' – presumably the first rays of a new age of religious zeal heralded by the curacy – is overshadowed by the consciousness of noon – the narrator's present – as a period of discomfort best slept through. Recent times are described as 'dusty, sun-burnt, hot, arid'. There is no explanation for these images; they suggest thirst, and perhaps a thirst unslaked, for the shower which has fallen is no life-giving moisture, but a species of blight, and its abundance is no virtue. The conclusion must be that these curates are lazy and useless for the furtherance of God's purpose. In the context, the idea of the shower of curates having 'fallen upon' the land suggests a rather different metaphor: something rather like one of the plagues of Egypt than any beneficent moistening of parched spirits. The satire becomes more personal with the reference to babes in net-caps and the subsequent comparison between the night-gown and the ecclesiastical surplice, implying immaturity in the curates who were the narrator's own contemporaries.

The discussion of the curacy is split by the second paragraph, from which emerge two other themes of significance in the novel. The more important of these is the clash between romance and realism. One reason for the presence of this clash is not available from the evidence in the novel. We know from contemporary documents that some of reviews of *Jane Eyre* were critical of many of its aspects, and particularly of its supposedly excessive romantic and sensational aspects; we know, too, that Brontë was sensitive to these criticisms, and that she intended *Shirley* as a riposte to them. The way in which Brontë digresses in this paragraph, to make, as it seems, a direct answer to at least some of her critics, is echoed in a double intention which runs throughout the novel: Brontë constantly tries to intertwine the romantic world of the female protagonists with the documentary and historical elements in the novel, which are more closely associated with some of the male characters, especially Robert Moore.

Another point that links paragraph two with the novel as a whole is the comparison between the novel and a meal. The use of food imagery for the content of the novel foreshadows its pointed use in later events, and is highly appropriate to the immoderate habits of the entertainingly repellent curates who eat and drink their way through the novel.

Let us turn our attention now to the second part of the extract. It is linked with the earlier paragraphs by the subject of the curacy, that evolution of the priesthood which is satirically described as a 'precious plant'. At last, in paragraph four, Brontë introduces three representatives of the genus – the horticultural metaphor is sustained with the description of their youth as 'in the bloom' – with whom the forthcoming narrative will have something to do. These are the clerical gentlemen to whom the chapter (entitled 'Levitical') is dedicated. There is irony in the reference to the 'favoured' area of the West Riding which can boast three such plants, while the reference to them as 'three rods of Aaron' invites comparison with the first priest of the Jews – by whose standard we will be unsurprised to find them fail. The rod of Aaron budded, blossomed and produced almonds: these curates seem more likely to turn into dry sticks. As earlier, there is a contrast with 'their moping old vicars' whose unreasonable expectation it is that the curates should devote their energies to pastoral work; the effect is to exhibit the shallowness of the 'youthful Levites' who easily dismiss this as 'dull work'. Here values are reversed: 'moping' is the curates' assessment of the vicars, and not the narrator's; 'dull work' is their assessment, too, but the satirical style ensures that we are not misled about the tendency of the writing.

There is no doubt here about the point of view of the narrator. She, clearly, is among those 'other eyes' whose perception of the curates' pursuits is a mixture of incomprehension and contempt. She describes vividly the extraordinary enthusiasm which the curates devote to their ceaseless round of visiting in all weathers, but fails to find a satisfactory justification for it. The periphrastic description of their behaviour as 'a course of proceeding' hints at its waste of lavished energy, while the parallel of the weaver at his loom reminds us that the weaver differs from the curates in producing something useful at the end of his labours. The most direct blow against the curates is struck in the middle of the last paragraph. The parallel sentence structure of 'It is not friendship . . . It is not religion . . .' highlights the conclusive point: 'theology they may discuss occasionally, but piety – never'. The effect is carefully worked: the leisurely, amplified playfulness of the paragraph builds incrementally – only to give way, in the final antithesis, to a deadly brevity.

A further change of tone takes place in the final sentences of the extract: the curates' meetings are reduced to the level of farce when seen through the eyes of their landladies who, in local accents, condemn the curates for 'giv[ing] folk trouble' for 'nought'. How the homeliness contrasts with the flights of the curates! The effect of changing the perspective in this way is to measure the curates' proceedings against ordinary experience: and they are found wanting, because their behaviour appears meaningless. Common sense is upheld here: the curates' 'system of mutual invasion' causes no significant stir, merely a 'fry' for the women. The war imagery is an apposite description of the quarrelsomeness of their meetings, as well as of the effect on the landladies. But there is an element of hyperbole about it, too: compared with the earthiness suggested by the use of dialect, there is something of the storm in the teacup about their activities.

The narrator presents herself in these opening paragraphs as a very prominent organising and commentating entity: she relates past and present, pointing out contrast and comparison; makes judgements about characters; discusses the action with us; introduces the speech and attitudes of landladies to support her views; and maintains throughout a mockingly ironic manner. Yet she is not part of the action, and even at the end of the novel, when she becomes more prominent, has only a geographical link with it – a link barely hinted at here in the reference to 'A certain favoured district in the West Riding of Yorkshire'.

It appears, at this point, that we are entering a totally different world from that of *Jane Eyre*, but, in fact, the impression is a little misleading. The second paragraph envisages the presentation of more romantic material later in the novel; the promise is fulfilled in frequent reference to the contrasting worlds of business and romance, and the contrast is stressed at the conclusion. Though there is a faithfully depicted backdrop of factual and documentary material in *Shirley*, the scenes which stay in the mind are cast very much in the theatrical and romantic mould of *Jane Eyre*.

The religious theme is almost as important as the conflict of business and romance. Although the curates have only a marginal role in the novel, the religious theme they help to establish has consistent significance, both as a backdrop and in the lives of Shirley and Caroline Helstone. As in the extract, the religious world is dominated by conflict. The military language used of the curates looks forward to the swashbuckling manner of Helstone, and to the Whitsuntide battle which we consider in a later chapter.

Conflict dominates the political world, too. It is adumbrated in this opening extract only in the background of a troubled, even sick England, thirsty for moral leadership but beset by parasites. The exploits of Napoleon and Wellington, and the problems arising from the Orders in Council are not otherwise approached until later in the opening chapter.

In addition to the political and religious interests, the novel reveals more general social interests. In introducing the voices of the landladies, the precursors of 'low persons' who play a role in the later action, Brontë shows a desire to broaden the social range of the novel. A voice like theirs will furnish the conclusion of the novel.

All this is perhaps too much. The element of confusion about the opening of *Shirley* sharply distinguishes it from *Jane Eyre*. Instead of urgency and purpose, we have a spacious and discursive style. What there is here of clarity of theme turns out to be in part misleading. The tone of the writing, however, is both complex and consistent. Humour, wit and irony colour every sentence, but do not disguise an underlying bitterness at the unproductive activity of curates, and a serious recognition of the hard work of parish clergy. The seriousness is a significant element in this opening: Charlotte Brontë is capable of witty, and very humorous writing, but she does not achieve consistent urbanity, try as she may; for her, psychological depth is always more important than social breadth; her heroines always tingle at her nerve-ends; the satirical fun is always, in the event, secondary to sympathetic insight.

III: *Villette*

With *Villette* Charlotte Brontë returns to first-person narrative. The novel begins in very low key. The narrator is involved in the action, but appears to be objective; the emphasis appears to be very much on the perceived rather than the perceiver, and we are not told her name until Chapter 2, in which Mr Home comes to visit his daughter, Paulina or 'Polly', at Bretton. The extract below is from Chapter 3 and describes his departure:

> On the morning of Mr Home's departure, he and his daughter had some conversation in a window-recess by themselves; I heard part of it.
> 'Couldn't I pack my box and go with you, papa?' she whispered earnestly.
> He shook his head.
> 'Should I be a trouble to you?'
> 'Yes, Polly.'
> 'Because I am little?'
> 'Because you are little and tender. It is only great, strong people that should travel. But don't look sad, my little girl; it breaks my heart. Papa will soon come back to his Polly.'
> 'Indeed, indeed, I am not sad, scarcely at all.'
> 'Polly would be sorry to give papa pain; would she not?'
> 'Sorrier than sorry.'
> 'Then Polly must be cheerful: not cry at parting; not fret afterwards. She must look forward to meeting again, and try to be happy meanwhile. Can she do this?'
> 'She will try.'
> 'I see she will. Farewell, then. It is time to go.'
> '*Now*? – just *now*?'
> 'Just now.'

She held up quivering lips. Her father sobbed, but she, I remarked, did not. Having put her down, he shook hands with the rest present, and departed.

When the street-door closed, she dropped on her knees at a chair with a cry – 'Papa!'

It was low and long; a sort of 'Why hast thou forsaken me?' During an ensuing space of some minutes, I perceived she endured agony. She went through, in that brief interval of her infant life, emotions such as some never feel; it was in her constitution: she would have more of such instants if she lived. Nobody spoke. Mrs Bretton, being a mother, shed a tear or two. Graham, who was writing, lifted up his eyes and gazed at her. I, Lucy Snowe, was calm.

The little creature, thus left unharassed, did for herself what none other could do – contended with an intolerable feeling; and, ere long, in some degree, repressed it. That day she would accept solace from none; nor the next day: she grew more passive afterwards.

On the third evening, as she sat on the floor, worn and quiet, Graham, coming in, took her up gently, without a word. She did not resist: she rather nestled in his arms, as if weary. When he sat down, she laid her head against him; in a few minutes she slept; he carried her up-stairs to bed. I was not surprised that, the next morning, the first thing she demanded was – 'Where is Mr Graham?'

(pp. 79–80)

Let us follow the usual sequence and begin by considering the structure of this extract. It is part of a conversation between Polly and her father which is framed by the perceptions of the narrator. The extract falls naturally into two sections, dividing at the departure of Mr Home. The first section, after the narrator's statement that she 'heard part of it', is largely dialogue reported without overt comment; it is a sharply realized piece of theatre; stage directions are minimised. Then, in the second, narrative half of the extract, the perceptions of the narrator become much more important as she describes and comments on the behaviour of Mrs Bretton and Graham in response to the situation; much that she says, or does not, expresses her own reactions, too. The changing of focus seems at first glance similar to the beginning of *Jane Eyre*, but the emotional tone, as we shall see, is very different.

The conversation of Polly and her father seems as if it is transmitted directly; yet we are conscious of the interpreting ear and eye, and the scene is a somewhat disturbing experience for the reader because the tone of the narrator seems ill-matched to the events which she is recounting. It is at once clear that we are dealing here with quite another species of double vision than in *Jane Eyre*.

Looking at the opening paragraph of the first, dramatic section, we are at once confronted with its strangeness of style. It contains one sentence, in which there are two bald statements about a conversation between Mr Home and Polly which the narrator 'heard part of', despite its being held in the window-recess. The earlier extract from *Jane Eyre* suggests that this is a rather private place, and Polly's whispering indicates a desire for secrecy. There may, therefore, be an implication of eavesdropping. Another, and a contrary, possibility is that the narrator is simply not interested enough to pay special attention and hear the whole conversation, and that she hears the whispering only because it is emphatic. The situation is characteristic of much of the earlier part of *Villette* in providing us with minimal or ambiguous clues about the narrator's role. No matter what our interpretation of what the narrator is doing, however, it is not clear that she is much moved by what she hears.

The conversation to which we are made privy by this strangely uninvolved narrator is, in fact, heavily emotional. The father bids a firm but sorrowful farewell to his young daughter; she would like to go with him on his travels, but trusts him and his judgement that she is too little, and despite her distress promises to be cheerful in his absence. The emotion is registered in the form the dialogue takes, and in the comments of the narrator, in action – and in silence. Polly's request to accompany her father is 'whispered earnestly', and his wordless shaking of his head expresses the sorrow he feels but cannot trust himself to speak. He asks her not to look sad because 'it breaks [his] heart'. Like a dutiful daughter she accepts his wishes, and claims, unconvincingly, that she is 'not sad, scarcely at all'; but the qualification, 'scarcely', and the repeated 'indeed' which precedes it, belie her statement. Here we are presented with a situation of much pathos: the child is striving to match the demands of a much-loved parent, no matter how cruel they may seem.

The unexpected switch to the third person at the end of Mr Home's speech – '. . . it breaks my heart. Papa will soon come back to his Polly' – is a way of controlling emotion by grammatical distancing; Polly soon catches on and copies him. It is a device which brings formal dignity to this touching scene: we miss – if only in the sense of noticing its absence – the kind of emotional temperature which a more sentimental writer might have created. The moment when Polly almost breaks – the repetition of the italicized '*now*' – is all the more powerful for the narrator's restraint; and the finality of the dead response, 'Just now', is all the more conclusive.

The physical signs of emotional stress are recounted in flat, brief phrases: 'She held up quivering lips. Her father sobbed . . .' The parting is formal and simple: Mr Home puts down his daughter, shakes hands with everybody, 'and departed'. The prose here verges on clinical: it contrasts violently with the kind of rhythmic transports to which we are treated later in the novel during the narrator's phases of hypochondria or delirium.

The observing eye in the first part of the extract, as in much of the rest of the prelude to the novel – the Bretton section which occupies the first three chapters, that is – is precise, lucid, detached, critical; it has upon us a chilling effect. It is, we may think, an effect peculiarly appropriate to a narrator with the surname Snowe.

'Lucy Snowe' is a name we should look at carefully, if only because Charlotte Brontë herself did. She changed the name from 'Frost' shortly before publication, thus making it clear that the resonances in the name were crucial to her: she wanted Lucy Snowe to appear cold. If the narrator seems unfeeling, unbending, unsympathetic, it is part of the author's intention. This seems on the face of it surprising, since we can see in Lucy's experience the shadows of Charlotte's education in Brussels; but, though the source of the novel may lie in Charlotte Brontë's life, she is not writing autobiography. Lucy Snowe, therefore, may be both unsympathetic, and based on Brontë's experience. The surname suggests other ideas, too. Snow carries overtones of purity and innocence which are missing from Frost; it may also be worth noticing that snow suggests, more than frost, the property of melting. Further resonances emerge later. Brontë gives particular emphasis to the name when in Chapter 5 she describes herself in mature years: 'my hair which till a late period withstood the frosts of time, lies now, at last white, under a white cap, like snow beneath snow' (p. 105). The portrait draws attention to a further property of snow: that it conceals or blurs the outlines of reality, or even buries them; this, too, we should keep in mind for future consideration.

Perhaps not all these ideas associated with snow will have a specific and thoroughgoing meaning in the text. It does not matter if we are wrong: at this stage we need to give our imagination freedom to roam over the possibilities as broadly as possible. We can leave until later the decision about which are valid, and which not.

The same applies to 'Lucy' as to 'Snowe'. It is an equally rich name, in respect of both its Latin origins and its sound associations: it may suggest to us variously light, lucidity, hallucination, loose, Lucifer, even lunacy – and it is hard to believe that Brontë could have been unaware of poems by Wordsworth which again support the idea of innocence. For Donne, of course, Lucy held far different associations, and it is possible that the proximity of the feast of St Lucy to the winter solstice is significant, drawing together the implications of both names; so also may be the vow of perpetual virginity for which St Lucy suffered martyrdom. It is for students who may wish to do so to think through these resonances or others that come to mind. Here we shall concern ourselves with the theme of coldness, which is at the heart of the mood of the narrative.

Coldness can be perceived in both parts of the extract. In the first part, it is apparent in the clipped narration, in the largely uncommented reporting of the scene. In the second half of the extract, Brontë stresses the point in the way Lucy comments on the situation at its emotional peak, where Polly, desolated at the loss of her father, drops to her knees with the cry of 'Papa!' on her child's lips. In this second part we need to be aware of manner as well as matter: to take particular notice of how Lucy comments, as well as what she says; consider what she does not comment on, as well as what she does. To take the latter point first, she gives no emotional reaction to what she has just witnessed; instead, she describes the cry: 'low and long'. This is the language of an amateur scientist engaged in study of an interesting experiment. Then Lucy compares the cry to that of

Christ on the cross – a comparison which, in its wild impropriety, might appear to suggest powerful feeling both in the observer and the object, were it not for the extraordinary introductory phrase, 'a sort of "Why hast thou forsaken me?"'. That phrase distances and even belittles by its vagueness the emotion witnessed, reducing it to a natural phenomenon of no special significance. The whole sentence shocks, because it places a moment of passionate intensity under a cold shower.

The remainder of the paragraph builds on this chill introduction subtly. When we read that Lucy 'perceived [Polly] endured agony', we note that the precise 'perceived' is appropriate for Lucy's reactions at this stage in the novel: she is much better at perceiving than at feeling, better at observing than at sympathising; we may recall the comparable word, 'remarked', a little earlier in the extract. There is no doubt that she understands: she knows that Polly feels things 'such as some never feel'; but at this point in the book, we may be inclined to think that Lucy Snowe herself is numbered among those who never feel. Here, too, we note the voice of an older Lucy, the one with white hair who introduces herself in Chapter 5. This older Lucy is philosophical: '[Polly] would have more such instants if she lived'. Of course, we also know, from the rest of the novel, that Lucy is compelled to grow accustomed to loss; yet, mellowed by experience though her remark may be, it retains the unattractive detachment that we associate with the younger Lucy.

The complexity of the narrator invites comparison with Jane Eyre. Both are youthful; both are outsiders; both view the action simultaneously as participants and as older commentators. Of course, as characters they are distinct: Jane is younger than Lucy; in the scene we have considered, we can see closer links, perhaps, between Polly and Jane than between Lucy and Jane. Despite the obvious differences from Jane Eyre, however, Lucy is beginning to look like very much the same kind of narrator in her complexity of vision. In both cases, the double perspective of a younger and of an older personality introduces an element of doubt – of unreliability – in the narrative. We are constantly invited to evaluate what we are being told because we can sense that it is only one side of a story which could be viewed from a different perspective: the implication of a second

narrator even implies the theoretical possibility of yet other narrators; and it stresses the incompleteness of the existing narrative.
What we read, therefore, is not history, but a narrator's experience:
subject and object are indissoluble.

Thus far, we have been considering the extract as a kind of play-
within-a-novel, noticing how the narrator plays the role of the audience reflecting upon the on-stage action, which, curiously, also
reflects her. Now we are confronted with the reactions of other
members of the audience attending this private performance, and we
need to be aware of another set of relationships. All the relationships
include the narrator merely by virtue of being narrated, and reflect
on her.

Lucy's reactions are explicitly compared with those of Mrs Bretton
and Graham, and the manner of the comparison is extraordinary in
both underestimating the strength of their feelings and nevertheless
representing them as stronger than Lucy's. One effect is that Polly
wins more sympathy with every sentence. Lucy appears almost
offensive in finding it necessary to explain away Mrs Bretton's shed-
ding merely 'a tear or two' by her being a mother – a condition
apparently likely, in Lucy's eyes, to unsettle the power of judgement
and render the emotions unstable. A similar effect is evident in the
description of Graham, who breaks off from his writing and 'lifted
up his eyes and gazed at [Polly]'. His reaction suggests a bleak emotional life, and we may be inclined to give weight therefore to Lucy's
initial description of Graham as 'faithless-looking' (Chapter 2,
p. 73): it already appears that in him we may have to deal with a
shallow personality. Mrs Bretton's muted reaction is prepared too:
Lucy describes her earlier as 'not generally a caressing woman', and
adds that 'even with her deeply-cherished son, her manner was rarely
sentimental, often the reverse' (Chapter 1, p. 64). What strikes us
most forcefully about this scene is the distance between Polly and
her observers: no one goes to comfort her, and no one speaks to her.
But worse is to come, for these brief comments on the other characters are merely a prelude to the final, self-congratulatory and self-
damning sentence in the paragraph: 'I, Lucy Snowe, was calm.' The
self-congratulation is evident in the deliberate form of the statement,
in which the use of apposition gives a regal stateliness to the 'I'. This

is not a practical matter of introducing the narrator's name: that has been done already, in precisely the same form of words, at the beginning of Chapter 2 (p. 69). No: this is the self-confidence of a quiet and somewhat introverted person who believes in her own superiority. The impression we receive in this scene is entirely consistent with what we have learned of Lucy Snowe earlier. We have watched her in her smug superiority criticising the Brettons for giving way to little Polly, whom clearly she dislikes with strange intensity; she has sneered at them for being misled by a mere child; she has sarcastically contrasted Polly's 'sudden, dangerous nature – *sensitive* as they are called' with her own 'cooler temperament' (Chapter 2, p. 70); and she has preened herself that she 'plead[s] guiltless of that curse, an overheated and discursive imagination' (p. 69). It is not an attractive personality, and few indeed are the readers who have liked Lucy Snowe; it was, in fact, her creator who led the charge in disliking her. Lucy Snowe seems to observe in order to criticise and judge; she has insight without sympathy; understanding without humanity.

The end of the extract is only superficially more sympathetic to Polly. Lucy's reference to her as 'The little creature' might appear sympathetic, were it not that Lucy, among other evidence of dislike for the child, has previously called her 'little busy-body' (Chapter 2, p. 72). The rest of the paragraph shows remarkably little feeling for her. It is represented as a virtue that Polly has been 'left unharassed' to reconcile herself to her loss in her own way, and certainly when she seeks comfort from the Brettons, she finds it readily enough. We see, perhaps, a more sympathetic side of Lucy Snowe here: she recognises that Polly is contending with 'an intolerable feeling', and notes that it is only 'in some degree' that she 'repressed' it; yet there is still the uncomfortable suspicion that Lucy Snowe is 'perceiving' again – it is one of her favourite words in the early chapters. This impression is borne out by Lucy's judgement of the new relationship between Graham and Polly: he comforts the child, who is described as 'nestled' in his arms, and she comes speedily to depend upon him; the first thing she asks in the morning is the whereabouts of Graham. Lucy's acid comment, 'I was not surprised', matches her earlier disparaging comments on the way the Brettons and Polly's father give way to, and thus, she supposes, spoil the child. In view of the disparity in age and circumstances between Polly and Lucy, it seems unlikely that we are confronting sexual jealousy here: rather, it is plain, simple meanmindedness.

From the point of view of narrative structure, the concluding paragraphs of the extract have a close connection with later events. Through the eyes of Lucy we will watch the development between Graham and Polly of the amorous thread which links the beginning and end of the whole novel, subordinate in uniting it only to the personality of the beady-eyed narrator. Lucy's education in repression in the course of the story is prefigured in Polly's experience in this episode, and the parallel makes Lucy's older self sensitive if not sympathetic to Polly's feelings.

Although she is another first-person narrator, Lucy Snowe seems very different from the narrator of *Jane Eyre*. Jane is a prominent character in every scene in the earlier novel, whereas in *Villette* Lucy most often presents herself as an observer, of the action as of life. It is only by degrees that we become aware that she is to be the focus of the action, and that it is her development that we are witnessing. *Villette* is in large measure the account of the thawing of this icy narrator. Her emotions are brought to life by force, and chiefly by tragic force. During the course of the novel, she is made to pass through just such partings as enervate Polly in this extract; she has to suffer the pain and bitterness of loss; she must be thwarted in love; in the end, she may emerge refined. The pattern – disgracefully oversimplified here for the moment – is mediaeval in its structural simplicity. It may be interpreted, likewise in the mediaeval manner, on more than one level.

Conclusions

1. Brontë is adept in using first-person narration to present a vivid account of an external situation, while at the same time using it to develop a rich impression of the narrator herself. In *Jane Eyre* our impression is sympathetic; in *Villette*, rather otherwise. Brontë does not need to use her narrator to explain; the narrative technique enacts, with intense vividness, the meaning of the events.
2. Brontë's use of third-person narration in *Shirley* appears less

sure, but the narrator has to perform a complex function: evaluating the characters, sketching in political and religious background, giving the point of view of common folk as well as the major characters, and discussing the novel with her reader.

3. In both narrative modes, scenes can be presented with theatrical sharpness. Dialogue and narrative are supported by use of natural setting and imagery to add detail and resonance to the narrative. Setting is used to express psychological dimensions in the writing.

4. In *Jane Eyre* and *Villette* in particular, but also in many individual scenes in *Shirley* – if not in the opening paragraphs – there is psychological depth. The writing is so rich as to suggest much beyond what can be easily expressed. We feel much more about characters and their situations than we are told in so many words.

5. All three novels inhabit more than one time-scale. The first-person narrators are complex, both old and young at the same time, particularly in *Jane Eyre*.

6. In *Jane Eyre* and *Villette*, there is tension between the inner and external worlds of the narrator. What the narrator describes reflects on the narrator herself, illuminating her personality and failings. The events narrated may often be interpreted as symbolic representations, prefigurings or recollections of events in the narrator's life.

7. Biblical and religious references are frequent, and sometimes ironic. There is evident familiarity with religious ideas, and in *Shirley*, an awareness of the religious dissension of the period.

8. In *Shirley*, irony is used freely to mock folly, and, by implication, uphold good sense – represented in the opening paragraphs respectively by curates and rectors.

9. Brontë's style is very variable: she can be florid or pithy, and can use local dialect when appropriate. She shows a fine mastery of pattern and rhythm in prose, using it cleverly to control the changing emotional temperature of her writing.

10. Names may have symbolic meaning, and in *Villette* the narrator's name is a broad clue to the interpretation of her behaviour. Similar points could be made about characters and places in all the novels.

Methods of Analysis

1. Begin with simple things.
   - Is the narration in the first or third person?
   - Are any specific narrative devices used, such as a letter, journal or diary?
   - Is the narrator describing events as they happen, or from a later time?
   - Is the narrator omniscient?
   - Is the narrator a participant in the action?
2. Go on to consider content.
   - Is the writing discursive, descriptive, meditative, narrative, or dramatic?
   - It is likely to be a combination of these, so have a look at the components: their balance, the relationship between them, as we have done with the extracts above.
3. Next look at the components which are not essential to the bare content, and which therefore say much more about the nature of the novel:
   - How are setting and imagery used? How do they express the narrator's personality?
   - Is any kind of symbolism used?
4. Now you can go on to consider details of style.
   - How does the language used reflect the narrator's personality?
   - Does the narrator make use of ambiguity or irony? Or are they used at the expense of the narrator?
   - Are there any authorial intrusions?
     (There are too many linguistic devices to list here: the best advice is to be alert to anything unusual, odd or striking. In Charlotte Brontë's novels, you will often find interesting uses of allusion, antithesis, periphrasis and personification. However, few people wish to know that you have memorised the technical terms: recognising effects is what matters.)
5. Think about the place of the extract in the whole structure of the novel.
   - How does the extract relate to the narrative approach of the rest of the book?

- Is the narrative voice the same as later?
- Is its style consistent with the rest of the book?
- How do the experiences in the extract compare with experiences elsewhere in the novel?

The effect of the analysis should, ideally, be a new, and more satisfying synthesis of your ideas about the book as a whole.

Further Work

Apply these methods of analysis to other early scenes in the books. I suggest looking at one or more of the following scenes, but by all means pick one of your own choice if you prefer:

Jane Eyre: The famous 'red-room' scene, which appears in the first five pages or so of Volume 1, Chapter 2 (pp. 19–22). The use of setting and imagery is particularly striking in this scene. Choose any one or two pages which seem interesting.

Shirley: Consider an extract from a later part of Chapter 1: say, the six paragraphs before Helstone's appearance (from 'The curates, meantime, sat and sipped their wine . . .', p. 42, to '. . . they would be sure to meet the best friends in the world tomorrow morning', p. 44). In large part, this will mean looking at the ways in which irony is used to flay the curates, but there is also some political material here.

Villette: Analyse the first seven paragraphs of Chapter 2, to the paragraph which ends, '. . . advanced to restore her to the house whence he had seen her issue' (pp. 69–70), or else try the first page or two of Chapter 4 (say, the first three paragraphs, or the first nine, finishing with Lucy's self-portrait, pp. 94–6).

2

Characterisation

It is as easy to underestimate the range and number of characters in *Jane Eyre* and *Villette*, as it is to overestimate the riches of *Shirley*. *Shirley*, with something under 150 characters, contains rather fewer than either of the other novels. Admittedly, many of these characters flit into the pages of the novels so briefly as not to linger in our memory; nevertheless, the feat of imagination involved in bringing this range of characters to life is remarkable.

We will be looking at a number of episodes which illuminate characters, and considering the ways in which Brontë's methods differ from one character to another. It is obvious that the degree to which characters are developed will vary; some will be foreground characters, others will play only a minor role. Less obvious is the variety in the treatment which more or less major characters are given, particularly in the first-person novels: the perceptions of a character-narrator are integral to the impact which other characters make, and the nature of those perceptions depends on many factors, including age, mood and situation.

With such large casts in her novels, Brontë makes full use of the faculty of characters for commenting, directly or indirectly, on each other. As the action evolves, there develop many contrasts and comparisons, and more extended parallels, which enrich the themes of the novels. As we shall see, the characters are carefully organised parts of the design of each novel.

As before, we will begin with *Jane Eyre*, and allow argument to emerge from analysis.

I: *Jane Eyre*

The destination of our discussion of *Jane Eyre* will be Edward Fairfax Rochester, but we will approach indirectly so as to see how Brontë's treatment of that famous figure compares with her treatment of other characters, in particular Mr Brocklehurst, who will be the focus of our analysis. We will always need to keep in mind that we see only through the eyes of Jane Eyre, either as a participant in the action, or as a commentator on it from a standpoint at least ten years later.

Jane is always central. In the early chapters of the novel, characters pass before us in rapid sequence: Mrs Reed, Bessie, Abbot, John Reed and his sisters, Eliza and Georgiana at Gateshead; Miss Temple, Miss Scatcherd, Helen Burns at Lowood. All these characters are defined and differentiated by reference to their attitude to Jane. All have a function in the novel which extends beyond simple 'character': they have thematic significance and emotional meaning for Jane.

Although these are not trivial characters – there are many other, minor figures who pass before us – it is their impact on Jane, rather than their individual qualities, which matters. There is clear evidence of this in an episode at the end of Volume 1, Chapter 2 when Mrs Reed, Abbot and Bessie react in sequence to Jane's hysterical behaviour when she is brought out of the red room. Bessie is the least hostile, simply inquiring the cause of Jane's panic; Abbot appears to believe that Jane is merely being naughty, and deplores the noise she is making; Mrs Reed, peremptory and dominating, expresses her detestation of Jane in her characteristic formal style, accusing her of 'artifice' and 'violence', and demanding 'perfect submission and stillness'. Thus, in reacting to Jane, each character expresses her own nature: Bessie feels an instinctive sympathy, but is bound to follow her mistress's lead; Abbot is trivially scolding, and apparently without feeling; Mrs Reed is the ring-master of this cruel circus, unchangeable in her conviction that Jane is a compound of all evils. Jane's mature comment is that 'I was a precocious actress in her eyes', and she recognises, with perhaps more sympathy than Mrs Reed deserves, that 'she sincerely looked on me as a compound of virulent passions, mean spirit, and dangerous duplicity' (all from p. 25). The technique used here links Brontë with earlier, and very different writers; Fielding and Austen both regularly used this technique for satirical ends. (Look at the coach ride in *Joseph Andrews*, for example, or the Box Hill episode in *Emma*). In Brontë's novel, however, satire is not the point: the focus is firmly on Jane herself, on her position as a victim, and on the impossibility of her coping with the heavy demands of the plight in which she is placed.

Of the minor characters, only two appear at both Gateshead and Lowood: Bessie and Mr Brocklehurst. The latter we shall look at in detail, for he will be useful later. He is thematically important, and the way in which he is presented shows some characteristic features of Brontë's approach to characterisation.

Mr Brocklehurst appears in Volume 1, Chapter 4 to interview Jane prior to her attending Lowood. Unsurprisingly, Jane is summoned to the breakfast-room with no inkling of what she is to find there:

> 'Who could want me?' I asked inwardly, as with both hands I turned the stiff door-handle which, for a second or two, resisted my efforts. 'What should I see besides aunt Reed in the apartment? – a man or a woman?' The handle turned, the door unclosed, and passing through and curtseying low, I looked up at – a black pillar! – such, at least, appeared to me, at first sight, the straight, narrow, sable-clad shape standing erect on the rug; the grim face at the top was like a carved mask, placed above the shaft by way of capital.
>
> Mrs Reed occupied her usual seat by the fireside: she made a signal for me to approach; I did so, and she introduced me to the stony stranger with the words: 'This is the little girl respecting whom I applied to you.'
>
> *He* – for it was a man – turned his head slowly towards where I stood, and having examined me with the two inquisitive-looking grey eyes which twinkled under a pair of bushy brows, said solemnly, and in a bass voice: 'Her size is small: what is her age?'
>
> 'Ten years.'
>
> 'So much?' was the doubtful answer; and he prolonged his scrutiny for some minutes. Presently he addressed me: –
>
> 'Your name, little girl?'
>
> 'Jane Eyre, sir.'

In uttering these words, I looked up: he seemed to me a tall gentleman; but then I was very little; his features were large, and they and all the lines of his frame were equally harsh and prim.

'Well, Jane Eyre, and are you a good child?'

Impossible to reply to this in the affirmative: my little world held a contrary opinion: I was silent. Mrs Reed answered for me by an expressive shake of the head, adding soon, 'Perhaps the less said on that subject the better, Mr Brocklehurst.'

'Sorry indeed to hear it! She and I must have some talk'; and bending from the perpendicular, he installed his person in the armchair, opposite Mrs Reed's. 'Come here,' he said.

I stepped across the rug; he placed me square and straight before him. What a face he had, now that it was almost on a level with mine! what a great nose! and what a mouth! and what large, prominent teeth!

(pp. 40–1)

As before, we will consider the general nature of the extract before proceeding to more particular points of interest. To begin with, we need to think about the social background which frames this passage, and about the ways in which it is rendered unique: that is, about those elements in it which we may consider ordinary, and those which are extraordinary.

Of course, we should remember that this novel is set in Victorian England. Children are not, in this social context, to be accorded the respect which they may command nowadays. It is therefore not expected that Mr Brocklehurst should be formally introduced to Jane; it is not remarkable that she should be spoken of, rather than spoken to ('Her size is small: what is her age?'), and perhaps not unexpected that she should be scrutinised like an object. The subjection of Jane is, therefore, not extraordinary. However, Jane's individual perspective brings to the episode a dramatic and emotional intensity far beyond the prosaic essence of the events. The point is made when Jane tells us that Brocklehurst 'seemed to me a tall gentleman; but then I was very little'; but the effect of her perspective goes much deeper than that. The extract is rich in the use of imagery, and we will need to look closely at that, as well as at style and mood, to understand the impact it makes.

The imagery associated here with Brocklehurst resonates throughout the novel, and has considerable thematic power. The initial image of the 'black pillar' which suddenly looms above Jane as she looks up from her submissive curtsey is developed at length. Brocklehurst is less a man than a piece of architecture, and he has all the unyielding qualities of a building, and none of the softness of humanity. The colour associated with him moves from black to 'sable-clad', and then, unexpectedly, to his 'grey eyes which twinkled under a pair of bushy brows'; and it matches his bass voice. He is straight, narrow, standing erect; his face is 'a carved mask' like the capital that tops a pillar. His movements are slow, portentous: 'bending from the perpendicular, he installed his person in the arm-chair'. We note here, particularly, the ponderous language which matches his manner – he is, after all, merely sitting down! He places Jane 'square and straight' in front of him to question her. His solemn style of speech matches his physique: abrupt, short, and occasionally stilted, as in his statement that 'Her size is small': Brocklehurst speaks in stone blocks.

Brocklehurst's appearance and voice are clearly intended to convey his character. Jane's initial doubt of his nature (pointedly resolved in 'for it was a man') is confirmed in the way in which Brontë describes him. The 'stony stranger' has a stony character: his face is 'grim', and its quality of a 'carved mask' expresses the repression of humanity in favour of a cold moral rectitude: 'all the lines of his frame were equally harsh and prim'. The emphasis on straightness and height suggests strict adherence to moral principle; but narrowness, too, suggests limitation in his ideas. The portrait is very sharply focused, perhaps edging towards the over-emphatic. But it is saved from parody by the presence of contrasting features: his twinkling eyes might suggest wit or goodwill as well as inquisitiveness; his large face and desire to confront Jane squarely may suggest straightforward-ness; the wolfishly large teeth hint at comic exaggeration. As a whole, however, Brontë bends her efforts here to portray Brocklehurst in speech, in actions, and in imagery as a stiff, cold-hearted man. There is no need for Brontë to express an opinion directly: it is all done dramatically.

In what follows the extract, Brocklehurst's character is explored in a more objective way as he questions Jane further. His character is no longer a matter of childish timorousness: it emerges from his own mouth. His question in the extract, 'are you a good child?', turns out to be intimately related to Brocklehurst's prejudices about religion, and about the Bible; it is to reduce his view to no greater absurdity than he does himself to say that love of the Psalms is good, and finding them uninteresting, as Jane admits she does later, 'proves [her] to have a wicked heart'. Brocklehurst's un-human nature emerges more clearly, too, for he shows no understanding of the kind of impact his words may have on Jane. His readiness to warn her of the threat of hell fire that awaits her when she dies, and his willingness to warn her of the likelihood of ill-health and death, show an extraordinary lack of tact, to say the least; and his story of the little boy who loves the psalms for ginger-nuts shows foolishness. We understand at this point that while Brocklehurst's corporeal frame may bend from the perpendicular, his principles – such as they are – never will.

It is evident that we, as readers, understand far more than is apparent to the child Jane in this episode. Brontë stresses Jane's little-ness: twice she has to look up at Brocklehurst; he 'seemed to me' tall; and when she is asked if she is good, she cannot say yes, because 'my little world held a contrary opinion'. The detail of her having to struggle with both hands against the resistance of the door-handle remind us that she is a child, small, not strong, and with cause to fear the large world she confronts, and the opening questions reveal Jane's apprehension. The whole extract is framed by fear – the form-less fear of a child trapped in a hostile world which she only partly understands. At the conclusion of the extract, her fear is vividly sym-bolised in Brocklehurst's 'large, prominent teeth'. Jane expresses the fear she cannot rationalise in a very direct and concrete way, and in a way peculiarly appropriate to a young child – in images; we interpret the imagery more subtly. This double vision is a function of the use of the complex narrator we considered in Chapter 1 – the younger, reacting, the older, commenting – and it produces a powerful effect here. With Brocklehurst's frightening fangs, we have entered, tee-tering on the brink of comedy, the world of Little Red Riding Hood, in which Brocklehurst plays the Wolf-Granny. At this point he becomes, briefly, a pantomime figure. We are tempted to laughter – as, indeed, an older Jane might be; but that does not make him any the less frightening for the immature Jane.

Jane does not have the advantage of meeting Brocklehurst when she is older, and in this respect, her reactions to him are very different from her feelings towards Mrs Reed, whom she finds it possible to pity when she visits her later in her last days. Brocklehurst, no matter how the older Jane may reinterpret him, is never in his own person other than the authority figure. Later, in the Lowood section, when Brocklehurst reappears, there are no new insights into his character. Some of his qualities are portrayed more emphatically, and the negative elements in his ideas are vividly dramatised. But he does not develop. There is no need, for he is what he appears to be – a representative of a harsh, Calvinist religiosity. The qualities which Jane sees in him – the stoniness, the blackness, the cold – are the qualities which the mature Jane sees in his religious standpoint. As the type of a particular religious view, he is important for his impact on Jane's development, and for the interplay between his and Rochester's and St John's attitudes to life.

If we now turn briefly to the impression Rochester makes on his first appearance, we find that a very different method is employed. He bursts into Jane's life in Volume 1, Chapter 12 as she listens, during an evening stroll, to the soft sounds of the natural world:

> A rude noise broke on these fine ripplings and whisperings, at once so far away and so clear: a positive tramp, tramp; a metallic clatter, which effaced the soft wave-wanderings; as, in a picture, the solid mass of a crag, or the rough boles of a great oak, drawn in dark and strong in the foreground, efface the aerial distance of azure hill, sunny horizon and blended clouds, where tint melts into tint.
>
> The din was on the causeway: a horse was coming; the windings of the lane yet hid it, but it approached. I was just leaving the stile; yet, as the path was narrow, I sat still to let it go by. In those days I was young, and all sorts of fancies bright and dark tenanted my mind: the memories of nursery stories were there amongst other rubbish; and when they recurred, maturing youth added to them a vigour and vividness beyond what childhood could give. As this horse approached, and as I watched for it to appear through the dusk, I

remembered certain of Bessie's tales wherein figured a North-of-England spirit, called a 'Gytrash'; which, in the form of horse, mule, or large dog, haunted solitary ways, and sometimes came upon belated travellers, as this horse was now coming upon me.

It was very near, but not yet in sight; when, in addition to the tramp, tramp, I heard a rush under the hedge, and close down by the hazel stems glided a great dog, whose black and white colour made him a distinct object against the trees. It was exactly one mask of Bessie's Gytrash, – a lion-like creature with long hair and a huge head: it passed me, however, quietly enough; not staying to look up, with strange pretercanine eyes, in my face, as I half expected it would. The horse followed, – a tall steed, and on its back a rider. The man, the human being, broke the spell at once. Nothing ever rode the Gytrash: it was always alone; and goblins, to my notions, though they might tenant the dumb carcasses of beasts, could scarce covet shelter in the common-place human form. No Gytrash was this, – only a traveller taking a short cut to Millcote. He passed, and I went on; a few steps, and I turned; a sliding sound, and an exclamation of 'What the deuce is to do now?' and a clattering tumble, arrested my attention. Man and horse were down; they had slipped on the sheet of ice which glazed the causeway. The dog came bounding back, and seeing his master in a predicament, and hearing the horse groan, barked till the evening hills echoed the sound; which was deep in proportion to his magnitude. He sniffed round the prostrate group, and then he ran up to me; it was all he could do, – there was no other help at hand to summon. I obeyed him, and walked down to the traveller, by this time struggling himself free of his steed. He efforts were so vigorous, I thought he could not be much hurt; but I asked him the question: –

'Are you injured, sir?'

I think he was swearing, but I am not certain; however, he was pronouncing some formula which prevented him from replying to me directly.

(pp. 128–9)

As in the Brocklehurst episode, Jane's feelings, and especially her feelings of fear, are all-important. To match the wolfish teeth of Brocklehurst, we have a reference to the nursery stories of Bessie; instead of the menacing black pillar, we have Jane's irrational terror of the Gytrash; instead of architectural imagery, we have the contrasting natural image of 'the solid mass of a crag'. To match the portrait of Brocklehurst himself, however, here we have almost nothing at all! Everything is impressions, mainly related to the horse or the dog; of Rochester himself we are told nothing except that he is good at swearing.

There is a great deal to consider – but we are not going to – about the ways in which the extract prefigures Rochester's character and behaviour, and how it relates to the rest of the novel. But here, and in what follows in the rest of this initial meeting of Rochester and Jane, we learn nothing definite at all about him. He is energy, he is mystery; but otherwise all is left to discover. Perhaps the most significant sentence in the extract is the opening sentence of the final paragraph: 'I think he was swearing, but I am not certain', for it illustrates Jane's function in the characterisation of Rochester. Here, as elsewhere, Jane obstructs our view of Rochester; we glimpse him over her shoulder, piecemeal. Where she is uncertain, so are we; what she does not know, we are ignorant of; and there is much about Rochester that falls into the regions of what Jane does not know.

The point is that these two characters, Brocklehurst and Rochester, are both considerable, but dealt with in very different ways because Brontë's intentions are entirely different. To put it most simply, in the case of Brocklehurst, she intends to reveal; with Rochester, to conceal. Brocklehurst is presented in a conceptual manner: there is little to develop, and subtlety of characterisation is not only not required, it would be actively obstructive. Brocklehurst holds no secrets. Rochester, on the other hand, is dealt with in a perceptual manner: his character emerges little by little, as Jane perceives more about him, or else is deceived about him, or corrects her earlier false impressions. He remains more or less mysterious for most, if not all, of the novel; even at the end, we still feel that there may be more to understand. In this process of character development, Jane is the medium through whom we perceive, gradually and with difficulty, the nature of the man. Rochester's development is, of course, more than a matter only of Jane's perceptions: Rochester himself changes, physically and morally, during the course of the novel, in ways which we shall refer to in a later chapter. None the less, his richness and fascination lie largely in his being presented as the invention of Jane's imperfect perceptions.

II: *Shirley*

From economy to amplitude. Whereas in *Jane Eyre*, characters are hurled before us, only to be brushed aside in the swift torrent of Jane's development, Brontë takes time in *Shirley* to introduce and round her characters in the manner of Dickens or Thackeray. Aside from the protagonists – Shirley Keeldar, Caroline Helstone, Robert and Louis Moore – a large cast takes the stage: Mr Yorke, Mrs Yorke, their children, Hortense, Mr Hall, William Farren, Joe Scott, Mrs Pryor, Mr Sympson, Mrs Sympson, Mr Helstone, Miss Mann, Miss Ainley, Sir Philip Nunnely, and the curates referred to in Chapter 1, among others, are all accorded space – sometimes, as with the Yorkes, to a point out of proportion to their impact on the action.

The kind of economical character parallelism which we noted in *Jane Eyre* in connection with the responses of Abbot, Bessie and Mrs Reed to Jane's behaviour is rare in the leisurely structure of *Shirley*.

Instead, Brontë evinces a talent for satirical tags, often alliterative. Mr Helstone is 'a clerical Cossack' (p. 68), Mrs Yorke a 'mighty matron' (p. 383), Mr Hall a 'Platonic parson' (p. 565). Equally vivid but without the alliteration, we have 'Corsican bandit' (Napoleon, p. 184), 'hired butcher' (Wellington, p. 391), and 'fat Adonis' (the Prince Regent, p. 391). Hard indeed to imagine such phrases finding a happy place in Jane Eyre's vocabulary. There is little opportunity in *Shirley* for the kind of partial revelation of character which Brontë uses for Rochester, since there is no actor-narrator who can felicitously obstruct our view; in *Shirley*, Brontë requires us to meet her characters face to face. Where mystery is generated about character, it is often as an effect of dialogue; look, for example, at the confrontation between Robert Moore and William Farren (towards the end of Chapter 8, pp. 156–7), which awakens our curiosity about Farren, and raises doubts in our minds about Moore's outlook. As in the other novels, Brontë sets us conundrums about her characters, but seems to find them harder to develop in third-person narrative.

A notable example is the mystery of Shirley's inconsistent behaviour towards Caroline, which is never resolved, and seems rather accidental than essential.

The difference between the two narrative perspectives is interestingly illustrated when Shirley herself is introduced. She does not appear until Chapter 11, by which time we have already come to know and sympathise with Caroline Helstone, and to know her 'Cossack' uncle, and it is as if from their implied point of view that we are invited to consider the heiress. There is something of a parallel with the interview between Brocklehurst and Jane Eyre in the last section: here, too, the protagonist is interviewed by a clergyman in the presence of another female; how different is the impression, however, as we shall see.

Our first perception of Shirley is filtered through the eyes of observers. Brontë opens her introduction of Shirley – it is a lengthy introduction, but the parts (pp. 210–11) we will need later may be briefly summarised – by saying that 'old Helstone felt' that there was 'real grace in ease of manner' when 'an erect, slight girl' walked up to him. She is shown with a 'silk apron full of flowers', and she speaks 'pleasantly'. There follows some discussion among Helstone, Mrs Pryor and Shirley about the orthodoxy of Shirley's religious views, at the end of which Helstone asks her to recite, as a proof of her rectitude, St Athanasius's creed. Shirley is saved from revealing the extent of her knowledge by the interruption of Tartar – 'a rather large, strong, and fierce-looking dog, very ugly, being of a breed between a mastiff and a bull-dog'. Shirley and Caroline co-operate in rescuing the flowers which Tartar has scattered, and thus is Shirley drawn to inquire of Helstone whether this young lady is his daughter. His niece, he responds, and the two women shake hands. The following description is prefaced by the words 'Caroline also looked at her hostess':

> Shirley Keeldar (she had no Christian name but Shirley: her parents, who had wished to have a son, finding that, after eight years of marriage, Providence had granted them only a daughter, bestowed on her the same masculine family cognomen they would have bestowed on a boy, if with a boy they had been blessed) – Shirley

Keeldar was no ugly heiress: she was agreeable to the eye. Her height
and shape were not unlike Miss Helstone's: perhaps in stature she
might have the advantage by an inch or two; she was gracefully made,
and her face, too, possessed a charm as well described by the word
grace as any other. It was pale naturally, but intelligent, and of varied
expression. She was not a blonde, like Caroline: clear and dark were
the characteristics of her aspect as to colour: her face and brow were
clear, her eyes of the darkest grey: no green lights in them, – trans-
parent, pure, neutral grey; and her hair of the darkest brown. Her features were distinguished; by which I do not mean that they were
high, bony, and Roman, being indeed rather small and slightly
marked than otherwise; but only that they were, to use a few French
words, 'fins, gracieux, spirituels:' mobile they were and speaking; but
their changes were not to be understood, nor their language all at
once. She examined Caroline seriously, inclining her head a little to
one side, with a thoughtful air.

'You see she is only a feeble chick,' observed Mr Helstone.

'She looks young – younger than I. How old are you?' she
inquired, in a manner that would have been patronizing if it had not
been extremely solemn and simple.

'Eighteen years and six months.'

'And I am twenty-one.'

She said no more; she had now placed her flowers on the table,
and was busied in arranging them.

'And St Athanasius's creed?' urged the Rector; 'you believe it all –
don't you?'

'I can't remember it quite all. I will give you a nosegay, Mr
Helstone, when I have given your niece one.'

She had selected a little bouquet of one brilliant and two or three
delicate flowers, relieved by a spray of dark verdure: she tied it with
silk from her workbox, and placed it on Caroline's lap; and then she
put her hands behind her, and stood, bending slightly towards her
guest, still regarding her, in the attitude and with something of the
aspect of a grave but gallant little cavalier. This temporary expression
of face was aided by the style in which she wore her hair, parted on
one temple and brushed in a glossy sweep above the forehead, whence
it fell in curls that looked natural, so free were their wavy undulations.

(pp. 211–12)

As we did with *Jane Eyre*, we will pay attention to the narrative perspective of the novel, and we will look at physical description, at relationships between characters and the parallels or contrasts which the author establishes; and we will try also to be aware of details of style which contribute to characterisation. We will try, too, to be alert to the thematic motifs which are touched on, and to links which may be made with the rest of the novel.

If we consider first the broad organisation of this description, we recognise a very clear structure. There is a brief discussion of Shirley's name and background; there is physical description at some length, and character is implied at times; there is a little dialogue, of a very straightforward kind – again perhaps implying a quality of character; there is a comparison between Shirley and Caroline; and there is a hint of some sort of opposition between religion and flowers, in that Shirley uses the flowers to divert attention from her ignorance of St Athanasius's creed. Let us consider these elements more closely, including, like Sherlock Holmes, the dog which does not appear there.

It is often noted that Shirley was a male name until Brontë turned it into a girl's. Here Brontë insists on its masculinity: Shirley's parents wanted a boy, so they made her into one. (It is an irrelevant but none the less diverting chance that has turned the name, thanks to the powerful influence of Shirley Temple, into one that is widely thought of as wholly unmasculine.) Later in this chapter, Shirley speaks of herself as 'an esquire . . . quite gentlemanlike', and says that she feels that her name 'is enough to inspire me with a touch of manhood'. She is interested in business, would like to be a church-warden, a magistrate and captain of yeomanry, a colonel or a justice of the peace. Here originates her playful style of 'Captain Keeldar', which is first used by Helstone. Shirley is in reality very feminine – a quality which this portrait stresses, as we shall see; but she has a toughness and self-reliance, and an independence of spirit which single her out from the generality of her sex, and which is sharply distinguished by contrast with Caroline's more conventional virtues. In the dialogue with Helstone in the extract we see independence and confidence in her unabashed but tactful avoidance of the Athanasian Creed.

Shirley's appearance is dwelt on. Brontë warns us that it is important in speaking of her features: 'their changes were not to be understood, nor their language all at once'. It is her intention to develop
here a complex and somewhat mysterious character who will hold
our interest. Fittingly, for she is to be the heroine, Shirley is an inch
or two taller than Caroline, though like her in build; she has a
stronger, dark and clear colouring, contrasting with Caroline's
weaker blonde. (We are left to guess at Caroline's feelings on being
dismissed as 'a feeble chick' by comparison with Shirley!) Her features suggest intellect and emotional liveliness in their 'varied expression . . . mobile . . . and speaking'. She has a 'thoughtful air', and a
manner 'extremely solemn and simple'. Everything about her suggests directness, openness, responsiveness. Her appearance, like her
manner, establishes an element of masculinity in her. At the end of
the extract she is given 'the aspect of a grave but gallant little cavalier', with hair to match; alliteration here illuminates the element of
paradox in Shirley's character.

An oddity in her physical description is that it begins with the
unwarranted negative statement that she 'was no ugly heiress'.
Brontë stresses that 'she was agreeable to the eye'. Whence the idea
of ugliness? Why should we expect her to be ugly? The idea seems to
be an echo of the appearance of Tartar, a decidedly ugly animal,
introduced only a few lines earlier as fierce-looking and strong as
well as ugly. The word suggests, that is, a link between Tartar and his
owner: not just of ownership, but of character, too. Thus the contrast between Shirley and the dog – which, after all, hardly requires
emphasis! – encourages us perversely to look for parallels between
them; and, sure enough, we can find them. Later in the novel, Tartar
and his owner will co-operate in routing the curates (Chapter 15).
Elsewhere Tartar shares Shirley's opinions about other characters: he
likes Sweeting better than Donne and Malone; he also likes Mr Hall
and Louis Moore. Eventually he even comes to look rather like Louis
Moore!

Much, then, emerges from the description of Shirley's appearance.
Let us turn now to what she says. In the dialogue of the extract,
Shirley's straightforwardness is evident along with her assumption of
superiority over Caroline, and equality with Helstone. If we make a

comparison with the *Jane Eyre* extract, some interesting differences emerge. Shirley examines Caroline in something of the manner of Brocklehurst, but her manner is much more straightforward and less pompous. Instead of Brocklehurst's 'Her size is small. What is her age?', we see Shirley rapidly moving to direct conversation in 'She looks young . . . How old are you?' Brontë stresses Shirley's sincerity by saying that her manner 'would have been patronizing if it had not been extremely solemn and simple'. We can compare Shirley with Jane, too, and see the advantage of her maturity. She is unabashed at her error about Caroline's relationship with Helstone, asks directly about Caroline's age, but is happy to speak of her in the third person to Helstone – thus assuming the role of an elder, as she does also with the words, 'And I am twenty-one', which set the seal on the impression the behaviour of the two girls has already given. Her diverting Helstone from St Athanasius's creed by offering him a nosegay suggests a balance of honesty and tact. She ignores – or refuses to acknowledge – Helstone's inquiry about whether she believes 'it all'. 'I can't remember' looks as if it may be a euphemism for rejection of, or lack of sympathy with, the principles enshrined in the creed.

Our final topic – the use made of nature – is referred to elsewhere and needs only brief discussion here. The association of Shirley with flowers is something which we may perhaps conventionally see as an expression of femininity. She appears first, before the extract begins, with 'her little silk apron full of flowers'. The feminine elements here are unmistakable: the apron, the silk, the 'little' all suggest the conventional view of a woman's role. By the end of the extract, however, the emphasis has changed: as Shirley delivers her bouquet into Caroline's lap, she bows slightly, like a cavalier giving a love token to a lady. The flowers for Caroline and Helstone are presented as a gesture expressive of Shirley herself, and thus she is associated with nature. The theme is developed at the conclusion of the extract, for her hair 'fell in curls that looked natural' – in contrast with the fashionable false curls such as Mrs Brocklehurst wears in *Jane Eyre*. The language used – 'free', 'wavy', 'undulations' – suggests different aspects of naturalness. In contrast, Helstone's obsession with St Athanasius and his creed is made to look distinctly unnatural, and perhaps a little unreasonable. Shortly before the beginning of the extract he has mocked Shirley as a 'Jacobin', and 'free-thinker', and, grasping her hands unthinkingly, caused her to 'let fall her whole cargo of flowers'; his role is thus to be an opponent of nature. In the extract, when Shirley sidesteps the creed and offers Helstone a nosegay, she is opposing more than the specific demand he here makes of her; she posits a different set of beliefs about life and the world; very generally, we may see this as offering the idea of nature as an alternative to, and perhaps opponent of, conventional religion.

Thinking about the relationship between the extract and the novel as a whole, we may begin to see the opposition between nature and religion in the extract as a parallel with the opposition between business and romance which we noted in Chapter 1. As if to confirm the implied link, the question of business is brought up immediately after the extract we have been considering (see pp. 214–15). It is clear that this extract is more carefully organised than might appear on a casual reading. Superficially no more than a description of Shirley, it shows Brontë developing a specific set of ideas about the nature of her heroine, and forging links between a number of different strands in the action and themes of the novel.

It is clear also that the ideas which emerge from the extract are beyond the knowledge or skill of the implied observers – Helstone and his niece – to communicate. Despite appearances, there can be no doubt that an omniscient narrator is at work; in contrast with *Jane Eyre*, there is no suggestion that one of the actors in the scene is looking back on past experience. The different narrative method helps to explain the use of French in describing Shirley: Brontë lacks here the discipline of the first-person narrator. The casual way in which French is introduced – 'to use a few French phrases'- looks like an astonishingly naive admission of its pointlessness; it is far from clear that the use of French contributes anything to our impression of Shirley that a few English words could not. The novel as a whole is peppered with French, but the effect is far from adding spice. It seems, indeed, a gratuitous intrusion, irritating in the extract as it is in general; only in the scenes involving Hortense, or Louis Moore, does it sound right. As if intent upon highlighting the contrast, Brontë caps her French epithets for Shirley's features with a livelier, English and rather Chaucerian cadence – 'mobile they were, and speaking'.

Aside from the gratuitous French, the portrait of Shirley is a complex piece of writing which prepares us for a subtle and central use of the character in the structure of the novel. Brontë ensures that Shirley is linked with the religious theme in the novel, and with the themes of trade, of feminism, and of nature, and that the parallel between her and Caroline is set up. It is an interestingly contradictory portrait, stressing an uneasy balance of feminine and masculine in Shirley, of politeness and wilfulness, gaiety and seriousness. The ambiguity persists to the end of the chapter when she vanishes from the scene with a wave of her hand 'white as a lily and fine as a fairy's': there is an element of idealisation here; but it is moderated because at the same time she is laughing joyously at having managed to ruffle Helstone's equanimity. In her relationships, too, the contradictory essence of Shirley is maintained in the later stages of the novel, when her independence of spirit demands the right to submit to a husband.

The simile of the fairy which is applied to Shirley might appear superficially to be a rather tired comparison, or at least conventional; but it is in fact pointed, for it suggests Shirley's association with the romance theme in the novel. She shares this association with Caroline, the 'wood-nymph' of Chapter 22. The point, however, does not become fully apparent until the fairy image becomes one of the keynotes of the conclusion of the novel, when the housekeeper refers to the vanished 'fairishes' and lost romance of yesteryear.

By no means all the characterisation of *Shirley* is equally rich. Like *Jane Eyre*, it has its less rounded characters: Joe Scott, for example, is comparable with Mr Brocklehurst in rather embodying a concept than showing the spontaneity of life; William Farren is an idealised figure, not an individual. All the major characters, however, are fully realised, rounded, and interesting individual portraits – not, perhaps, as complex as Shirley, but none the less convincing and interesting.

III: *Villette*

With *Villette*, we move beyond, rather than back to, the perceptual
world of *Jane Eyre*. The imperfect observation which we noted in
connection with Rochester is more evident here. No character is
fixed: we are constantly shown a new side – a complementary aspect,
or a contrasting quality – of a character already introduced. Everything is dominated by the viewpoint of Lucy Snowe, and her perceptions change from moment to moment. Not only that, but her
honesty about her perceptions is in question from an early stage; it is
many pages before she admits that she has understood from the first
that 'Dr John' and 'Graham Bretton' are one and the same, and that
she recognised him as soon as he appeared at Madame Beck's pensionnat. The portrait of the drunken Irish woman – Mrs Sweeny –
at the beginning of the Belgian phase of the novel (Chapter 8) is
exceptional in being self-contained. Elsewhere the characters range
into new dimensions with the unpredictability of actuality. It is hard
in this novel to find anything comparable to the portrait of Mr
Brocklehurst in *Jane Eyre*.

The presentation of Monsieur Paul is typical. We get to know him
by degrees, as Lucy does; thus he constantly surprises us with new
facets. He is a character whom perhaps most of us find a little inade-
quate as the focus of Lucy Snowe's romantic feelings. Tetchy, irrational, demanding, conventional, sulky, and self-immolatingly
Catholic, he is far less the romantic hero than Rochester. There is
about the smell of the cigar which advertises his presence, as there is
about Rochester's, a hint of the fishy fume which heralds Satan in
Book IV of *Paradise Lost*; but there is nothing epic here – the smell
is, after all, only a cigar. Paul Emanuel is a *little* man: energetic, even
violent, yet he has nothing elemental about him. It is none the less
evident that Monsieur Paul Emanuel is a rich character. Although
we find it hard to see him as the hero, we continue to feel that he
has a potential as yet unrevealed; he has the depth, and the promise,
of actual people whom we know; we can never say that we have
plumbed his depths. Here is Monsieur Paul's reaction to Lucy's
increased social activity when she begins to study German with Polly
(Chapter 26):

That . . . self-elected judge of mine, the professor in the Rue Fossette, discovering by some surreptitious, spying means, that I was no longer so stationary as hitherto, but went out regularly at certain hours of certain days, took it upon himself to place me under surveillance. People said M. Emanuel had been brought up amongst Jesuits. I should more readily have accredited this report had his manoeuvres been better masked. As it was I doubted it. Never was a more undisguised schemer, a franker, looser intriguer. He would analyze his own machinations: elaborately contrive plots, and forthwith indulge in explanatory boasts of their skill. I know not whether I was more amused or provoked by his stepping up to me one morning and whispering solemnly that he 'had his eye on me: *he* at least would discharge the duty of a friend and not leave me entirely to my own devices. My proceedings seemed at present very unsettled: he did not know what to make of them: he thought his cousin Beck very much to blame in suffering this sort of fluttering inconsistency in a teacher attached to her house. What had a person devoted to a serious calling, that of education, to do with Counts and Countesses, hotels and chateaux? To him I seemed altogether "en l'air." On his faith, he believed I went out six days in the seven.'

I said, 'Monsieur exaggerated. I certainly had enjoyed the advantage of a little change lately, but not before it had become necessary; and the privilege was by no means exercised in excess.'

'Necessary! How was it necessary? I was well enough, he supposed? Change necessary! He would recommend me to look at the Catholic "religieuses", and study *their* lives. *They* asked no change.'

I am no judge of what expression crossed my face when he thus spoke, but it was one which provoked him: he accused me of being reckless, worldly, and epicurean; ambitious of greatness and feverishly athirst for the pomps and vanities of life. It seems I had no 'dévouement', no 'recueillement' in my character; no spirit of grace, faith, sacrifice, or self-abasement. Feeling the inutility of answering these charges, I mutely continued the correction of a pile of English exercises.

'He could see in me nothing Christian: like many other Protestants, I revelled in the pride and self-will of paganism.'

I slightly turned from him, nestling still closer under the wing of silence.

A vague sound grumbled between his teeth; it could not surely be a 'juron': he was too religious for that; but I am certain I heard the

word *sacré*. Grievous to relate, the same word was repeated, with the
unequivocal addition of *mille* something, when I passed him about
two hours afterwards in the corridor, prepared to go and take my
German lesson in the Rue Crécy. Never was a better little man, in
some points, than M. Paul: never, in others, a more waspish little
despot.

(pp. 386–8)

As with the other novels, we need to look carefully at the narrator's
role in the portraiture, and it is well worth spending a few moments
considering the tone of this scene in general before proceeding to
detail. An immediate response, I think, is to feel that the impact of
the portrait is oddly distanced by the use of reported speech – which
masquerades here, as often in the novel, as direct speech: Monsieur
Paul whispers 'that he "had his eye on me . . ."'; Lucy tells us that 'I
said, "Monsieur exaggerated"'. In the reported speech, Lucy Snowe
adopts linguistic forms which Monsieur Paul would have used. The
effect is to stress that the whole trivial episode is located in Lucy
Snowe's memory. There is vividness, but not the immediacy of *Jane
Eyre*; the meeting is glimpsed through a veil created partly by time,
partly by Lucy's intermediacy. As a result, what we as readers experience here is not the impact of Monsieur Paul himself, but Lucy's
feelings about his impact. The whole extract is framed by Lucy's
opinions about Monsieur Paul as a 'self-elected judge' and a 'waspish
little despot'. What she says about his behaviour in the extract supports her opinion.

The portrait which emerges is very coherent. What Lucy says
about Monsieur Paul is matched by the brow-beating style of his
speech, with its repetitions and rhetorical questions, and by his
angry mutterings and 'jurons' when he fails to win his point. The
portrait is, if anything, too coherent to be realistic.

Lucy, indeed, does not pretend to be objective, nor does she
pretend to be accurate. On the contrary, she tells us repeatedly of her
uncertainties: 'I doubted' his having been brought up among Jesuits,
'I know not whether I was more amused or provoked' by his behaviour, 'I am no judge of what expression crossed my face' at his
behaviour. Her perceptions are, then, incomplete. Her opinions, on

the other hand, are thoroughly decided: 'Never was a more undisguised schemer'; 'Never was a better little man . . . never . . . a more
waspish little despot.' We know from the rest of the novel that Lucy's
ignorance of Monsieur Paul is much greater than she imagined at
the period of which she is writing – and her narrative, though ema-
nating from a more mature point of view, does not see fit to tell us
what she later discovered.

The clues to the 'real' Monsieur Paul are there, but Lucy Snowe at
this stage does not recognise their meaning. At this point, it is hard
to imagine that Monsieur Paul is to be her romantic hero. She fails
to see the significance of his attempt at tyranny; she fails to see what
religion means to him; and she fails to see that he is a serious person:
very different from herself in outlook and habits, but none the less
with valid and valuable ideas about how he – and she – should
conduct their lives. Her repeated use of the word 'little' to describe
him is difficult to interpret. To be sure, Monsieur Paul is not tall;
but 'little' may imply a whole range of emotional responses to him,
from fondness to contempt, and including bitterness, vexation and
unwilling respect on the way. It is hard to know from this extract the
precise feeling which underlies the word; and that perhaps reflects
Lucy's ambivalent feelings about him. She admits that she did not
know 'whether to be more amused or provoked' by Monsieur Paul's
behaviour in the extract, and her doubt looks like a heavy clue to her
uncertainties about him in general.

What emerges most strongly for us from the episode is the comic
side of Monsieur Paul. He may be a schemer, but he is openly so:
'undisguised' is how Lucy – usually in disguise herself – puts it. Her
mixed amusement and anger at his statement that he is keeping an
eye on her sets the tone of our response. His 'whispering solemnly',
however, stresses the comic element: this is a stage intriguer. Lucy
pursues the comic aspect of his behaviour when she apes his style of
speech in 'On his faith'. Though she may claim to be no judge of the
expression which crosses her face at his words to her in paragraph
four, that it is one of amusement is suggested by its provoking him
to wilder transports of criticism. His accusations that Lucy is 'epicurean, ambitious of greatness, and feverishly athirst for the pomps
and vanities of life' are so distant from the nature and possibilities of

her situation as to be self-evidently foolish: she has no money to be epicurean, no route to fulfil ambition, and there is little temptation to pomp and vanity in the gloomy corridors of the Pensionnat. Lucy's use of French for key points in his criticism shows her feelings: she understands what he is saying, but takes no notice. Her failure to translate implies unwillingness to accept. (How different is the effect from the use of French in *Shirley*! Here it is central to the impact of the characterisation.)

Monsieur Paul's accusations become outrageous in the fourth paragraph, when he claims to find nothing Christian in Lucy's behaviour, and broadens his attack to include 'many other Protestants'. He becomes, with his dark mutterings in the final paragraph, as much a pantomime figure in Lucy's mature eyes as Brocklehurst, for different reasons, was in Jane Eyre's. Not until the last sentence does the eye of Lucy Snowe melt when she admits Monsieur Paul's virtues; but it is only a partial thaw, for the repeated 'little' reinforces his comic aspects, his stature so ill matching the violence of his transports. Later in the novel, the word becomes less ambiguous when Lucy, having accepted Monsieur Paul as an honest and virtuous man, and her lover, calls him her 'dear little man' (Chapter 35, p. 490).

Let us look now more closely at how this episode relates to the novel. We will begin with Monsieur Paul's character, and then consider themes.

The ambiguities in Monsieur Paul which appear in the extract are exaggerated when we look at the whole novel, which shows him often acting in a manner similar to his behaviour towards Lucy in the extract. He is repeatedly interfering, obtrusive, despotic, inquisitive, repressive. In the same way that he lumps her in with 'other Protestants', he includes her in his tirade against 'les Anglaises' in Chapter 29 (p. 428). He rummages in her desk as a matter of custom, according to Lucy, who in Chapter 29 claims that 'that hand of M. Emanuel's was on intimate terms with my desk' (p. 430). He tells her which pictures are suitable for her to look at in the gallery in Chapter 19 (this episode is discussed in Chapter 6 of this book); he demands in Chapter 30 (pp. 444–5) that she take a test, and carries out his threat in Chapter 35 (p. 495). He objects to the colour of her dress on the picnic in Chapter 33 (p. 471); characteristically, he chooses to consider its pink shade almost adulterously violent. We should not forget, however, that he has the virtue associated with this vice: he can spur Lucy to do what she has not done before, and it is only because of his despotic behaviour that she is pushed to play a role in the school play in Chapter 14 (p. 202) – and is thus enabled to discover more in herself than she knew existed.

Throughout the extract the theme of religion is linked with Monsieur Paul. Lucy seems not to acknowledge its importance because the religion in question is not hers. Lucy shows great fear, but little understanding, of the emotional power of Catholicism, and fails to recognise the nature of the influence which it can exert over the lives of its adherents. It is a belief which she distrusts because she senses in it something too passionate for her own nature to contend with; in Chapter 15 she derides the Catholic church into which she wanders as 'a Babylonish furnace' (p. 235), and the faith, patronisingly, as 'honest popish superstition' (p. 235). Only by degrees does she become aware of its real importance for Monsieur Paul.

The religious theme has diverse aspects in the extract. Lucy's amusingly acid reference to Jesuitical machinations is a negative aspect: it reflects Lucy's indiscriminate suspicion of Romish practices; more specifically, it looks forward to what Lucy sees later in the novel as the evil power of the unholy trinity comprising Madame Walravens, Père Silas and Madame Beck. The tirade of Monsieur Paul is less negative, for it grows out of convictions which are later discovered to be genuine. His criticism of Lucy as 'en l'air' (out of touch with reality) is perhaps understandable, if not persuasive, coming from a man who is shown later to possess remarkable constancy and self-discipline in his devotion to the memory and family of his dead, and saintly, wife. In the light of his self-abnegation, the reference he makes in the extract to 'the Catholic "religieuses"', and the demand he makes for 'grace, faith, sacrifice, or self-abasement' may appear less unreasonable. The florid terms in which he piles these abstractions on each other appear more like the zeal of strong conviction, less like empty pomp. In contrast, the continuing chill of Lucy Snowe, persevering with correcting English exercises while

Monsieur Paul rants, or turning from him, 'nestling still closer under the wing of silence', begins to look unfeeling, or perhaps like a retreat from emotion; she seems too comfortable in her cocoon. Lucy would never be guilty of muttering imprecations as he does; perhaps she is also incapable of feeling as strongly as he does about another person. So violent, indeed, is the contrast between Monsieur Paul and his observer that we are inclined to wonder what he sees in her. He is volatile, she is reserved; he is talkative, she silent; he is Catholic, she Protestant; he is emotional, she cold. The criticisms which he launches at her amount to reiterations of their essential difference. He speaks to her here in a language far more foreign to her emotionally than his French. Equally, the manner of Lucy's account, like her observation of Polly which we discussed in Chapter 1, savours of a naturalist reporting the behaviour of a hitherto unknown species, and reinforces the strong impression of her separateness, and even aloofness.

The portrait of Monsieur Paul, like other portraits in *Villette*, turns back to the narrator. When we look at her vision of Monsieur Paul closely, we notice that the sheer energy of her criticism of him – 'self-elected judge', 'waspish little despot' – derives at least in part from her own inadequacy. That repeated 'little' reveals unwillingness to recognise his real virtues, especially when we note the unbalance in the extract between her cataloguing of his faults, and the single compliment she pays him. In this novel, the characters and the narrator are held in uneasy equipoise, constantly commenting on each other, never allowing us to feel that we fully know either the observer or the observed.

Conclusions

1. Brontë employs different methods of characterisation. Some characters are merely sketched in as part of the necessary authentication of background. Others are used to embody concepts which are important to the novel, and do not develop. The major characters are revealed gradually, are developed, and undergo change.

2. Brontë uses imagery and symbolism, setting, speech, gesture and action, and appearance to communicate character.

3. Even in *Shirley*, Brontë seems to be happiest when she is exploring character through the medium of an observer. In the other novels, the narrator's perceptions are essential to the process of characterisation.

4. In *Jane Eyre* and *Villette*, the method of characterisation reveals as much about the observer as it does about the observed. Jane and Lucy express themselves in the process of describing others.

5. In the three portraits we have considered, as in Brontë's approach to characterisation in general, religion plays a role in one way or another.

Methods of Analysis

1. Remember, first of all and last of all, that a character in a novel has no independent life: he is part of a fictional structure. If we are dealing with a character, we are dealing with him in relation to the other characters that he talks to, and in relation to the themes and mood of the novel as a whole. We cannot see Brocklehurst independently from Jane Eyre, for example: they are parts of a whole, and thus, when we speak of Brocklehurst, we must also speak of Jane, and of the religious theme, and of links between Brocklehurst, Rochester, and St John.

2. Consider the points mentioned in the second of the conclusions, and how they express character:
   - what a character does – including posture, gesture and deeds
   - what a character says – meaning and intention
   - how he says it – vocabulary and syntax can reveal nuances which are not expressed directly
   - how a character looks, either by nature or by mood
   - imagery or symbolism associated with the character.

3. Look at the interplay between character and other elements:
   - the relationship between character and setting
   - the relationship between character and theme
   - the relationship between character and mood
   - especially, the relationships between characters.

4. Seldom in written work will you have time to comment on all these subjects. Selection will be necessary, using all the judgement and imagination which you can command.

5. Last, but certainly not least:
   • Pay special attention to the observer of the character, or the narrator: how do the observer's prejudices and interests affect the portrait? How does the portraiture help to bring the observer or narrator to life?

Further Work

Here, as everywhere, you must exercise judgement. You will not be able to consider all the points outlined above, but must select those you think are most appropriate. First of all, you will need to select what to work on from a lengthy list here: the opportunities for analysis of character or study of characterisation are plentiful!

Jane Eyre: You might look at a portrait, such as that of Helen Burns or of Miss Temple in Volume 1, Chapter 8; or you might wish to look at a character who occupies a larger role in the novel, such as St John Rivers, considering in particular the page in Chapter 30 in which he offers Jane the post of school-mistress (from where Jane says, 'I thank you for the proposal . . .' to the point where he leaves and she says that '. . . still he puzzled me', pp. 381–2). Alternatively, you might prefer to look at how character emerges from a more social scene, such as the visit of the Ingram party to Thornfield in Volume 2, Chapter 2 (possibly the introduction of the visitors, beginning with 'There were but eight . . . and concluding a page later with the paragraph which ends, '. . . with a truly imperial dignity', pp. 200–1).

Shirley: Try Mr Yorke in the first four paragraphs of Chapter 4 ('A Yorkshire gentleman . . . a man in whom awe, imagination, and tenderness lack', pp. 76–7), or Caroline Helstone in the first four paragraphs of Chapter 6

('Mademoiselle Moore, . . . the idea was not logical, but Hortense had perfect faith in it', pp. 102–3); or look at how character emerges from the conversation between Caroline and her uncle in Chapter 7, when they discuss marriage ('"Uncle," said she, "whenever you speak of marriage . . ."' down to the end of the first paragraph of narrative following the dialogue, ending '. . . but it was years since they had first made their cells in her brain', pp. 124–5). The portraits of Miss Mann and Miss Ainley (Chapter 10) deserve analysis, too, either independently or in comparison.

Villette: Madame Beck is a particularly rich character, but it is not easy to choose from the wealth of material to hand. The opening of Chapter 19 is a brief but interesting passage to explore; the first three paragraphs (pp. 270–1) are sufficient. You may prefer to consider the diverting and irritating Ginevra Fanshawe, who has an entertaining conversation with Lucy at the beginning of Chapter 27 (from the beginning of paragraph 3, 'As Miss Fanshawe and I were dressing . . .' down to the end of the conversation nearly two pages on, pp. 393–4). A little later in the chapter, there is a comparison between Ginevra and Paulina, both from Lucy's and from Dr Bretton's points of view ('At dinner that day, Ginevra and Paulina each looked, in her own way, very beautiful . . .' down to the end of the paragraph a little over two pages later, '. . . by what a good and strong root her graces held to the firm soil of reality', pp. 397–400); this would make an interesting but complex exercise.

3

Setting

Setting is the environment in which the action in a novel takes place. It is linked with characterisation, because it is the background against which the characters are placed, and is an important part of the illusion of actuality in Brontë's novels; it can also be used to support thematic ideas. Setting is much more than the natural world: it includes other aspects of physical environment such as houses and rooms, sea or land, country, and all the associations of these; it also includes the emotional environment – the tone, mood and atmosphere which are generated partly by description of the physical environment.

One preliminary point which we must be clear about is that setting is essential to the impact of a novel. It is not something added on, which could conceivably be removed. In the course of reading a novel, most of us perhaps have been tempted to skip the descriptive bits, and, in point of fact, there is no law against skipping. Studying is more than reading, however, and in studying a novel we should give special attention to precisely those parts of the book which are not action and dialogue. Those are passages in which the ideological world of the novel is likely to be most clearly expressed.

In Brontë's novels, the setting is always richly depicted and powerfully felt. Places are tangible and authentic; the characters are conscious of them. The Pensionnat is as convincing as Lowood – and, of course, both grew directly out of Brontë's own experience. Place names are often as important as the names of characters, and have powerful emotional associations: consider the different feelings evoked by 'Thornfield', 'Fieldhead', and 'Labassecour' (farmyard); the names of places far across oceans – India and the West Indies – have romantic associations for Brontë. In this chapter we focus on three extracts which use the natural world in distinct ways. We could equally well have used three rooms, or three houses, or three churches – and such examples are suggested in the section at the end of the chapter on further work – but in Charlotte Brontë's novels the natural world stands out as the most important aspect of setting. All the novels draw deeply on nature, and use it to generate symbolic meanings. Also, there is plenty of evidence that for Brontë the concept of nature has meanings far beyond its use simply as setting – a point which our discussion should bring out.

I: *Jane Eyre*

From *Jane Eyre* we take the prelude to Rochester's declaration of love, when Jane is walking in the garden at Thornfield, in Volume 2, Chapter 8.

I walked a while on the pavement; but a subtle, well-known scent – that of a cigar – stole from some window; I saw the library casement open a handbreadth; I knew I might be watched thence; so I went apart into the orchard. No nook in the grounds more sheltered and more Eden-like; it was full of trees, it bloomed with flowers: a very high wall shut it out from the court, on one side; on the other, a beech avenue screened it from the lawn. At the bottom was a sunk fence; its sole separation from lonely fields: a winding walk, bordered with laurels and terminating in a giant horse-chestnut, circled at the base by a seat, led down to the fence. Here one could wander unseen. While such honey-dew fell, such silence reigned, such gloaming gathered, I felt as if I could haunt such shade for ever: but in threading the flower and fruit-parterres at the upper part of the enclosure, enticed there by the light the now-rising moon cast on this more open quarter, my step is stayed – not by sound, not by sight, but once more by a warning fragrance.

Sweet-briar and southernwood, jasmine, pink, and rose have long been yielding their evening sacrifice of incense: this new scent is neither of shrub nor flower; it is – I know it well – it is Mr Rochester's cigar. I look round and I listen. I see trees laden with ripening fruit. I hear a nightingale warbling in a wood half a mile off; no moving form is visible, no coming step audible; but that perfume increases: I must flee. I make for the wicket leading to the shrubbery, and I see Mr Rochester entering. I step aside into the ivy recess; he will not stay long: he will soon return whence he came, and if I sit still he will never see me.

But no – eventide is as pleasant to him as to me, and this antique garden as attractive; and he strolls on, now lifting the gooseberry-tree branches to look at the fruit, large as plums, with which they are laden; now taking a ripe cherry from the wall; now stooping towards a knot of flowers, either to inhale their fragrance or to admire the dew-beads on their petals. A great moth goes humming by me; it alights on a plant at Mr Rochester's foot: he sees it, and bends to examine it.

'Now, he has his back towards me,' thought I, 'and he is occupied too; perhaps, if I walk softly, I can slip away unnoticed.'

I trod on an edging of turf that the crackle of the pebbly gravel might not betray me: he was standing among the beds at a yard or two distant from where I had to pass; the moth apparently engaged him. 'I shall get by very well,' I meditated. As I crossed his shadow, thrown long over the garden by the moon, not yet risen high, he said quietly, without turning –

'Jane, come and look at this fellow.'

I had made no noise: he had not eyes behind – could his shadow feel? I started at first, and then I approached him.

'Look at his wings,' said he, 'he reminds me rather of a West Indian insect; one does not often see so large and gay a night-rover in England: there! he is flown.'

The moth roamed away. I was sheepishly retreating also: but Mr Rochester followed me, and when we reached the wicket, he said: –

'Turn back: on so lovely a night it is a shame to sit in the house; and surely no one can wish to go to bed while sunset is thus at meeting with moonrise.'

(pp. 278–80)

We will be looking at many different elements in the extract. In particular, we should consider how the setting appeals to the senses – the use of colour, sound, smell, taste, and texture; the choice of language and other aspects of style; the use of imagery and symbolism; and the relationship between these things and the characters in the extract. We will look also at the powerful moral implications in the extract and, finally, at how the extract relates to the rest of the novel.

Let us first distinguish bones and flesh. The context of this extract is easily outlined. The scene is the garden at Thornfield. The passage introduces a critical moment in the relationship between Jane and Rochester. She is drawn, almost unwillingly, towards Rochester; she has sensed his attraction to her, but has no understanding of him, or of the nature or extent of his interest in her. He is to her a conundrum. Thus later she is unsurprised, though distraught, at the plan which he is shortly to propose of sending her to Ireland. Equally, it is no surprise when he embraces her and declares his love – if not his intentions.

This bare summary makes the novel sound like a simple romance. It is much more, as the extract makes clear. Attached to the bones of the relationship there is a wealth of emotional and moral resonance which emerges from the use of setting. That is what we shall explore.

Let us begin by noticing the components of the passage. It is a description of the natural world, but it is not only the natural world. This is a garden and, moreover, an orchard; it is, therefore, manmade, and not the wilder nature which Jane confronts, half-fearfully, on her departure from Thornfield later on in the novel. There are two characters, one walking in the garden, the other interrupting her thoughts; there is, thus, if we wish to view it in this light, an echo of the first meeting of Jane and Rochester, which we considered in Chapter 2. She tries to avoid notice; yet, with what seems to her almost supernatural perception (but we, perhaps, guess that he has been watching for her) he divines her presence, and catches her attention at the very moment when she thinks to escape unnoticed. The elements of the passage suggest that she is quarry, he hunter. There is no 'sex' as such in *Jane Eyre* – nor is there in the other novels. Yet the sense of sexual feeling is as powerful as it is subtle here, as it is in many other scenes.

Next, we should consider the kind of impact the setting makes on the heroine. The passage is sensuous – it is full of the scent of many flowers, the encompassing silence before the dialogue is reinforced by the sweet song of the nightingale; there is the sweetness of honey-dew, the riotous colour of flowers including jasmine, pink and rose; the weight of the fruit ripening on the trees and bushes. Brontë uses all her senses; but there is more to the natural world described here than sensuous appeal. Nature is here alive, sentient: muscular linguistic forms crowd upon us ('fell', 'reigned', 'gathered', 'yielding', 'laden', 'warbling', 'humming'), giving the garden a sense of urgent life. There is fecundity here, with fruit 'large as plums' on the gooseberry bushes, the cherries ripened; the garden oozes honey-dew and dew-beads.

The setting is rich indeed. But what strikes us most forcefully is not the wealth of scent and colour, but the sense of retreat: Jane tells us that she 'went apart'; the nook she flees to is 'sheltered', 'screened'; she thinks she is 'unseen', wishes to be 'unnoticed'. We may be reminded here, perhaps, of Jane's earlier retreat, the window-seat behind the red curtains in the breakfast-room, which we looked at in Chapter 1: on one side of her shelter there is 'a very high wall', while on another 'a beech avenue screened it from the lawn', and on a third 'was a sunk fence; its sole separation from lonely fields'. Jane steps 'aside into the ivy recess'. Here, she communes with herself, shut off from her (comparatively) busy world, composing her mind and calming her body. Jane is happy here: 'I felt as if I could haunt such a shade for ever' – though perhaps it is only unquiet spirits which engage in haunting, and a confident one does not need to seek the shade. Again, it is the notion of retreat and concealment which appeals to Jane.

Let us remember, now, that she is not really alone in her retreat: Rochester comes too, and he knows that she is there. She, however, does not know that he knows, and her instinct is to remain hidden. The tremor that his arrival causes is recognised in the switch to present tense from near the end of the first paragraph ('. . . my step is stayed . . .') until the end of the third paragraph. Rochester's arrival is heralded by the insistent, insinuating scent of his cigar: first it is 'a subtle, well-known scent [which] stole from a window'; then it is the 'warning fragrance' which alerts her to his presence; and finally it is a 'perfume' which increases, until Rochester himself appears in person. There is something sinister in the manner in which his smoke approaches by degrees. That he is a foreign element in this world is indicated by the oxymoron used to describe the aroma of his cigar: 'a warning fragrance'. Let us keep in mind, however, that in Brontë's terminology, the cigar and the fruit are equally fragrant. Does she intend us to see Rochester's cigar as of a kind with the natural world, or as an intrusion into it? Certainly he takes a much more active, less humble approach to nature than does Jane: where she notices and enjoys, Rochester lifts, takes, stoops to inhale; nature is not, for him, sacred – it is to be used and enjoyed. She is passive: he active.

The sacred quality nature is given arises from the imagery and language used in the passage, which are intensely religious. The religious motif is introduced early in the extract, by the description of the orchard as 'Eden-like', and we may find many echoes of religious or biblical language elsewhere. For example 'wander unseen' reminds us of Adam and Eve after the Fall; the flowers are spoken of as 'yielding their evening sacrifice of incense'.

What part does Rochester play in this scene? Is he Adam? Or is he, rather, the serpent? Brontë knew her Milton (as the extract from *Shirley* in the next section indicates), and could not have been unaware of the smell which heralds the arrival of Satan in the garden in Book IV of *Paradise Lost*. The scent of Rochester's cigar is described first as 'subtle': the word means, very roughly, 'faint'; but it also echoes the archaic meaning of cunning, treacherous and wicked associated with the serpent in the Garden of Eden (Genesis, iii.1). There is in the extract no clear meaning associated with these hints; that is to emerge from the sequel, when the natural world registers its offence at what next passes between Jane and Rochester in the garden.

If we think a little further about the doubt in which we are left over the nature of Rochester, we discover that it is no accident. At one moment, his walking in the garden while Jane vainly tries to evade notice, recalls Adam and Eve hiding after the Fall from 'The Lord God walking in the garden in the cool of the day' (Genesis, iii.8). At another, he is the subtle serpent, tempting her to 'Turn back'. His dual status, as god and devil, exactly reflects Jane's response to him. Her Christian devotion is, for a time at least, obscured by the 'idol' she sets up for herself. He becomes for a time her god: for she cannot see the deep flaws in him. The ambiguity about him is, indeed, essential to the impact of the extract, and reflects the confusion in Jane's mind. That opening oxymoron used to describe the aroma of his cigar – 'warning fragrance' – reflects Jane's inability to distinguish the natural odours of the garden from the stink of evil. It points also to the moral blindfolding which the power of Rochester's attraction has induced in her.

The integrity of character and theme with setting is striking here. The passage is based on the narcotic appeal the garden makes to Jane's senses; and the sensuous appeal is used to communicate moral ideas central to the characters and their development. The ambiguity over Rochester's moral status remains unresolved, because his narcotic power has rendered Jane incapable of judgement.

Let us move on to think further about how the imagery in the extract develops later in the novel. Two other, more specific images in the extract show the variety of Brontë's writing: the moth, and the chestnut tree.

The moth appears towards the end of the passage, where Rochester calls to Jane to observe 'this fellow'. It is rather more than simply a piece of the rich mosaic of sights and sounds in the garden. In its habits, the moth, a nervous creature of the night, but drawn to the light, is like Jane, who points out the parallel when she says, 'The moth roamed away. I was sheepishly retreating also'. This simple parallel may prompt us to think of further links between the moth's world and Jane's. Oddly, too, the moth reminds Rochester of 'a West Indian insect'; the moth may thus be seen as another foreign element in the garden, and perhaps as a forewarning of the moment when a visitor from the West Indies will bring about the end of the relationship of Jane and Rochester.

The other image – given less emphasis here, although it turns out to be the more important one – is the 'giant horse-chestnut'. We may see it as a parallel for the Tree of Knowledge if we wish to carry the religious imagery to such a point – but it does not need that interpretation to develop power. Little is said of it in the extract, but it recurs again and again later in the chapter. When Rochester asks Jane to sit with him on the seat which surrounds its bole, he suggests, disingenuously – he has just revealed his Irish plans for Jane – that 'we will sit there in peace to-night, though we should never more be destined to sit there together' (p. 282–3). A little later, after Rochester has declared his deceitful love, the tree responds before Jane can: 'A waft of wind came sweeping down the laurel-walk, and trembled through the boughs of the chestnut: it wandered away – away – to an indefinite distance – it died' (p. 285). The lonely song of the nightingale which has been introduced in the extract is then the only sound for a few moments, as Jane weeps. It is not until Rochester calls for Jane to be his wife, claims that he is right in the eyes of God and defies the opinion of men, that the natural world – in the figure of the tree – registers offence. Jane wonders first, 'what had befallen the night? . . . we were all in shadow' (p. 287), and then focuses on the tree: 'what ailed the chestnut tree? it writhed and groaned' (p. 287). Here the use of nature is akin to the pathetic fallacy with which we are familiar in Shakespeare, and at the conclusion of the chapter develops an additional range of symbolic meanings. There occurs a great storm in which 'the rain rushed down' (p. 287), 'the thunder crashed, fierce and frequent as the lightning gleamed' (p. 288), and in the morning Adèle comes to tell Jane that 'the great horse-chestnut at the bottom of the orchard had been struck by lightning in the night, and half of it had split away' (p. 288). The meaning is clear, and as simple as in Shakespeare: a wrong in the human world is mirrored by disturbance of the natural world. But the emotional and poetic richness of the parallels are Brontë's own. We may see the chestnut tree as a parallel for the relationship between Rochester and Jane, or as a symbol of conflicts within either Rochester or Jane – and in Jane there is a range of conflicts or divisions to consider.

That is not the end of the horse-chestnut. Elemental in Volume 2, Chapter 8, it becomes, two chapters later, a symbol of the seeming destruction of the relationship between Rochester and Jane: she 'faced the wreck of the chestnut-tree'. Superficially it appears destroyed, 'black and riven: the trunk split down the centre'. But then she realises that 'The cloven halves were not broken from each other, for the firm base and strong roots kept them unsundered below' (all p. 309). Under a blood-red moon, Jane apostrophises the cloven parts of the tree in a passage which we may perhaps view as a gloomy precursor of her final relationship with Rochester:

> . . . the time of pleasure and love is over with you: but you are not desolate: each of you has a comrade to sympathise with him in his decay.

> (p. 310)

Rochester's decay – his semi-blind state at the conclusion – is the location of the final reference to the chestnut-tree. In the penultimate chapter, set at Ferndean, Rochester, now as he thinks useless, rather self-pityingly compares himself with that same cloven wreck:

> 'I am no better than the old lightning-struck chestnut-tree in Thornfield orchard . . . And what right would that ruin have to bid a budding woodbine cover its decay with freshness?'

> (p. 493)

The tree has become something rather less potent than earlier, because it is more specific. The language is metaphorical, as often in Brontë at moments of heightened emotion. The budding woodbine to which Rochester refers is, of course, Jane, who reassures him that he is 'green and vigorous' (p. 493) despite his partly disabled condition.

There is not space to discuss fully all the imagery used in the extract, and we already have enough evidence to show the integrity of the extract with the rest of the book: it is not just a matter of character and plot; the imagery is consistent and sustained, too. It would be possible to look at the use made of other images in the extract – the nightingale, which links with other bird images, or the moon – in much the same way. The extract looks towards future events in both incident and imagery. It echoes the past, too: we have already noticed the birds in Bewick's book, for example; the ambiguities surrounding Rochester echo the ambiguities of some of the images in Bewick. The motifs we have followed through thus illustrate a broader imaginative consistency in the whole novel.

Brontë worked hard at her writing, but there is more than hard work at the root of the setting in *Jane Eyre*; she uses nature to bind the action together in a rich web of varied and interrelated imagery and symbolism. This scene, this chapter indeed, is a remarkably consistent and richly realised piece of writing, utterly convincing in its psychological and poetic power. The writing here is inspired, and it is not unique in *Jane Eyre*. Explore some of the passages suggested in the Further Work section; you will discover that Brontë's inspiration is by no means limited to one chapter.

II: *Shirley*

The beginning of Chapter 18 of *Shirley* is largely a discussion between Shirley and Caroline which ends with an echo of *Jane Eyre* in making reference to Milton. There is some description of the setting at the start, but the extract finds a place here mainly because of the way the discussion develops the ideas implicit in the setting:

> The evening was still and warm; close and sultry it even promised to become. Round the descending sun the clouds glowed purple: summer tints, rather Indian than English, suffused the horizon, and cast rosy reflections on hill-side, house-front, tree-bole; on winding road, and undulating pasture-ground. The two girls came down from the fields slowly: by the time they reached the churchyard the bells were hushed; the multitudes were gathered into the church: the whole scene was solitary.
>
> 'How pleasant and calm it is!' said Caroline.
>
> 'And how hot it will be in the church!' responded Shirley; 'and what a dreary long speech Dr Boultby will make! and how the curates will hammer over their prepared orations! For my part, I would rather not enter.'
>
> 'But my uncle will be angry, if he observes our absence.'
>
> 'I will bear the brunt of his wrath: he will not devour me. I shall be sorry to miss his pungent speech. I know it will be all sense for the

Church, and all causticity for Schism: he'll not forget the battle of
Royd-lane. I shall be sorry also to deprive you of Mr Hall's sincere
friendly homily, with all its racy Yorkshireisms; but here I must stay.
The grey church and greyer tombs look divine with this crimson
gleam on them. Nature is now at her evening prayers: she is kneeling
before those red hills. I see her prostrate on the great steps of her
altar, praying for a fair night for mariners at sea, for travellers in
deserts, for lambs on moors, and unfledged birds in woods. Caroline,
I see her! and I will tell you what she is like: she is like what Eve was
when she and Adam stood alone on earth.'
      'And that is not Milton's Eve, Shirley.'
      'Milton's Eve! Milton's Eve! I repeat. No, by the pure Mother of
God, she is not! Cary, we are alone: we may speak what we think.
Milton was great; but was he good? His brain was right; how was his
heart? He saw heaven: he looked down on hell. He saw Satan, and
Sin his daughter, and Death their horrible offspring. Angels serried
before him their battalions: the long lines of adamantine shields
flashed back on his blind eyeballs the unutterable splendour of
heaven. Devils gathered their legions in his sight: their dim, dis-
crowned, and tarnished armies passed rank and file before him.
Milton tried to see the first woman; but, Cary, he saw her not.'

                                                              (pp. 314–15)

This extract is easier to deal with in some ways than the one from
Jane Eyre, but we will adopt the same approach. We will look at the
components of the extract, and consider its style and its use of
imagery, and the relationship between the characters and their
setting. We will need to look particularly at the links between the
descriptive first paragraph and the subsequent dialogue. As we did in
the last section, we will try finally to see its place in the novel as a
whole.

There are three components clearly distinguishable in the extract:
the natural world, and the church, which together comprise the
sense of a native locality; and the discussion – a rather one-sided discussion – of Milton. Shirley, who usually plays the lead in her talk
with Caroline, uses these disparate elements to develop a theory
about the nature of womanhood. As with *Jane Eyre*, we find that the
setting is linked with theme.

Let us look at the description of the natural locality first. The pastoral world and the church are both part of it, yet the relationship between them is uneasy. Brontë tries to communicate a feeling of the scene by appealing to the senses in different ways: 'still and warm; close and sultry'; the atmosphere is complex, with a graduation of warm colours from the purple clouds to 'rosy reflections'. There is something exotic here, in the reference to the 'Indian' tints of summer, as there was in the garden in *Jane Eyre* when the moth brings a recollection of the West Indies. The language is heightened, with clouds which 'glowed', colours which 'suffused' the horizon. It is not only the reflections, but the whole scene which is rosy, to a degree that makes Caroline's exclamation, 'How pleasant and calm it is!' sound, in the hush after the church bells are silenced, like understatement. However, it is in the end ordinariness, and not the exotic, with which Brontë is most concerned. The comparison with Indian tints stresses, paradoxically, the Englishness of the scene: there is an intensity, as it were, unnatural about the colours she has described, and Brontë stresses then the homeliness of the scene with references to 'hill-side, house-front, tree-bole'. The placing of the house between hill and tree assumes an easy conference of nature and man which extends to the 'winding road, and undulating pasture-ground'.

Nature here is locality, and much stress is laid in the novel on the locality of Yorkshire. Both Caroline and Shirley are proud to have grown from Yorkshire stock, and they take a pride in their Yorkshire heritage – see, for example, Chapter 12, where Shirley claims with evident pride, that 'Five generations of my race sleep under the aisle of Briarfield church'. That does not mean that they adhere to all the standards of their countrymen, and the opening paragraph concludes with a contrast between 'the multitudes' in the church beneath silenced bells, and the 'solitary' scene which the two girls, late for church, now have to themselves. The clamour of the bells, it is implied, like the church itself, is at odds with the natural world. In this conflict between crowd and solitude, noise and quiet, we may perhaps see an echo of the conflict of public and private worlds which we have noticed in *Jane Eyre*.

In *Shirley*, however, the contrasting of public and private has a different significance which is developed in the dialogue that occupies most of the extract. Brontë's ideas are picked out in precise detail. The natural world is 'pleasant and calm', and the grey church and tombstones look 'divine' with the 'crimson gleam' of natural light. However, the power of light transforms only externals. Inside the church, everything is unnatural or oppressive: it will be unbearably hot; Shirley imagines a 'dreary' sermon from Dr Boultby, and is wearied at the thought of the curates' orations. There is an implicit criticism of mechanical, brow-beating rhetoric in the use of the brutal 'hammer' to suggest the style in which the curates deliver their sermons. While the emphasis in the description of the natural world is on spontaneity, calm and relaxation, with the two girls coming 'slowly' down from the fields, the reference to the curates' 'prepared' orations suggests stilted delivery and threadbare ideas.

Nature and Church are in conflict here. Shirley, brushing aside the nervous concerns of Caroline about her uncle's anger, and offering herself as a bulwark against him, imagines all too vividly how the clergymen will strike familiar attitudes. She knows Helstone's 'pungent speech' and Hall's 'racy Yorkshireisms', and it is hard to read of her sorrow at missing them without sensing irony. Fittingly, Mr Hall's style links him with the landscape and its people, but he is exceptional. The church of Shirley's imagination seems all too imperfectly human, all too mundane; while the world of nature is 'divine'. Nature is personified: she is 'at her evening prayers', she is 'kneeling', she is 'prostrate'; the personification points to the communion of man and environment. For Shirley, it seems, sensitivity to nature is a more attractive, and more sincere, form of worship than what goes on inside the church. This outlook helps to make her an attractive character: Shirley has a spontaneity and independence which we warm to and admire. It is also what prompts Caroline to call her, a little later in the chapter, a pagan. Here, then, the conflict of nature and religion which we noted in the portrait of Shirley in the last chapter is presented more emphatically.

The meaning of nature is taken a step further in the extract. Shirley's conclusion is remarkable in identifying nature with Eve, and through her, with the nature of women. Men, she implies, are rationalists, driven by argument and conflict, like the clergy in the church; women, on the other hand, are at one with the natural

world, and more at ease with their own nature. She has already dismissed man as 'the Troubler' (Chapter 14, p. 265). Her ideas are,
naturally enough, not cast in stone. She also sees some men as 'lords
of the creation' and Robert Moore as 'a noble being' (both in
Chapter 12, pp. 225–6). At the same time, she feels that 'the
cleverest, the acutest men are often under an illusion about women'
(Chapter 20, p. 343). She is willing in the end to welcome Louis
Moore as her master, but it is important that he is a man peculiarly
sensitive to nature.

The discussion of nature takes a new turn when Caroline introduces Milton's portrayal of Eve, startling Shirley into a repeated
exclamation. The transition is perhaps not an easy one, yet it has the
effect of expanding, not of changing, the subject. Shirley sees the
greatness in Milton's conception of heaven and hell and their inhabitants, but she thinks he failed in his conception of Eve; his physical
blindness, she implies, did not permit him to see the original woman
as a reality. His universe, like the minor world of Briarfield church,
is a world in conflict and his Eve is a projection of a male notion of
woman's place in that conflict. Milton, undoubtedly, is among those
'cleverest, acutest men' who are under an illusion about the nature of
women. Although she claims to be 'ignorant as stone' (Chapter 20,
p. 343), Shirley shows a balanced mind in acknowledging the
virtues, while recognising the faults, of men – Milton among them.

The use which Brontë makes of the natural setting in this brief
extract is characteristic, but more than usually pointed. Beginning
with what appears to be a straightforward piece of description of
location the extract moves rapidly to a discussion of the meaning of
nature as a theme. Nature has moral significance: it is always good in
Shirley's eyes, and usually in Caroline's, too: what is natural is what
is best in human nature. Nature is a touchstone throughout the
novel. Tartar, Shirley's dog, shares her tastes in people, and his liking
for Louis Moore is a signal that Louis is to be regarded as a person
with heart and sense. Louis's love of painting nature is another indicator: he is a man who values nature and natural feeling, and it is
this quality more than any other which makes him a suitable partner
for Shirley in the end. The theme of nature bears upon two other
themes of central significance in *Shirley*: the divisiveness of religion,

and the position of women in society – topics which we discuss later; suffice it to say here that when Brontë takes us inside churches elsewhere in the novel it is with a critical eye (see Chapters 9 and 34). The extract considers also the practical relationship between man and his natural environment, and we may wonder, looking forward to the conclusion of the novel, whether Robert Moore's plans and achievements form part of the rural idyll which the first paragraph of the extract proposes. These themes are not the subject of barren discussion: they are brought to life by a vividly dramatic style, with the sharp contrast between nature and church, with pointed use of personification, and with an appropriately poetic attempt to capture in brief the brilliance of Milton's universe. Setting is far from decoration here. It is deeply felt, and integral to the texture of the novel.

III: *Villette*

From *Villette* we take the beginning of Chapter 12, which introduces the legend of the nun reputed to haunt the garden and corridors of the pensionnat:

> Behind the house at the Rue Fossette there was a garden – large, considering that it lay in the heart of a city, and to my recollection at this day it seems pleasant: but time, like distance, lends to certain scenes an influence so softening; and where all is stone around, blank wall and hot pavement, how precious seems one shrub, how lovely an enclosed and planted spot of ground!
>
> There went a tradition that Madame Beck's house had in old days been a convent. That in years gone by – how long gone by I cannot tell, but I think some centuries – before the city had overspread this quarter, and when it was tilled ground and avenue, and such deep and leafy seclusion as ought to embosom a religious house – that something had happened on this site which, rousing fear and inflicting horror, had left to the place the inheritance of a ghost story. A vague tale went of a black and white nun, sometimes, on some night or nights of the year, seen in some part of this vicinage. The ghost must have been built out some ages ago, for there were houses

all round now; but certain convent-relics, in the shape of old and huge fruit-trees, yet consecrated the spot; and, at the foot of one – a Methusaleh of a pear-tree, dead, all but a few boughs which still faithfully renewed their perfumed snow in spring, and their honey-sweet pendants in autumn – you saw, in scraping away the mossy earth between the half-bared roots, a glimpse of slab, smooth, hard, and black. The legend went, unconfirmed and unaccredited, but still propagated, that this was the portal of a vault, emprisoning deep beneath that ground, on whose surface grass grew and flowers bloomed, the bones of a girl whom a monkish conclave of the drear middle ages had here buried alive, for some sin against her vow. Her shadow it was that tremblers had feared, through long generations after her poor frame was dust; her black robe and white veil that, for timid eyes, moonlight and shade had mocked, as they fluctuated in the night-wind through the garden-thicket.

Independently of romantic rubbish, however, that old garden had its charms. On summer mornings I used to rise early, to enjoy them alone; on summer evenings, to linger solitary, to keep tryste with the rising moon, or taste one kiss of the evening breeze, or fancy rather than feel the freshness of dew descending. The turf was verdant, the gravelled walks were white; sun-bright nasturtiums clustered beautiful about the roots of the doddered orchard giants. There was a large berceau, above which spread the shade of an acacia; there was a smaller, more sequestered bower, nestled in the vines which ran all along a high and gray wall, and gathered their tendrils in a knot of beauty, and hung their clusters in loving profusion about the favoured spot where jasmine and ivy met, and married them.

(pp. 172–3)

In this passage, as in our previous two examples, the discussion of setting at anything beyond the simplest level is impossible to divorce from theme and character. The description of the garden opens important elements in the plot, touches on several themes in the novel – the religious theme, and the theme of the conflict of passion and duty, which are important in the other novels, too – and in every line expresses the personality of the narrator. Lucy Snowe stamps herself on the passage from the beginning when she makes it plain that this is a selective description. The details are selected by her memories from years hence, and her phrasing emphasises the distance in time: 'to my recollection' throws the whole experience back into a past rendered mistier by 'at this day'. She alludes to the well-known line from Thomas Campbell's *The Pleasures of Hope*, ''Tis distance lends enchantment to the view', characteristically omitting the magical element. Enchantment, Lucy would have us believe, plays little part in her life, and is here moderated to 'an influence so softening'. From that point Lucy gives her opinion about, rather than simply describes, the garden in which she found solace.

The components of the extract are not hard to isolate. Lucy carefully contrasts stone and garden, in a manner which implies a parallel, in her life at the pensionnat, between the dullness of her daily routine, and the moments in the garden when her spirit could flourish more freely. Her discussion of the legend of the nun both attracts and repels, for it shows us the sides of her which chill, and those with which we feel sympathy. And, as we will see in our analysis, the odd concluding paragraph expresses a depth of loss which borders on the tragic.

Let us begin by looking at the description of the garden, and see how the choice of language develops a powerful emotional impact. The emotional power of the garden is evident from the beginning. It lies at 'the heart of the city', and has a 'softening' quality. In contrast, around it are 'stone . . . blank wall, and hot pavement'. The opposition suggested here is as yet blurred; but the 'blank' and 'hot' imply lack of feeling, lack of sympathy, pressure and stress. The garden, on the other hand, suggests repose.

A significant feature of the garden is that it is 'enclosed' and 'planted'; it is the remnant of the 'leafy seclusion' of earlier days. That is, it is a man-made retreat, and the discussion of the nun is a natural sequel which sets up a parallel between her and Lucy. The nun by, perhaps, religious conviction, and Lucy, by force of economics, are both shut off from the world. Both confront time and destiny – which are symbolised by the 'Methusaleh of a pear-tree, dead, all but a few boughs' – in isolation. The garden contains, but covers, the hardness and relentlessness of stone, for beneath the roots of the pear-tree, you can scrape away moss and earth to reveal 'slab, smooth, hard, and black . . . the portal of a vault'. Here, the legend goes, are imprisoned the bones of a girl. Similarly, we may say, Lucy is imprisoned in the pensionnat. She feels at risk in a hostile, spirit-less and barren world, as the girl was buried by a 'monkish conclave of the drear middle ages'. Lucy is guilty of no obvious crime, and the girl is buried for 'some sin against her vow' – the 'some' seems to mean more than 'an unknown'; rather, perhaps, 'a sin of little signifi-cance'. From this point, at intervals throughout the novel, encoun-ters occur between Lucy and the nun – or what appears to be a nun – until the truth about the mysterious materialisations of the figure is finally revealed. However, the actuality of the nun, and the anti-climactic truth about her nature, do not diminish the symbolic meaning of the nun story for Lucy.

The meaning of the nun is not diminished, either, by Lucy's apparent scepticism. She is at her sourest in despising the 'tremblers' who feared the apparition. and their 'timid eyes'. For her, it seems, the nun is no more than a 'vague tale' of a story 'built out some ages ago' – that is, a silly and unconvincing concoction; thus far, Lucy appears to be a scornful critic. But, now, look at the final phrases of the second paragraph: 'her black robe and white veil that . . . moon-light and shade had mocked, as they fluctuated in the night-wind through the garden-thicket'. This sounds far from scornful: it is a poetic conclusion, and a conclusion showing a personal knowledge of the nameless fears and fancies which darkness can make the human mind prey to. Is Lucy here simply mocking the tremblers? Surely not. The ambiguous language suggests that there are real fears here which Lucy is unwilling to acknowledge openly, but which are powerfully suggested in the terrifying 'night-wind'. Lucy, it would appear, is here saying one thing while feeling another.

Ambiguity affects the religious imagery in the paragraph, too. The nun story seems to be treated in a mildly sceptical manner: Lucy is not scornful of the rule which destroys the young nun, yet it is clear that her natural sympathies lie with the victim – 'the bones of a girl' – of a 'drear' era. At the same time, however, the natural world of the garden is presented as sacred, perhaps sanctified by the sacrifice of the young nun. The old fruit-trees are 'convent-relics' which 'conse-crated' the spot; 'grass grew and flowers bloomed' in the earth above the vault. The effect recalls the passage we considered from *Shirley*, in which nature holds a religious ceremony parallel with the one in the church. The way in which religion is treated in the extract reflects the way it is treated in *Villette* as a whole: Lucy is often drawn to criticise, is to some degree fearful of the emotional element in Catholicism, and is deeply suspicious of Catholics; yet she is strangely drawn to it and them, even to the point of confession – even to the threshold of marrying an adherent of that alien faith. These contrasting sides of her nature are suggested in the extract in the clashing of nature and stone images, of sterile and fertile. Lucy's contradictory character is easily visible in her evident fascination with a mere 'ghost story' which she pretends to dismiss as 'a vague tale . . . unconfirmed and unaccredited'. The sacred aspects of the garden setting thus support both theme and character here, as they do in the novel as a whole.

The ambiguity of feeling is clearer still in the description of setting in the final paragraph, in which the manner of expression communicates meanings far beyond Lucy's superficial intentions. At the beginning, Lucy strikes her acid pose when she dismisses the whole nun business roundly and alliteratively as 'romantic rubbish'. This is the quality in her which leads Ginevra to call her Diogenes, Timon, 'crusty and crabbed'. She refers with the assumed contempt of familiarity to 'that old garden' which 'had its charms'. But her pose is belied by the nature of the writing that follows, which is romantic to a fault: intensely romantic, sensuous, poetic. The description is full of colour – white gravelled walks, sun-bright nasturtiums, as well as the implied colours of the plants, moon and so on. The sense of touch is used in 'fancy rather than feel the freshness of dew' (how 'fancy' awakens thoughts of the romantic poets! and how vivid is the alliteration in suggesting the merest breath of a touch); she can 'taste one kiss' of evening. The language is exotic with the names of plants, both familiar and continental, not only jasmine and nasturtium, but acacia and vines. The whole paragraph is verdant as the turf itself.

But there is more here, a subtle imagery which reflects Lucy's feelings more intimately. The whole description uses the language of love. Lucy used to linger in the evenings to 'keep tryste' with the rising moon, to 'taste one kiss' of the breeze; the language used here – especially 'tryste' – is surely just the stuff of the 'romantic rubbish' which Lucy affects to scorn. The 'sequestered bower' recalls the theme of seclusion picked out earlier, but it also suggests a place of privacy, where she can be 'nestled', among the 'tendrils in a knot of beauty' as in a lover's arms. There is more than a suggestion of human hair in the way the vines 'hung their clusters in loving profusion'. At the end of the paragraph the plants are joined in pagan matrimony where 'jasmine and ivy met, and married them'. There is a logical progression here from 'solitary' to 'keep tryste' to 'taste one kiss' to 'married', and no doubt it is possible to interpret the details of setting in the paragraph in specific Freudian-sexual terms. We need not go so far. Clearly, however, the garden reflects the emotional and sexual nature of the observer, which has no outlet in her everyday life, and which she herself denies. The garden shows us the more human, and more attractive, and sadder – because repressed – elements in Lucy Snowe. It reveals the longing for 'enchantment', which the opening of the extract appears to deny by omitting that key word of Campbell's line.

The basic opposition in the extract grows out of the contrast between nature and stone, but Brontë develops the opposition with enormous power. There is the literal opposition between Lucy's harnessed academic life and her moments of freedom; there is, as in *Shirley*, an opposition between the rule of religion and the spontaneity of human nature which constitutes one of the major themes of the novel; and there is the spiritual clash in Lucy Snowe between the cynical stone she wills herself to be, and the volatile emotions which stir her being. We are vividly shown the contrast between the tight-lipped sterility she presents to the world, and her inner yearnings.

As in *Jane Eyre*, a tree is central to the impact of the passage. The ancient pear-tree, Methusaleh, is nearly dead. Like other great trees in the orchard, it is 'doddered': the word means that the topmost branches have been removed or lost, but also suggests decay and fragility. Yet still it has a fertile element, expressed in its blossom, richly described as 'perfumed snow in spring', and in the pears, which are turned into jewels in 'honey-sweet pendants in autumn'.

'Pendant' is especially apposite in the coincidence of its literal and metaphorical meanings. As for the blossom, it recalls the description of Lucy herself as capped with snow. The tree thus expresses Lucy's nature – during her time at the pensionnat, but still more fittingly later, from her point of view looking back on her life; at both periods, she shares its superficial sterility, and inner fertility. 'Snow in spring' suggests either the promise of life renewing itself after winter, or budding life destroyed by unexpectedly late cold; and either of these ideas, depending on our perspective, we may associate with Lucy Snowe.

Conclusions

1. Setting is intimately associated with other structural elements in the novels. It can express subtle aspects of character and theme.
2. Brontë is particularly sensitive to natural setting, and description of nature plays an important part in the impact of all the novels. She uses personification and alliteration freely, appeals to the senses, and is always aware of the symbolic possibilities in setting.
3. Brontë's close sympathy with the natural world often finds expression in the use of religious language in describing it.
4. Setting is used to express emotional states as well as ideas. As in *Jane Eyre*, it can express feelings about a relationship as well as individual feelings.
5. Brontë often uses setting as a subtle counterpoint to theme or character, expressing ideas beyond, or in conflict with, surface meanings.
6. Nature is more than setting: it is also a theme in the novels. Brontë, like Shirley, is something of a pagan in her pantheistic sense of the natural world, even though her values are Christian.
7. Remember that setting is not always sympathetic. It may clash with the human events which are set against it in an ironic, or perhaps a tragic or amusing way.
8. As in all the examples we have considered, Brontë uses setting to develop subtly important oppositions, conflicts and ambiguities in the meanings of her novels.

Methods of Analysis

1. Setting in isolation matters little. Look at the characters who are set against it, and try to see the interplay between them and their background. Look for elements in setting which reflect the emotions of characters, or their personality. Look, equally, for contrast between character and background.
2. Setting is particularly effective in generating strong emotional responses. Study the language used for its richness or starkness, its use of imagery, and its use of exotic or unusual language.
3. Imagery is often significant in descriptions of setting, and deserves particular attention. Look for ways in which images express ideas or feelings within or about characters.
4. Pay special attention to contrasts between different elements of setting – such as the church and the natural world in the extract from *Shirley*. Such contrasts are likely to offer insight into the meaning of the novel, and into the author's ideas.
5. Remember that the use of language is important only for its effect. There is no value in spotting simile or alliteration, or any other device, outside the context of meaning.

Further Work

Jane Eyre: Volume 1, Chapter 9, in which Helen Burns dies, is a good example of the use of nature to counterpoint human events. Study paragraphs three to seven (from 'April advanced to May' to 'a handful of herbs and blossoms to put in a coffin', pp. 89–90).

An important section of the novel is the part of Volume 1, Chapter 11 in which we read Jane's first impressions of Thornfield; the six paragraphs beginning with the end of her first conversation with Mrs Fairfax would be interesting ('"But I'll not keep you sitting up late"' to 'its old tower-top looked over a knoll between the house and gates', pp. 112–15).

Alternatively, you could look at Jane's arrival at Ferndean in Volume 3, Chapter 11, from the beginning of the chapter, until she sees Rochester just over a page later (pp. 478–81).

Shirley: Setting is perhaps less important in *Shirley* in general than it is in the other novels, yet there are several passages of very considerable interest. One is the description of Nunnely dale and wood which begins about three pages from the beginning of Chapter 12 (from 'They both halted on the green brow of the Common' to '"Miss Keeldar, I could guide you"', pp. 219–21).

An alternative passage is the account of the walk taken by Caroline and Mrs Pryor in the second section of Chapter 21, about six pages from the beginning (from 'The day being fine' for four paragraphs, ending 'a graphic charm as pleasant as it was unpretending', pp. 360–1).

Villette: A short passage which will repay close study is the episode in which Lucy wanders lost in the streets in the final two paragraphs of Chapter 15 (from 'Twilight had passed into night' to the end of the chapter, pp. 235–6).

A longer extract which would be suitable is Lucy's account of her escape from the seeming imprisonment of the pensionnat in the middle of Chapter 38 (the five paragraphs beginning, 'The other day, in walking past, I had seen, without attending to the circumstance, a gap in the paling' and concluding, 'for myself, I have scarce made an effort', pp. 547–8).

4

Dramatisation

In this chapter we look at the quality which, above all others, made Charlotte Brontë's writing distinct from the work of her predecessors and contemporaries. Her work was admired, as it is still today, for its vivid realisation of experience, and in particular for her ability to put the souls of her characters before us. Where other writers exerted themselves to depict social conditions or manners, Charlotte Brontë chose instead to delve into the mysterious and deceptive world of the psychology of her heroines. This was not solely a matter of choice: she had not, she felt, the experience to write about the world at large; but she knew that she understood the heart.

The subject of this chapter is a development of ideas we have considered earlier. By 'dramatisation' I mean the fusion of character, setting, imagery and other elements to create a vivid, convincing and psychologically profound narrative. We will be including some of the ideas we have looked at in earlier chapters, and introducing new ones. We will, in particular, be looking more closely at the interplay between characters in dialogue, and at Brontë's use of symbolism. Above all, our approach must be inclusive, since every aspect of the text contributes to the depth of truth which Brontë's writing can express.

There are four elements to consider in each section of the chapter:

a) The context of the extract. We need to look at what leads up to the episode, to have a chance of understanding its meaning.

b) The narrative content of the extract. This will be brief. But we must be sure that we understand what is happening.

c) Analysis of the language of the passage, so as to understand the use of symbolism, or allusion, or other devices which may be used in it. This is the point to which most of our energy will be directed, and it should generate clear ideas about meaning, theme and character.

d) A glance at the outcome of the episode. We will attempt to understand its significance in the development of the whole novel.

In practice, of course, it will not be quite as neat as that. Interpretation will to some extent take its own course.

I: *Jane Eyre*

We have already considered some of the symbolic and psychological implications of scenes in *Jane Eyre*. We noticed, for example, the significance of the chestnut tree which expresses aspects of Rochester, and represents some of his feelings about himself. But the dramatisation in the novel is richer. There are many other images, incidents, conversations and settings which express the feelings of Jane herself, and her relationships with other characters. Here we look at a critical moment in Volume 2, Chapter 10 when Jane recounts to Rochester, how, two nights preceding her wedding to him, she was startled out of her sleep to see an apparition in her room. She has just told him about her strange dreams, which she calls the 'preface' to her story:

> 'All the preface, sir; the tale is yet to come. On waking, a gleam dazzled my eyes: I thought – oh, it is daylight! But I was mistaken: it was only candle-light. Sophie, I supposed, had come in. There was a light on the dressing-table, and the door of the closet, where, before going to bed, I had hung my wedding-dress and veil, stood open: I heard a rustling there. I asked, "Sophie, what are you doing?" No one answered; but a form emerged from the closet: it took the light, held it aloft, and surveyed the garments pendent from the portmanteau. "Sophie! Sophie!" I again cried: and still it was silent. I had risen up in bed, I bent forward: first surprise, then bewilderment, came over

me; and then my blood crept cold through my veins. Mr Rochester, this was not Sophie, it was not Leah, it was not Mrs Fairfax: it was not – no, I was sure of it, and am still – it was not even that strange woman, Grace Poole.'

'It must have been one of them,' interrupted my master.

'No, sir, I solemnly assure you to the contrary. The shape standing before me had never crossed my eyes within the precincts of Thornfield Hall before; the height, the contour were new to me.'

'Describe it, Jane.'

'It seemed, sir, a woman, tall and large, with thick and dark hair hanging long down her back. I know not what dress she had on: it was white and straight; but whether gown, sheet, or shroud, I cannot tell.'

'Did you see her face?'

'Not at first. But presently she took my veil from its place; she held it up, gazed at it long, and then she threw it over her own head, and turned to the mirror. At that moment I saw the reflection of the visage and features quite distinctly in the dark oblong glass.'

'And how were they?'

'Fearful and ghastly to me – oh, sir, I never saw a face like it! It was a discoloured face – it was a savage face. I wish I could forget the roll of the red eyes and the fearful blackened inflation of the lineaments!'

'Ghosts are usually pale, Jane.'

'This, sir, was purple: the lips were swelled and dark; the brow fur-rowed; the black eye-brows widely raised over the blood-shot eyes. Shall I tell you of what it reminded me?'

'You may.'

'Of the foul German spectre – the Vampyre.'

'Ah! – What did it do?'

'Sir, it removed my veil from its gaunt head, rent it in two parts, and flinging both on the floor, trampled on them.'

'Afterwards?'

'It drew aside the window-curtain and looked out: perhaps it saw dawn approaching, for, taking the candle, it retreated to the door. Just at my bedside, the figure stopped: the fiery eyes glared upon me- she thrust up her candle close to my face, and extinguished it under my eyes. I was aware her lurid visage flamed over mine, and I lost consciousness: for the second time in my life – only the second time – I became insensible from terror.'

(pp. 316–18)

This is a vivid scene, one of those which most closely defines that 'Gothic' element in the novel which readers either abhor or delight in. We need to look carefully, according to our plan, at the context in which it occurs, its subject matter, what it reveals of Jane herself and of her relationship with Rochester, and its links with the rest of the novel.

When Jane tells Rochester about her experience, he has recently returned to Thornfield in an episode which seems to recapitulate in brief their first meeting – she hears his horse's hooves, he is accompanied by Pilot, and wildly waving his hat. Barely giving him time to draw breath, Jane launches into the 'preface' of the apparition. Over-wrought and excited at the prospect of her impending wedding, she has had a dream immediately before waking: a dream of bats and owls, and of nursing a terrified infant; in the dream was, yet again, the galloping of a horse – a night-mare, no doubt. Thus we are prepared for the apparition by trappings associated with conventional Gothic yarns: there are the bats, the disturbing dream of the child, and Rochester refers to finding 'poison, or a dagger in the veil besides its embroidery', while Jane tries to communicate to him her strange sense of oppression and foreboding.

This context is important, for it lends authenticity to the subject, and helps to define the mood of the passage. The incident itself is lurid; Brontë takes pains to ensure that it is cast against a backdrop of anxiety which lends it conviction. It is also, perhaps, an incident better reported in conversation than narrated directly. We notice a sharp contrast in mood between speaker and listener: Jane is voluble; Rochester's responses are laconic, or mocking. Though he is concerned because she looks unwell – her eyes glitter feverishly – he wishes to diminish her concern over her experience. He appears on one level to be the voice of reason which brings a measure of normality to the episode. For us, Jane's nervous excitement is all the more real for being thrown in relief against the cold rationality – as it appears – of Rochester.

Having stamped a degree of authenticity on the incident, Brontë feels free to give rein to her darkest imaginings. Tension is developed step by step by recounting the perceptual uncertainties to which Jane is prey. She is dazzled by a gleam, unsure whether it is daylight or a candle. There is a mysterious rustling in the closet. The rustling becomes a 'form' almost as mysterious – an 'it' and not a person. Jane assumes that it is Sophie she sees, and questions her urgently and with simplicity – her habitual intricacy of syntax forgotten in increasing fear: 'Sophie, what are you doing?', then repetition of the name only. We are given Jane's emotional responses now, in rapid crescendo, before we know what she perceives – 'first surprise, then bewilderment'; and finally 'my blood crept cold through my veins' uses alliteration and personification to communicate Jane's horror at recognising (as it were) her intruder as a stranger. Thus far, the reader is made, by lack of information, to share Jane's bewilderment.

At this point the tension eases momentarily. Rochester attempts to dismiss her fears with his disingenuous interruption ('It must have been one of' the familar inhabitants of the house), but Jane contradicts him with the physical description of the woman. Then anxiety emerges again in the uncertainty with which Jane describes the woman's dress. She is wearing something indeterminate – 'gown, sheet, or shroud': is the apparition dressed for wedding, sleep, or funeral? The doubt opens the way to more impressionistic writing which communicates Jane's feelings more directly. As the woman puts on the veil, Jane sees in the mirror a strange image of a face 'Fearful and ghastly . . . discoloured . . . savage', and she recalls 'the roll of the red eyes and the fearful blackened inflation of the lineaments!' The brevity of Rochester's seemingly sceptical responses ('Describe it, Jane', 'You may', 'Afterwards?') does nothing to halt the flow of Jane's vivid account, and she continues to focus on the grotesque aspects of her experience: furrowed brow, black eyebrows, eyes bloodshot or dark and swollen. When Jane concludes that the figure reminded her of the vampire, no doubt remains about which territory we are in. These are the murky regions of the sensational novel.

It is not yet enough. Brontë presses on with yet more melodrama. The apparition rends the veil in two and tramples it, leans towards Jane with 'fiery eyes'. Brontë develops the fire image when the woman's 'lurid' face 'flame[s]' over Jane, who at that point loses consciousness.

This is one of those scenes, such as the death of Little Nell, which for some of us are impossible to read without laughter. The reaction is understandable. The episode can appear so overblown in both language and subject-matter as indeed to be risible from a rational point of view.

Reason, however, does not govern here. Most readers sense this, and, recognising the exaggeration as an effect Brontë was consciously aiming at, are able to take a sophisticated position. They can enjoy the element of parody in this episode, and see, equally, its serious side. The dual response makes sense. Despite the tendency towards farce in this scene, Brontë uses it to express real and deep feelings in Jane, which it would be hard, and surely less effective, to narrate directly. 'Despite', in fact, gives the wrong impression: it is precisely because of the exaggeration that the scene works. It is a dream-like episode both in arising out of sleep, and in drawing with a very broad brush. Brontë takes care to stress the exaggeration by giving Rochester coolly ironic commentaries, such as his response to Jane's wild picturing of the 'roll of the red eyes and the fearful blackened inflation of the lineaments' that 'Ghosts are usually pale, Jane'. Thus Brontë is able to suggest that she is dramatising things which lie below the threshold of conscious thought.

The effects which Brontë achieves are particularly clearly illustrated in three features of the imagery: the obvious reference in the veil and the gown to wedding, the effect of the mirror, and the use of fire imagery to suggest passion.

The wedding imagery moves from the impressionistic to the factual, from Jane's feelings to specific physical description. The woman is wearing something white which Jane thinks is either a gown, or a sheet, or a shroud; the ceremonial gown is thus linked with the more private and physical fact of the bed, and the shroud we may interpret, if we wish, as suggesting the disturbing strength of Jane's fears about the effects of marriage upon her – there is more than one way in which this marriage can be a kind of death for Jane. When the gruesome intruder takes the veil and throws it over her own head, she represents a terrible amalgamation of ceremonial and savage.

Were Jane sleeping, we might attribute the vision simply to her over-excited imagination struggling with prospects new and strange to her restricted life. But, of course, she is not, and the events are 'real'. What Brontë does here is to present an actual incident with a logic of its own, but one so exaggerated as to give it – even if it did not take place as an interruption in Jane's sleep – a dream-like or nightmarish quality. The real is made unreal, and thus becomes surreal. This is in direct contrast with the rational episodes in the novel, in which Brontë notes, with authentic detail, the nature of day-to-day life at Thornfield (or Gateshead, or Lowood): in this episode she intends us to see ideas which underlie the surface texture of Jane's life. The surreal lives off the real. It steals an air of authenticity by association with the very fully recorded details of everyday life in the novel.

There is other evidence of Brontë's intention here in the imagery of the extract. The use of mirror images is frequent in *Jane Eyre*, and it is always pointed. It appears, for example, in the red-room episode in Volume 1, Chapter 2, which is specifically recalled by this extract: it was there that Jane lost consciousness for the first time in her life. Here, the mirror helps to create the sense of nightmarish distortion which colours the whole scene; mirrors are a popular Gothic device, and of considerable importance in some variants of the vampire legend, for in a mirror a vampire is invisible. The mirror also implies an identification between the intruder whom Jane sees, and Jane herself: Jane looks in the mirror, and sees a stranger dressed up for a wedding.

How are we to interpret this mirror-image? The woman seems so different from Jane: large, brutishly physical, swollen black and purple, glaring violently, where Jane is small, neat and demure. That, then, must be the point. The intruder is an intruder in Jane's hitherto ordered existence. Her violence suggests the violence with which Jane's world is disrupted. Above all, she represents Jane's apprehensions, from the limited perspective of her narrow experience, about the world of sexual passion, physical intercourse, and sensual violence which she feels she is on the point of entering into. The image is grotesque because Jane's fears are of the unknown; she does not know quite what to expect of marriage to Rochester, but she knows that it will not be an arctic scene from Bewick's *Birds*.

Passion is the keynote of this scene. It appears in the portrait of the intruder in violent and ugly form. It appears, also, in the imagery of fire which is often used in the novel to suggest passion. The fire image here develops, as the scene does, to an extravagant climax. It begins with the 'gleam [which] dazzled my eyes' that Jane mistakes for daylight, but which is actually the candlelight by which Jane first sees her visitant. It continues with the woman taking the candle from the dressing table, and holding it so as to show her features 'quite distinctly in the dark oblong glass'. Then the image modulates into 'the fiery eyes [which] glared upon me' as the apparition thrusts the candle close up to Jane's face and then extinguishes it, leaving Jane with an impression of the 'lurid image [which] flamed over mine'. The fire imagery here has both a practical and thematic effect: it enables Jane to see what she has to see; and it supports the sense of violent passion which is created by the description of the intruder.

The fire image makes a useful starting-point for thinking about the place of the extract in the structure of the novel. Fires and fire imagery are central to the novel. It is easy enough to point to the fire in Rochester's room, and the conflagration of Thornfield as the most obvious instances elsewhere, but there are many examples of the use of the image; In *Language of Fiction*, David Lodge alludes to one hundred and fifty-four references to fire of various kinds in *Jane Eyre*. Fire, be it noted, is not always used to suggest passion; it also means the comfort of the fireside to Jane – for example when she and Helen Burns are entertained by Miss Temple (Volume 1, Chapter 5), or when Bessie tells stories by the nursery hearth (Volume 1, Chapter 1). Brontë is never mechanical in her use of symbolism.

Another obvious implication of the scene stems from the tearing of the veil in half, and its trampling underfoot by the intruder. Clearly, this looks back to the betrayal of marriage by Rochester in keeping his wife a prisoner in the attic and thus almost denying her very existence; it also looks forward to the impending betrayal implicit in his bigamous intention towards Jane; we may also like to see in it a pre-figuring of the catastrophe of the marriage service.

At a somewhat deeper level, the tearing of the veil symbolises Rochester's betrayal of the principles of fidelity and honesty which should be enshrined in marriage. Indeed, his behaviour throughout the scene, as he humours Jane, encouraging her to give voice to her impressions so that he can, while appearing solicitous, gently ridicule her for giving way to what he describes a little later as 'mental terrors', is quite appalling. Depite the superficial impression his words give, rationality is very far from his mind; what he says to Jane derives from murky guilt. After seeing the veil, he makes a drama of embracing Jane, and giving thanks that she herself is unharmed, before insisting that what she has experienced was 'half dream, half reality', and that the woman was Grace Poole. The contempt Rochester reveals in this scene for both his wife and Jane is not redeemed until late in the novel when he injures himself in the attempt to save his wife from the fire at Thornfield.

This scene works on many levels. It is horrific, entertaining and amusing, yet it shows us Jane's fears: it dramatises what she feels, but would be unable to express so vividly, about her situation and her future. At the same time, it shows us that her fears are justified, if not quite as she thinks, by revealing Rochester's duplicity. Imagery and action here are used, as they often are in the novel, to throw the nerves of the heroine in patterns on the screen of the imagination.

II: *Shirley*

It would be reasonable to predict that in *Shirley*, with its broad canvas, Brontë would be less likely than in *Jane Eyre* to use the kinds of psychological drama analysed above. In fact, the later novel shows just as wide a variety of techniques to expose the inner feelings of characters. Caroline is given soliloquies from time to time; the interplay between Shirley and Caroline throws light on both characters; dialogue is used very effectively, for example, in Robert Martin's conversation with Mr Yorke in which he reveals his change of heart (Chapter 30); setting is used, of course; the symbolism of water is important in the characterisation of Caroline and Shirley; personifications are used to dramatise mental conflict in several characters, especially Caroline; *Coriolanus* is alluded to at length to develop the character of Robert Moore; most obvious of all is the device of Louis

Moore's journal. Although these techniques are often part of the process of characterisation, there are episodes in which they touch more deeply on the structure of the novel. What Brontë makes less use of in *Shirley* is the Gothic style which is so important a part of the effect of *Jane Eyre*.

We will study the episode of Shirley's being bitten by a supposedly rabid dog, and the aftermath. Practically speaking, it turns out to be a trivial incident, but it has a thematic bearing on the novel as a whole.

Shirley's encounter with Phœbe occurs in Chapter 28, offstage, and is recalled in Chapter 36. Approaching Fieldhead after a walk at the beginning of Chapter 28, Shirley separates from her party for a period of twenty minutes to give directions to her foreman. When she reappears, her mood is changed from 'joyous' to 'quite pale, very thoughtful, almost sad'; she misses luncheon and spends an hour alone in her room. There is no immediate explanation for the darkening of Shirley's spirits. The biting itself is not described until Shirley recounts it to Louis Moore towards the end of the chapter:

> 'I heard a panting sound; a dog came running up the lane. I know most of the dogs in this neighbourhood; it was Phœbe, one of Mr Sam Wynne's pointers. The poor creature ran with her head down, her tongue hanging out; she looked as if bruised and beaten all over. I called her; I meant to coax her into the house, and give her some water and dinner; I felt sure she had been ill-used: Mr Sam often flogs his pointers cruelly. She was too flurried to know me; and when I attempted to pat her head, she turned and snatched at my arm. She bit it so as to draw blood, then ran panting on. Directly after, Mr Wynne's keeper came up, carrying his gun. He asked me if I had seen a dog, I told him I had seen Phœbe.
>
> '"You had better chain up Tartar, ma'am," he said, "and tell your people to keep within the house; I am after Phœbe to shoot her, and the groom is gone another way. She is raging mad."'
>
> Mr Moore leaned back in his chair, and folded his arms across his chest; Miss Keeldar resumed her square of silk canvass, and continued the creation of a wreath of Parmese violets.
>
> 'And you told no one, sought no help, no cure: you would not come to me?'
>
> 'I got as far as the school-room door; there my courage failed: I preferred to cushion the matter.'

'Why? What can I demand better in this world than to be of use to you?'

'I had no claim.'

'Monstrous! And you did nothing?'

'Yes: I walked straight into the laundry, where they are ironing most of the week, now that I have so many guests in the house. While the maid was busy crimping or starching, I took an Italian iron from the fire, and applied the light scarlet glowing tip to my arm: I bored it well in: it cauterised the little wound. Then I went up-stairs.'

(pp. 477–8)

The incident appears in the event a fuss about nothing – no harm results, and later, in Chapter 36, it is suggested that the dog might have been merely ill-used, and perhaps not mad; but neither Shirley nor Louis is yet aware of that. For them it is a significant event, and the telling of it a significant confidence.

Our method will be to consider what the episode means for the characters; to consider the symbolic meanings of the episode, and to look at its links with the rest of the novel. All three pillars of our analysis will show how the incident reveals much about Shirley herself and dramatises some major themes.

The manner in which the incident reflects Shirley is in some lights straightforward. We can see here the interesting mix of masculine toughness and feminine tenderness which typifies her behaviour and language throughout the novel. Her intention is kindness to the animal, which looks 'bruised and beaten all over'. She is bitten, and explains that because her 'courage failed' she did not seek Louis's help. There is no lack of courage, however, in the direct action she takes with the red-hot iron: here we see that 'Captain Keeldar' is more than simply a style which Shirley likes to affect; there is steel in her heart. In her speech, too, Shirley resembles a model soldier in terseness and objectivity. The simplicity of the final three statements in the extract serves to support the sincerity of Shirley's estimate of her wound as 'little' in importance as in size. Louis's horror at what she has done – expressed in his folding his arms across his chest, and in the single exclamation 'Monstrous!' – stresses the singularity of Shirley's behaviour. He – even such a man as he – is nearly offended at her wilful self-reliance, even while he respects deeply her strength of mind and will.

Looking further into the incident takes us at once towards more symbolic interpretations. We may consider it significant, in particular, that the instrument which Shirley uses for her act of bravery is an iron. The iron is much used at this point in the novel because of the quantities of washing and ironing generated by Shirley's guests. She is a good housekeeper as well as a great lady and understands the implications of her social activities well. There is also, however, a conflict between her deed and the tool she uses. Bravery is traditionally, if not wholly correctly, associated with masculinity; the iron, on the other hand, is conventionally associated with homely, domestic, feminine activities. An Italian iron is a narrow design specialised for use on pleats and frills, and thus may be seen as a more than usually feminine implement. (Of other implications of the 'Italian' nature of the iron I have nothing to say, despite several hints in the novel of a passion in Shirley for things Italian – such as 'Parmese' violets. Let those who wish to develop the idea do so!)

There is also about Shirley's handiwork with the iron a suggestion of feminine self-immolation as opposed to masculine self-abnegation. The description of the 'light scarlet glowing tip' of the iron has something of the lovingness of Cleopatra with her asps, and that impulse has interesting implications. What she performs is essentially a private act: she tells none of the guests, not even Louis, and waits until the maid is occupied elsewhere. When Shirley claims that her behaviour was intended to 'cushion the matter' it is not entirely the irony that it appears: she indeed prefers her self-violence to laying her weakness before others. She needs, in addition, to perform an act of self-punishment, or self-discipline. There is that in Shirley which needs to perform this spectacular act hidden from the eyes of the world, and for her own perverse satisfaction: she needs to punish herself; and it is, evidently, very much more than a dog's bite which Shirley wishes to cauterise.

If we now try to see the pattern of symbolism in the episode which Shirley describes we can begin to perceive something of the deeper meaning of her deed. Clearly, it has to do with Shirley's good will, and her rapport with the natural world. She has described herself as essentially a pagan, and her judgements are founded in nature, and not in religion; this is an opposition which we have analysed in an earlier chapter. Here nature is represented by Phœbe – as elsewhere by Tartar, whose behaviour towards men seems to imply the judgement of nature on them.

In this episode, nature – as expressed by the dogs – gives contradictory signals. Mr Wynne's keeper tells Shirley to 'chain up Tartar'; Phœbe is 'ill-used', is 'too flurried to know' Shirley and thus bites the arm which is trying to give comfort; Phœbe is described – though erroneously, it later appears – as 'raging mad'. Nature, it seems, is upset; but how seems unclear. We could enter into more minute detail in analysis of this episode. We might, for example, try to develop the gender element here: Phœbe is a bitch, mistreated by Mr Sam Wynne; Phœbe is the moon-goddess (identifiable with Artemis), and the moon is traditionally a female symbol. We do not need, however, to be so specific, but may allow what is imprecise to remain so.

The general theme is nature, and more particularly the nature of Shirley. Here, it is as if nature is turning against itself, or against her. From that point of view, her auto-surgery with the iron may be seen as a way of curing an invisible but real sickness in her: we may interpret it as a symbolic enactment of her decision to accept her femininity and what it conventionally implies. She associates herself in this episode with traditional female or feminine roles: she uses the iron, though to rather unusual purpose; and she has on her lap, and is working on, some sewing – 'the creation of a wreath of Parmese violets'. The schooling to which she subjects herself symbolically in this episode is matched a little later in action when she disciplines herself to adopt the role of female to Louis's male – tutoring him in his role, too. The violence which Shirley performs on herself with the iron symbolises an equally violent change in her outlook and behaviour. This is almost the last act of 'Captain Keeldar'.

We have already been speaking about the links between this episode and the book as a whole. The significance of nature as theme and setting, the use of Tartar, and the theme of the social status of women have already been mentioned, and it is not necessary to say more. A further point which is of importance, however, is the opposition in the novel between water and aridity, between fertility and sterility. It appears in the episode, of course, in the phantom hydrophobia of Phœbe, which Shirley at this point fears she may die from. This theme goes right back to the ironic 'shower' of curates who fall in Chapter 1 (p. 39); it continues in the picture of barren uselessness which Caroline sees in the Misses Mann and Ainley, and in her own future; it appears in the quotation and discussion of Cowper's "The Castaway" (Chapter 12, pp. 231–3); Caroline, seeing Robert in intimate conversation with Shirley in Chapter 13, thinks of talking to him herself at the Hollow, at the edge of a 'deep ravine, from whose rifted gloom was heard a sound like the spirit of the lonely watercourse, moaning amongst its wet stones' (p. 239); disappointed in her hopes of Robert, she succumbs to a fever, 'hot, parched, thirsty, restless' (Chapter 24, p. 399); we are told that 'the breath of Asiatic deserts parched' her lips (Chapter 25, p. 419); almost the last view we have of Caroline, however, is of her giving her plants a 'refreshing shower' from her watering-pot, and pausing to watch Venus – 'a silver point – the Star of Love' – as Robert Moore steals upon her to rest his hand at her waist (Chapter 37, pp. 592–3). We may therefore choose to see Shirley's encounter with Phœbe as pointing to a kind of moral hydrophobia: independent, intelligent, commanding, she has a natural aversion from the kind of submission which love and marriage to Louis would involve; however, aware of the sterile future to which she may be condemning herself, she deliberately disciplines herself to accept his love. The situation is paradoxical, in keeping with the conflicting indications of the Phoebe episode. The effect of it is that, in order to be natural, Shirley has to behave in a way which is to her unnatural: this is the point which is enacted in branding herself with her maid's Italian iron.

Charlotte Brontë, as we have already noted, is no revolutionary. Shirley rejoices in her independence, and in her superiority to most of the men of her acquaintance; but the best she can do, in the end, is to give up her independence for Louis.

III: *Villette*

The range of methods used to dramatise Lucy's experience in *Villette* is as wide as those used in the earlier novels. The use of personification, in particular, is of great importance, developing to the brink of full-blown allegory in the style of *The Pilgrim's Progress*. We have already considered how setting may be used to express character. As in *Jane Eyre*, mirror images are used very effectively. So frequent are the parallels between characters that it is possible to see many as shadows of the possible lives of Lucy. The novel is a veritable fairground for the modern critic. Every incident seems to be open to interpretation on a variety of levels.

The following extract, from Chapter 26, 'A Burial', which deals with the fate of Lucy's letters from Dr Bretton, is a good example:

> I then made a little roll of my letters, wrapped them in oiled silk, bound them with twine, and, having put them in the bottle, got the old Jew broker to stopper, seal, and make it airtight. While obeying my directions, he glanced at me now and then, suspiciously, from under his frost-white eye-lashes. I believe he thought there was some evil deed on hand. In all this I had a dreary something – not pleasure – but a sad, lonely satisfaction. The impulse under which I acted, the mood controlling me, were similar to the impulse and the mood which had induced me to visit the confessional. With quick walking I regained the pensionnat just at dark, and in time for dinner.
>
> At seven o'clock the moon rose. At half-past seven, when the pupils and teachers were at study, and Madame Beck was with her mother and children in the salle à manger, when the half-boarders were all gone home, and Rosine had left the vestibule, and all was still – I shawled myself, and, taking the sealed jar, stole out through the first-classe door, into the berceau and thence into the 'allée défendue.'
>
> Methusaleh, the pear-tree, stood at the further end of this walk, near my seat: he rose up, dim and grey, above the lower shrubs around him. Now Methusaleh, though so very old, was of sound timber still; only there was a hole, or rather a deep hollow, near his root. I knew there was such a hollow, hidden partly by ivy and creepers growing thick round; and there I meditated hiding my treasure. But I was not only going to hide a treasure – I meant also to

bury a grief. That grief over which I had lately been weeping, as I wrapped it in its winding-sheet, must be interred.

Well, I cleared away the ivy, and found the hole; it was large enough to receive the jar, and I thrust it deep in. In a tool-shed at the bottom of the garden lay the relics of building-materials, left by masons lately employed to repair a part of the premises. I fetched thence a slate and some mortar, put the slate on the hollow, secured it with cement, covered the whole with black mould, and, finally, replaced the ivy. This done, I rested, leaning against the tree; lingering, like any other mourner, beside a newly-sodded grave.

(pp. 380–1)

At first glance, this appears to be a straightforward piece of narrative writing. It will reveal its meaning fully only after thorough examination. As before, we will need to look at the background to the episode, then at the events narrated, and finally at the details of the way in which the events are presented. Style is particularly important in this extract.

The key to the episode is the letters. Ordinary enough in themselves, they mean a great deal to Lucy. Five in all, they were written to her by Dr Bretton. She has earlier described them as 'kind letters enough – pleasing letters'. Time, she explains, has 'mellowed them to a beverage of . . . mild quality', but when, lonely and hopelessly devoid of friendship at the pensionnat, she first 'tasted their elixir', their content seemed 'a divine vintage' (all p. 334). These quotations come from Chapter 23, in which Lucy's visit to the theatre is brought to a premature end by an outbreak of fire. The stirring performance, and the dangerous conclusion, seem to match the intensity with which Lucy savours the letters, reading into them much more than they contain. Not knowing Dr Bretton well at this stage, she fails to make sufficient allowance for his shallowness.

The pathos of Lucy's situation is redoubled by her inability to keep the letters to herself. Madame Beck, the eye and ear of the pensionnat, borrows them for her own perusal, and is not dismayed to be discovered (see p. 377). When, in Chapter 22, Lucy thinks she has lost the first of the letters, having carried it from place to place in a vain endeavour to find a private moment in which to read it, she is distraught – 'I groped on the floor, wringing my hands wildly' – and describes the event as a 'Cruel, cruel doom!', bewailing in a rare moment of self-pity '[having] my bit of comfort preternaturally snatched from me, ere I had well tasted its virtue' (p. 326). The letter means much to her: in so restricted a life as Lucy lives, the merest glimpse of sunlight is a great treasure. The later loss she takes with greater patience: she is able to '[take] heart of grace' and wait for Madame Beck to return what she has purloined. At this point, she has recognised Dr Bretton's love for Polly, and has accepted the disappointment of her own hopes of him.

The letters suffer a third invasion, this time by Monsieur Paul. He has been more circumspect than Madame Beck, but Lucy notices that the ribbon in which the letters are held has been retied, and finds other signs of tampering with her drawer (see p. 378). It is then that Lucy thinks hard about a secure hiding-place for these 'mementos'. She has given up hope of Dr Bretton, but nevertheless cannot give up thoughts of him. She speaks with understanding of the paradoxical behaviour of the grief-stricken, of the habit of 'people who have undergone bereavement always jealously [to] gather together and lock away mementos: it is not supportable to be stabbed to the heart each moment by sharp revival of regret' (p. 378). This paradox – the need to forget mementos – points to the heart of the episode, as we shall see.

Let us return now to the events narrated in the extract. It begins with details of the wrapping up of the letters – in oiled silk, bound with twine, in an airtight bottle. By the light of the moon, while all is quiet, Lucy 'shawl[s] herself' and steals out to the 'allée défendue'. There she discovers a hole at the base of the old pear-tree, lodges the bottle inside, covers it with a slate, cements it in, and then conceals her handiwork with a covering of earth and ivy. The events are briefly summarised: but the manner of their dramatisation attaches to them a wealth of psychological and thematic significance.

It is obvious, firstly, that Lucy's deed is a ceremonial one. The chapter is entitled 'A Burial', and the episode celebrates the interment with an attention to detail, and a control of mood, which might match the entombment of a person. The use of 'little' to describe her roll of letters recalls our earlier discussion of the word:

here it suggests fondness and intimacy – and perhaps an element of self-deprecation. The ceremonial mood is supported by a religious tone in the passage, in its implicit denial that 'there was some evil deed on hand', its allusion to 'the mood which had induced me to visit the confessional', and its strange use of 'relics' to refer to the building materials left recently by masons. Even the name of the tree, Methusaleh, makes a minor contribution to the effect. The language used is appropriate to a formal funeral, with references to weeping, the winding-sheet, interment, and Lucy as a 'mourner, beside a newly-sodded grave'. The mood is one of controlled grief: Lucy feels a 'dreary something – not pleasure – but a sad, lonely satisfaction' as she parcels up the letters; she has lately been weeping, but is now more resigned; she lingers beside the grave like a mourner, but one capable of action. Methusaleh matches her mood: 'dim and grey', but 'of sound timber still'. All this follows naturally from the beginning of the passage, when the wrapping up of the letters is recounted with the dignified detail appropriate to a laying-out.

The point of the ceremonial is complex. The extract makes clear that a double meaning is intended: to 'hide a treasure' and 'to bury a grief'. There is a psychological, as well as a narrative, element in what happens here. That double meaning carries a double emotional weight. The 'treasure' is so only because Lucy wishes to see it in that light; there is no evidence in the novel to suggest that Dr Bretton considers his letters to Lucy important. For Lucy, nevertheless, those letters represent the square of daylight which tantalises a prisoner incarcerated in his cell; they promise, if not freedom, then the possibility of it; they reassure her that there is a world outside the pensionnat. They are very much hers – almost the only private property she has; thus they are part of her identity. The retention of those letters constitutes declaration of Lucy's emotional investment; and that makes them a very dangerous treasure.

Lucy's intention in burying this treasure is also to bury the feelings – or at least the display of them – associated with it. There is a curious mirror image between Lucy and the 'old Jew broker' with suspicious eyes under his 'frost-white eyelashes': we recall, inevitably, Lucy's white cap of hair, and that 'Snowe' was, for a time, 'Frost'.

Thus Brontë stresses the collusion of broker and customer in the stoppering, sealing, and making airtight of the jar. The detail makes final, it would appear, the sealing up of Lucy's emotions, in the same sort of way that a death is followed by a viewing, a service and a burial. The reference to the confessional indicates the private nature of what is proceeding. Secrecy is essential to this episode, too: there is emphasis on the absence of Madame Beck, the boarders, the pupils, teachers and Rosine; Lucy 'stole out' into the berceau into a forbidden (défendue) place; the letters, at last, are shut away from prying eyes.

The psychological importance of this episode is not hard to explain, but it is not straightforward. Clearly, Lucy has determined that her love for Dr Bretton shall be forever concealed. What is not clear is whether she hopes by burying to destroy it. Clearly, again, if that is her intention, it fails; for part of the point of the episode is that the letters, and with them her love, are preserved – buried, yes, but sealed up and thus protected from decay: why else must the container be airtight? The mirroring of Lucy in the old Jew broker's eyelashes reminds us of one of the implications of snow which we noticed in Chapter 1, that it may blur and cover up reality: but it does not destroy what lies beneath. The grief of her loss is put out of mind, but will never leave her heart, for a part of her is buried with the letters.

The episode is a key moment in the novel. Its significance is stressed when, as at other critical points, the strange Gothic nun appears, in another odd mirroring of Lucy herself. The nun 'had no face – no features: all below her brow was masked with a white cloth' (p. 381). Equally, Lucy has no face and no features: this is part of the point of the burial: Lucy has buried herself away from public gaze as far as she can, and her vivid emotional life is known to us, her readers, better than to any of her acquaintance. That is to say, she is herself a species of nun; the place where she buries the letters is close to the place where the bones of the mediaeval nun are rumoured to be buried. Lucy lives a secret life, pretending to be like other people, behaving as Madame Beck would wish her to, while within lurks a different creature entirely.

The symbolic meaning of this episode is clearer than its narrative outcome. It is not certain that the letters remain interred. That she obtains her jar from a pawnbroker may perhaps alert us to the idea of redemption – to the possibility, if not the fact – and, speaking of the letters in Chapter 23, Lucy tells us that 'I read them in after years' (p. 334); but how she might have done so is not explained.

Lucy's grief, however, is never forced out of its hiding place. Her self-discipline is iron. In a peculiarly harsh scene (Chapter 32), she is made to confront the reality of Polly's relationship with Dr Bretton. Letters are important here, too: Graham Bretton's letter to Paulina, which she finds among twelve addressed to her father, makes an interesting link with Lucy's. Like Lucy, Polly refers to her letter, in which Graham declares his love for her, as a 'treasure', but her actions are the reverse of Lucy's. Instead of vainly attempting to conceal her letter, she displays it. The seal, she says, was 'too beautiful to be broken, so I cut it round with my scissors'. She makes much of Graham's hand-writing, 'like himself . . . clear, firm, and rounded', and breaks off to ask Lucy if she knows 'his autograph'. Beneath Lucy's steel response, 'I have seen it: go on', lie a world of implicit pain and, at this point, a closer knowledge of Graham's character than Polly yet has (all pp. 464–5). Later, in Chapter 37, when Polly talks to Lucy about Graham's 'firm, marble chin . . . straight Greek features', we may feel that she has picked on the only firm thing about him, and think how she may live to regret her choice. Lucy, however, secretly shares her admiration and is dismayed at this death-blow to her wild hopes, and stuns Polly into silence by saying that she makes it a point never to see him, because 'I value vision, and dread being struck stone blind'. In response, Polly, saying more than she knows, compliments Lucy on being a 'Spartan girl! Proud Lucy!' (all pp. 519–20). For Polly, proud of her treasure, secure in being the 'little treasure' of Monsieur de Bassompierre (p. 525), 'a pearl . . . pure and of price' (p. 522), life seems to be a simple, serene sequence of success and security. For Lucy, poor, unvalued by those around her, and unregarded by Graham Bretton, life is a secret struggle to survive by camouflage and concealment.

This is the point implied in the burial scene. Like the Spartan boy who refuses to confess to his theft of the fox, Lucy will keep her secret, gnawing at her heart though it is, until death. Monsieur Paul does not learn of it; Lucy herself does not acknowledge it as she turns from Graham to Paul Emanuel as the partner of her life.

In the burial scene, then, a simple action is used by Brontë to develop psychological facets of Lucy which are deep, complex and more powerfully communicated by symbolism than by discussion. Lucy's feelings do not respond well to clinical analysis; they speak more directly to our own feelings through the medium of image and implication.

Conclusions

1. Vivid dramatisation is the key to Brontë's success. She is able to make her characters psychologically convincing, and explores them more deeply than is usually understood by characterisation. She is also able to generate thematic resonances from the surface meaning of the events she narrates.

2. The major themes, and the psychology of her major characters are portrayed by a variety of means. In this chapter we have looked mainly at the use of imagery and symbolism. Other techniques include personification of abstract ideas, literary allusions and parallels, and the use of setting to sympathise with or contrast with events and characters.

3. Brontë's preference for the use of imagery and action to express psychology enables her to communicate emotional states more vividly and directly than she could do by explanation.

4. Because her method is imprecise, it does not limit our responses: instead, she encourages us to explore her themes and characters in an active and creative way, and we participate in the creative process.

5. Brontë makes frequent use of symbolism to develop the meanings of incidents; each novel has a distinctive vein of symbolism, alongside features common to all the novels.

6. Brontë's method also generalises. The interaction of character and event points to common experience, to universal human feeling.

Methods of Analysis

1. It is important in discussing the dramatisation of specific scenes to remind ourselves of the context of their actions; thus we have summarised briefly the context of each of the extracts.
2. Next, look at the events narrated, or the dialogue recounted, and at the implications of what happens.
3. Then you will be able to consider the meaning and resonance of the imagery and symbolism used in the extracts, and what it reveals about the characters.
4. Consider the way language is used by Brontë to develop a rich and complex mood, tone, or atmosphere against which the events in the extracts are set.
5. Think about how these episodes reflect themes, and how the content of the episodes relates to images, events, symbols and themes elsewhere in the novel.
6. Finally, try on the basis of your analysis to arrive at an interpretation of the full meaning of each extract, and attempt to summarise it.
7. Remember that this is essentially a creative process. We are looking at what the language of the novels implies, without concerning ourselves initially about the possible dangers of misinterpretation. We endeavour, however, to check our interpretation against the pattern of each novel as a whole, and to be aware of how our analysis of the scene is consistent or inconsistent with the whole.

Further Work

Jane Eyre: A scene which uses methods similar to those we have discussed is the fire in Rochester's bedroom in Volume 1, Chapter 15, pp. 167–70. Choose an extract of sensible size and explore the way in which language and image are used to develop the significance of the scene – for example, as an expression of Jane's passions. The symbolism of fire is central to this discussion.

Shirley: You could try now a rather different approach to the communication of emotional states. Consider how personifications are used in the first four paragraphs of Chapter 7 to express the psychology of Caroline Helstone (pp. 121–2). If you would prefer a passage more akin to the one we have discussed, look instead at Martin Yorke's meeting with Caroline in the woods in the first two pages of the second section of Chapter 32 (pp. 527–9).

Villette: A suitable scene is that in which Lucy retires to the attic at the pensionnat to learn her part in the play (Chapter 14, pp. 203–5). This is a very rich episode; you may wish to focus on its context, and look at the implications of her agreeing to perform at all, as well as the manner in which she does so.

5

Protestantism, Popery and Other Persuasions

Religion is part of the texture of Charlotte Brontë's novels as it was of her mind. The daughter of a clergyman, with strong Wesleyan connections on her mother's side, and throughout most of her life frequently in the society of churchmen, one of whom she eventually married, brought up in a God-fearing household, educated at schools where religious principles were strongly upheld, she could hardly have ignored religion; it was the medium in which she lived. The impact on her writing is subtle but profound. Her novels do not discuss faith or theology, or argue principle. They do not even concern themselves with simple morality. But her characters are generally conscious of the demands of conscience; they are concerned with right behaviour. There is always, in her work, the sense of an enfolding providence, and her characters think of their lives as having purpose and direction. The concern with religion is therefore a general one: though her characters sometimes worry themselves over doctrinal differences, it is not apparent that they cause the author much anxiety. Only in *Villette* is the clash of Rome and Canterbury crucial: the earlier novels treat religion less specifically. The powerful influence of religion comes across most clearly in her style. Brontë's language is part of a culture of which the religious heritage forms an important component, and shows how deeply her religious ideas are embedded in the habit of her mind. Her writing is steeped in allusions to, and echoes of, the Bible and other texts with a religious significance, especially *The Pilgrim's Progress* and *Paradise Lost*; the cadence of her writing, and its poetic qualities in her heightened moments, owe much to the style of the Authorised Version.

The treatment of religious behaviour in the novels covers a spectrum from deep seriousness to trivial comedy. We see characters ranging in their response to religion from St John Rivers's self-immolation to Martin Yorke's heedlessness. Religious adherence is no guide to moral quality: Brontë sees Mr Hall, Mr Helstone, Mr Brocklehurst and all her other clergymen as individuals; and perhaps none of them is as saintly as Helen Burns. Brontë does not make simple moral judgements; rather, she invites us to contemplate the behaviour of her characters in terms of its effect on others. Hers is a surprisingly – given her background – pragmatic view of the world.

Our business in dealing with the extracts which follow is to look at the part religion plays in each novel, and we will need to refer more widely to the novels than previously. Comparisons between characters, and their views of each other, will form an important part of our exploration. Though the topic is a large one, we do not need to fear it, because we will be making no attempt to deal with it comprehensively. We will content ourselves with picking out the major issues which affect the characters and help us to understand Brontë's ideas. We need not be pedantic about discriminating, from moment to moment, which aspects of religion we are referring to; we can treat the topic broadly, and refer to whatever seems useful within its general framework. Novels, after all, are not philosophical or ethical treatises; they deal with the complex, mixed, and often confused moods and feelings of characters.

I: *Jane Eyre*

Jane Eyre may be viewed as a sequence of moral judgements. From the beginning, when she is locked in the red-room for wickedness, to Lowood where she is branded a liar, to Thornfield where she comes near to being drawn into an adulterous relationship with Rochester, to Marsh End, where she comes within an ace of becoming a missionary, Jane is made to view herself and her life in moral terms. It is in her intense and troubled relationship with St John Rivers, who has his own difficult moral choices to make, that she is required to focus her judgement most sharply. This is a passage from Volume 3, Chapter 4 in which Jane listens to a sermon by St John:

> But besides his frequent absences, there was another barrier to friendship with him: he seemed of a reserved, an abstracted, and even of a brooding nature. Zealous in his ministerial labours, blameless in his life and habits, he yet did not appear to enjoy that mental serenity, that inward content, which should be the reward of every sincere Christian and practical philanthropist. Often, of an evening, when he sat at the window, his desk and papers before him, he would cease reading or writing, rest his chin on his hand, and deliver himself up to I know not what course of thought: but that it was perturbed and exciting might be seen in the frequent flash and changeful dilation of his eye.
>
> I think, moreover, that Nature was not to him that treasury of delight it was to his sisters. He expressed once, and but once in my hearing, a strong sense of the rugged charm of the hills, and an inborn affection for the dark roof and hoary walls he called his home: but there was more of gloom than pleasure in the tone and words in which the sentiment was manifested; and never did he seem to roam the moors for the sake of their soothing silence – never seek out or dwell upon the thousand peaceful delights they could yield.
>
> Incommunicative as he was, some time elapsed before I had an opportunity of gauging his mind. I first got an idea of its calibre when I heard him preach in his own church at Morton. I wish I could describe that sermon: but it is past my power. I cannot even render faithfully the effect it produced on me.
>
> It began calm – and indeed, as far as delivery and pitch of voice went, it was calm to the end: an earnestly felt, yet strictly restrained zeal breathed soon in the distinct accents, and prompted the nervous language. This grew to force – compressed, condensed, controlled. The heart was thrilled, the mind astonished, by the power of the preacher: neither were softened. Throughout there was a strange bitterness; an absence of consolatory gentleness; stern allusions to Calvinistic doctrines – election, predestination, reprobation – were frequent; and each reference to these points sounded like a sentence

pronounced for doom. When he had done, instead of feeling better, calmer, more enlightened by his discourse, I experienced an inexpressible sadness; for it seemed to me – I know not whether equally so to others – that the eloquence to which I had been listening had sprung from a depth where lay turbid dregs of disappointment- where moved troubling impulses of insatiate yearnings and disquieting aspirations. I was sure St John Rivers – pure-lived, conscientious, zealous as he was – had not yet found that peace of God which passeth all understanding: he had no more found it, I thought, than had I; with my concealed and racking regrets for my broken idol and lost elysium – regrets to which I have latterly avoided referring; but which possessed me and tyrannized over me ruthlessly.

(pp. 393–4)

The structure of the extract is not as simple as it may appear at first sight. It is an analysis of St John Rivers himself, which has been introduced a little earlier by contrasting him with his sisters. It includes also, in the first and third paragraphs, Jane's sense of the mystery of his character, some material in the second paragraph about St John's attitude to nature, and a description of the impression made on Jane by his style of sermon. Jane has found it easy to get on with the sisters, but has found that the 'Incommunicative' brother presented much more of an obstacle. As we have seen elsewhere, Brontë makes a point of the limitations of the narrator, who says that St John did not 'appear' to enjoy peace of mind, notes him sinking into 'I know not what' reverie, and comments that he did not 'seem' to love nature. The extract therefore uses the outward signs of expression, gesture and voice to express St John's character and his religious ideas. The focus on the narrator becomes much stronger during the course of the extract: at the beginning she observes St John's behaviour in general; the following description of his sermon in Morton church is not only an indicator of his mind, but chiefly, and finally, an expression of his powerful impact on Jane. We will begin by considering the portrait of St John himself, then look at the light he throws on Jane, and turn finally to his contribution to the religious theme of the novel.

The impression given of St John here is of a man divided. Brontë presents him by simple statement, but also dramatises his demeanour. 'Zealous' in his ministry, 'blameless' in his life, St John is a good man and a good pastor. Jane's respect for him is everywhere apparent. Yet she is also sensitive to the hidden aspect of his character: he has a 'brooding nature', is a stranger to 'serenity' and 'inward content'; she notes his 'perturbed' and agitated glances, which both indicate how Jane is struck by him, and suggest that the inner man is at odds with his outer demeanour. The picture she presents of him as he sits at the window, 'his desk and papers before him', is of a man confronting his work but torn from it, 'chin on his hand', by unruly thought. Conflict is central to his character. The first two paragraphs show him as a man uncomfortable with his vocation, yet unable to surrender to the gentler invitations of nature. He is presented as a restless wanderer. The description of his feeling about his house – 'the dark roof and hoary walls he called his home' – stresses his alienation. Ill at ease in his habitation as in the natural world outside it, he nourishes a spirit equally ill at ease in its corporeal frame. The implication of his failure to find solace in nature is a subject we shall need to consider a little later; for the moment, let us note simply that St John's unease is both with the external natural world and with his own nature; for Brontë, the two are closely connected.

The sermon matches St John in being righteous, yet disturbing. The tone is calm throughout, but the content crushes. The whole is fiercely disciplined: earnest, 'strictly restrained,' 'distinct', 'nervous', 'compressed, condensed, controlled', 'stern' – the language expresses emphatically the iron regulation he has imposed on himself and his life. There is, however, no attractiveness in his discourse. The problem is summed up in a succinct antithesis: 'The heart was thrilled, the mind astonished . . . neither were softened.'

It is in the idea of softening that Jane, in contrast with St John, sees the virtue of religious faith. Serenity and 'inward content' should be 'the reward of every sincere Christian and practical philanthropist'. This is more than a conventional courtesy to the norms of Christian faith: it is an expression of the principles which Jane has learned from Helen Burns at Lowood. In the two terms used here – sincerity and philanthropy – we can discern ideas which Jane shares with her inventor. Though she makes no overt criticism, Jane has no interest in the cornerstones of Calvinism – election, predestination and reprobation. She notes the absence of 'consolatory gentleness' in St John's sermon. She refers with misgiving to his sternness, to his ideas of sentencing and doom. There is nothing in his sermon to suggest 'that peace of God which passeth all understanding'; nothing which matches Jane's ideas about the rewards of religious faith.

Her own 'softness' – we may interpret the word as having to do with tolerance or sympathy – is nowhere more evident than in her ability to feel the spiritual troubles of one so unlike herself as St John, and even to see him as like her in his inner conflicts. Her response to him – a primitive emotional response, for it is 'past [her] power' to describe his sermon as she feels it deserves – is one of 'inexpressible sadness' for the deep pain from which she feels his eloquence derives. She senses in him something akin to her own pain, and her language becomes heightened poetically with alliteration and parallelism as she picks out in him the 'turbid dregs of disappointment' and refers, with the knowledge of her own rebellious will, to 'troubling impulses', 'insatiate yearnings', 'disquieting aspirations'. Conversely, though Jane perceives these qualities in him, it is hard for us to imagine in St John the capacity for the same kind of sympathy with Jane. Indeed, the sequel shows that he has none of her kind of insight, and that duty to his image of God is all that rules his heart. In Chapter 34, St John demands that Jane shall accompany him as a missionary to India and, even though he argues with unconscious brutality that she is insufficiently handsome for secular life, still insists that she shall, for the sake of moral rectitude as well as propriety, be married to him.

It is characteristic of Jane, of the novel, and of Brontë, that nature should be used as an indicator of the limitations of St John's perspective. He knows the countryside well, and is sensitive to his surroundings in his own gloomy way, but the natural world is not 'that treasury of delights it was to his sisters' – or, we may add, to Jane. His is a gloomy response: gloomy towards nature as towards the destiny of man. He does not walk among the hills to find 'soothing silence', nor for their 'thousand peaceful delights'. We note here the same kind of language that Jane uses of religious consolation.

Nature, like religion, brings peace and tranquillity to those who are pure in heart. St John's problem is that, like Brocklehurst earlier, he believes that nature is to be disciplined, or even extinguished. He will discipline his own nature by resolutely turning away from Rosamond Oliver, whose first name, rose of the world, is chosen to symbolise not only the temptations of the flesh which St John's spirit must reject in the quest for true purity of devotion, but all those delights of the world which, though they be perfectly innocent or inspiring, he cannot allow himself to enjoy. St John Rivers is, of course, not another Mr Brocklehurst, and their difference is as illuminating as their similarity. St John is worthy of respect; Brocklehurst is not. Where Brocklehurst delights in punishing others, using the promise of 'divine Consolations' as an excuse for starving the mortal bodies of his charges and inflicting on them as much as possible of the sufferings of the early Christians and the torments of the martyrs (Volume 1, Chapter 7, pp. 74–6), St John's first victim is himself.

Jane's reliance on nature rather than principle suggests that there is an element of the pagan about her as there is about Shirley Keeldar. Despite her temptation – vocation she realises it is not – later in the novel to join St John in his missionary work, the implication of the extract is that his faith is too narrow to satisfy her. As their relationship develops, we as readers seem better aware than Jane how dangerous is her position. She needs a more open and more generous faith, without the minatory and castigatory harshness from which she suffered so desperately in childhood.

Ironically, the origin of her sympathy with St John derives precisely from her pagan aspect. Jane's dregs of disappointment are the failure of her relationship with Rochester; her inner troubles are the self-doubt and sense of loss arising from that catastrophe; her longings are for the man she has been compelled to cast off. She uses the strongest possible language to describe her state of mind. Rochester she describes as 'my broken idol'. The words are carefully chosen to recall the biblical account in which Moses, coming down from the mountain to find his people under the leadership of Aaron worshipping a golden calf, breaks in his disgust the two stone tablets bearing the commandments: thus we are to see Jane's idolatry as contrary to the Christian code. We note, too, that the ambiguity of her feelings towards Rochester is reflected in the phrase, for it was the tablets which Moses broke, not the idol (which he later destroys comprehensively and variously – but initially by fire). The point is that she sees herself as setting Rochester up in opposition to her Christian God; and having done so is a measure of his importance to her, as it is of her sense of wrong. Her idol is broken because he has been shown to be morally flawed. The effect is to make her feel that she has been banished from paradise; but it is not a Christian paradise which she has lost; it is 'elysium' – a pagan heaven. Her regrets, she says, 'possessed' her and 'tyrannized over' her, as ruthlessly as, earlier at Thornfield, did her obsession with Rochester. The degree to which she is not herself suggests, indeed, possession by devils: it seems as if it is not she who controls her emotions.

Jane's powerful feelings towards Rochester show us a further dimension in her sympathy with St John. At the point from which the extract is taken, she has yet to perceive his involuntary feeling for Rosamond Oliver, and to see how he disciplines himself 'as a resolute rider would curb a rearing steed' (Volume 3, Chapter 5 p. 407), yet she already has a certain understanding of him. The source of at least some of their common disquiet is sexual: Jane does not know it yet, but she senses it. When she is later drawn closer to St John, it is partly because she feels compelled to admire the resolution with which he schools his heart.

Despite the sympathy in their natures, the religion of St John is seen in this extract to be wanting. Jane does not pretend to be able to understand St John's ideas: she cannot describe the sermon, nor even 'render faithfully' its effect upon her. But she shows how his faith fails to produce the fruits which she feels it should nurture, in the most effective manner: by using biblical language to point the vacuum in his soul when she says that St John 'had not yet found that peace of God which passeth all understanding'.

What is the alternative to St John's version of faith? Although Jane sets against him the pagan consolation of nature, it is not with any confidence of setting right against wrong. She is very suspicious of nature in the moral dimension, after all, because her own nature has betrayed her. No absolute judgements are made, therefore. Brontë's treatment of religion here is far from simple: faith is a matter of feeling, doubt, seeking and slow discovery.

St John's place in the novel is essential – and, as we shall see, he ends it. We are constantly drawn to see him in relation to other characters. The parallel with Brocklehurst's attitude to nature is obvious. The comparison of St John curbing the horse of his passions, quoted a little earlier, suggests links with Rochester, who literally and metaphorically fell off his horse when he met Jane. St John's Calvinistic side recalls Jane's victimisation at Gateshead and Lowood – two versions of hell for her in her early years. Against his philosophy, Helen Burns's stoicism offers a brighter version of Christian faith; in her painful existence, she looks forward to the hereafter as a 'region of happiness' where she will be 'received by the same universal mighty Parent' (Volume 1, Chapter 9, p. 95). St John is thus one among many influences – they include, for example, the Reeds, Miss Temple and St John's sisters in addition to those we have briefly outlined – which pull Jane this way and that in her long search for independence and maturity.

For Brontë, religion is not simply a matter of principle and rule. Faith grows from sincere, conscientious exploration of self, and, in lesser beings than Helen Burns, from the alchemy of experience.

II: Shirley

In Chapters 16 and 17 of *Shirley* occur Whitsuntide, the School-Feast, and – our topic – the Whitsuntide procession of twelve hundred children. Of the three bodies of four hundred souls, with a band at the rear of each regiment, each led by the teachers and one of the curates, Caroline and Shirley lead the Briarfield group with Mr Malone. The whole army is headed by Helstone, Hall and Boultby. Their march in Chapter 17 is contrasted, as they set out, with the manœuvres of real soldiers, cavalrymen, who are spied on the brow of Stilbro' Moor. The army is united under the generalship of Helstone, the clerical cossack who slips easily into his military role when they pass into the narrow defile of Royd-lane, to be confronted by a rival procession, 'headed also by men in black' and accompanied with music:

[Mr Hall] pointed with his staff to the end of the lane before them. Lo and behold! another, – an opposition procession was there entering, headed also by men in black, and followed also, as they could now hear, by music.

'Is it our double?' asked Shirley: 'our manifold wraith? Here is a card turned up.'

'If you wanted a battle, you are likely to get one, – at least of looks,' whispered Caroline, laughing.

'They shall not pass us!' cried the curates, unanimously: 'we'll not give way!'

'Give way!' retorted Helstone, sternly, turning round; 'who talks of giving way? You, boys, mind what you are about: the ladies, I know, will be firm; I can trust them. There is not a churchwoman here but will stand her ground against these folks, for the honour of the Establishment. What does Miss Keeldar say?'

'She asks what is it?'

'The Dissenting and Methodist schools, the Baptists, Independents, and Wesleyans, joined in an unholy alliance, and turning purposely into this lane with the intention of obstructing our march and driving us back.'

'Bad manners!' said Shirley; 'and I hate bad manners. Of course, they must have a lesson.'

'A lesson in politeness,' suggested Mr Hall, who was ever for peace: 'not an example of rudeness.'

Old Helstone moved on. Quickening his step, he marched some yards in advance of his company. He had nearly reached the other sable leaders, when he who appeared to act as the hostile commander-in-chief – a large, greasy man, with black hair combed flat on his forehead – called a halt. The procession paused: he drew forth a hymn-book, gave out a verse, set a tune, and they all struck up the most dolorous of canticles.

Helstone signed to his bands: they clashed out with all the power of brass. He desired them to play 'Rule, Britannia,' and ordered the children to join in vocally, which they did with enthusiastic spirit. The enemy was sung and stormed down; his psalm quelled: as far as noise went, he was conquered.

'Now, follow me!' exclaimed Helstone; 'not at a run, but a firm, smart pace. Be steady, every child and woman of you: – keep together: – hold on by each other's skirts, if necessary.'

And he strode on with such a determined and deliberate gait, and was, besides, so well seconded by his scholars and teachers – who did exactly as he told them, neither running nor faltering, but marching with cool, solid impetus; the curates, too, being compelled to do the same, as they were between two fires, – Helstone and Miss Keeldar, – both of whom watched any deviation with lynx-eyed vigilance, and were ready, the one with his cane, the other with her parasol, to rebuke the slightest breach of orders, the least independent or irregular demonstration, – that the body of Dissenters were first amazed, then alarmed, then borne down and pressed back, and at last forced to turn tail and leave the outlet from Royd-lane free. Boultby suffered in the onslaught, but Helstone and Malone, between them, held him up, and brought him through the business, whole in limb, though sorely tried in wind.

(pp. 300–1)

This entertaining passage of arms recalls the eighteenth century: Fielding, Swift and Pope watch from the wings. Shirley's manner of expressing her surprise at the confrontation, 'Here is a card turned up', evokes the game of cards in the third canto of *The Rape of the Lock*. The tone is mock-heroic; the spirit, one of fun – the episode is appropriately introduced by Caroline's whispered laughter. There is irony, here, of course, as there must be in the clashing of two such Christian armies as these; but the irony is allowed to emerge naturally, while Brontë enjoys with us the action, noise and spectacle. We will begin with that, and move on later to consider the more serious implications of the extract and its place in the novel.

An obvious feature of the extract with which to begin our analysis is the balance of dialogue and narrative. It is the dialogue, initially, which communicates the good-humoured excitement of the clash. Brontë focuses on individual characters effectively to express the mood of the whole group. The exclamations from the curates ('They shall not pass us!') and from the pugnacious Helstone, here more cossack than cleric ('Give way! . . . who talks of giving way?'), set the bellicose mood, developed later in the more active 'Now, follow me!'. Of course, the heroism is mock: and contrary to convention, the soldiers here are women and children. It is a minor joke that Helstone appears to place more faith in the firmness of his churchwomen than of his 'boys' (the context seems to suggest that he means the curates!) – '. . . the ladies, I know, will be firm; I can trust them'. Later, as the column makes its final advance upon the hostile force, Helstone and Shirley – here Captain Keeldar in act as well as in character – keep order, 'the one with his cane, the other with her parasol'. The incongruity of cane and parasol again recalls *The Rape of the Lock*.

When she turns to narrative, Brontë maintains the mock-heroic style, and develops the action with fine attention to sequence and rhythm when she writes that 'the Dissenters were first amazed, then alarmed, then borne down and pressed back, and at last forced to turn tail'. The language is muscular ('borne', 'pressed', 'forced', 'turn') and full of consonantal sounds of conflict, while the movement writhes like an El Greco ('down', 'back', 'turn tail'). Hard on the heels of this martial passage comes comedy with the bathos of Boultby, breathless in the 'onslaught', supported by the fitter Helstone and Malone.

The manner of presentation of this episode is crucial to its religious point. Let us look first at the individuals who participate, before proceeding to think about the significance of the whole.

In keeping with the eighteenth-century mood, Brontë uses an eighteenth-century technique – such as we have noted already in *Jane Eyre* in Chapter 2 – of comparing the behaviour of different characters. Here the fiery temperament of Helstone is contrasted with the more practical outlook of Shirley and the mildness of Mr Hall. Helstone calls the roll of the forces assembled against him: 'The Dissenting and Methodist schools, the Baptists, Independents, and Wesleyans', which together he terms an 'unholy alliance', claiming that it was the clear intention of these opponents to obstruct his own procession. Clearly, his view is exaggerated, born of bigotry and suspicion, and it is immediately reduced to absurdity by Shirley's response, 'Bad manners!', which, though superficially supportive, is actually in conflict with Helstone's assessment. Finally comes Mr Hall's suggestion (it is, of course, no more than that: a demand would be out of keeping with his character) that what Helstone's group should do is to offer their opponents an example of polite behaviour and, presumably, freely make way for the other procession. Naturally enough, this voice of Christian meekness is ignored by everybody else, and 'Old Helstone moved on'. Helstone is perhaps too 'Old' in experience – too embittered, too corrupted – to be moved by such lily-livered sentiments as Mr Hall's.

What Brontë picks out here, then, is conflict: doctrinal conflict, and conflict of personalities. The Whitsun battle is a metaphor for the religious dissension which we commented on in dealing with Chapter 1. Brontë does not take Helstone's side in the debate. The curates shout unanimously, 'we'll not give way!', but their unanimity is as weak as their will, and they are able to maintain their firmness only by being caught 'between two fires' – the military phrase neatly refers also to personalities – Helstone and Shirley, who are of sturdier mettle. Clearly, Brontë has no axe to grind. She makes no attempt to distinguish the rights and wrongs of one party in relation to another: she merely observes the differences, viewing each 'unholy alliance' as a mirror-image of the other – the opposition is 'our double . . . our manifold wraith', as Shirley puts it. Brontë's mother and father might well have been aligned, had they been moved to engage in such activities, on opposite sides in this doctrinal conflict.

There is no judgement made, either, about the implications of the music, which is an important weapon in the battle. The choice of music is appropriate to the standpoints of the different armies. The dissenters sing 'the most dolorous of canticles', while the established church strikes up 'Rule, Britannia'. It is hard to imagine that Brontë supports the latter against the canticle, no matter how dolorous it is, or its rendition. Brontë's point of view is indicated in the conclusion of the musical battle, when 'The enemy was sung and stormed down; his psalm quelled: as far as noise went, he was conquered'. The pointlessness of this mock-heroic conflict is revealed in the bathos of 'as far as noise went'. A further implication here is that the doctrinal battle is being fought in the wrong medium: the outcome of the musical jousting will not change anyone's mind about which place of worship he attends. Again, Brontë is a detached observer, amused by the antics of her puppets: the conflict is, in her eyes, ultimately meaningless.

Brontë takes, therefore, a much broader view than we might expect from the religious experience of her childhood. There is no suggestion here of sympathy with one side or another; nor, despite the comedy, is there any sign of contempt for the protagonists in the battle; there is certainly no scorn of the 'enthusiastic spirit' with which the children sing. There is consciousness both of the littleness of this battle and of the more serious conflicts it symbolises: as in *The Rape of the Lock*, the mock-heroic strikes in two contrary directions, both aggrandising and belittling. We may be reminded here of those glittering Miltonic armies which Shirley has spoken of in the extract we discussed in Chapter 3. The Miltonic view of the spiritual world seemed to Shirley unrealistic; so, too, it seems, to Brontë did the doctrinal conflicts of her times.

The Whitsuntide battle dramatises the religious environment of the novel. From the beginning, when the visiting of the curates is described as a 'system of mutual invasion' religious behaviour is seen as a series of social events characterised by conflict or aggression. As she does here, Brontë carefully refrains elsewhere in the novel from making doctrinal or sectarian judgements: her view throughout is tolerant. In Chapter 9, she is happy to describe the lusty singing in the Wesleyan chapel at Briarfields (pp. 163–5), but she is just as happy to describe the secular domestic joys of the Yorkes' home at Briarmains: 'if Briar-chapel seemed alive, so also did Briarmains' (p. 165). The singing in the church, though spirited, is all of struggle and fight, and the congregation appears to respond with joy and hope to the most appalling visions of 'slaughter and blood' or 'tumult and war' (both p. 163) expressed in the hymns; the Yorkes' mansion, on the other hand, is lit by a homely fire instead of the sulphurous fume of hell, and, instead of resounding with loud hymns, murmurs with the gentler 'sound of voice and laughter' (p. 165). Much later in the novel, in Chapter 34, Martin Yorke, 'the young cynic' (p. 548), who harbours in his heart 'an irreligious reluctance to see the approach of Sunday' (p. 545) but attends church with the aim of seeing Caroline, characterises an ordinary insensitivity to religion and its practices; his mind is on anything and everything but God. Yet his is the voice which Brontë chooses to express her ironic observations about the occasion. At first he is alone in the church except for one old woman, and, in the event, 'not one affluent family attended, not one carriage party appeared'. The church is peopled only by 'grey-haired elders and feeble paupers', and Brontë comments that 'It is always the frailest, the oldest, and the poorest that brave the worst weather, to prove and maintain their constancy to dear old mother Church' (both p. 547). But there is no judgemental frowning. Brontë has every sympathy with the sincere church-goer, is amused by the behaviour of the average, and, despite the fondness and familiarity of the reference to church as 'dear old mother', is not convinced that the goal of man's existence is necessarily to be found inside any of the houses dedicated by the various doctrines to the worship of the Creator.

The effect is to present religious difference as petty *sub specie aeternitatis* – an amusing but fraught diversion from the practicalities of Christian life. For Brontë's own religious views, we must look elsewhere than in the man-made temples, and turn instead to God's own creation.

III: *Villette*

In approach to religion, as in other things, Brontë's novels are quite distinct. *Villette* alone stresses the chasm that yawned between the Roman and English churches. Remarkably little is said directly of Lucy Snowe's own religious views, yet she constantly must contend with those endemic to Brussels. There are several episodes which it would be interesting to analyse, including Lucy's confession, and her confrontation with the Madame Walravens/Père Silas coalition, not to mention several cruces in her relationship with that knight of Rome, Monsieur Paul Carl David Emanuel. The religious theme is equally important, however, in many less obvious passages, such as this from Chapter 13, in which Lucy describes a daily evening custom of the pensionnat – the 'lecture pieuse':

> The scene of the 'Etude du soir' was always the refectory, a much smaller apartment than any of the three classes or schoolrooms; for here none, save the boarders, were ever admitted, and these numbered only a score. Two lamps hung from the ceiling over the two tables; these were lit at dusk, and their kindling was the signal for

school-books being set aside, a grave demeanour assumed, general silence enforced, and then commenced 'la lecture pieuse'. This said 'lecture pieuse' was, I soon found, mainly designed as a wholesome mortification of the Intellect, a useful humiliation of the Reason; and such a dose for Common Sense as she might digest at her leisure, and thrive on as she best could.

The book brought out (it was never changed, but when finished, recommenced) was a venerable volume, old as the hills – gray as the Hôtel de Ville.

I would have given two francs for the chance of getting that book once into my hands, turning over the sacred yellow leaves, ascertaining the title, and perusing with my own eyes the enormous figments which, as an unworthy heretic, it was only permitted me to drink in with my bewildered ears. This book contained legends of the saints. Good God! (I speak the words reverently) what legends they were. What gasconading rascals those saints must have been, if they first boasted these exploits or invented these miracles. These legends, however, were no more than monkish extravagances, over which one laughed inwardly; there were, besides, priestly matters, and the priest-craft of the book was far worse than its monkery. The ears burned on each side of my head as I listened, perforce, to tales of moral martyrdom inflicted by Rome; the dread boasts of confessors, who had wickedly abused their office, trampling to deep degradation high-born ladies, making of countesses and princesses the most tormented slaves under the sun. Stories like that of Conrad and Elizabeth of Hungary, recurred again and again, with all its dreadful viciousness, sickening tyranny and black impiety: tales that were nightmares of oppression, privation, and agony.

I sat out this 'lecture pieuse' for some nights as well as I could, and as quietly too; only once breaking off the points of my scissors by involuntarily sticking them somewhat deep in the worm-eaten board of the table before me. But, at last, it made me so burning hot, and my temples and my heart and my wrist throbbed so fast, and my sleep afterwards was so broken with excitement, that I could sit no longer. Prudence recommended henceforward a swift clearance of my person from the place, the moment that guilty old book was brought out. No Mause Headrigg ever felt a stronger call to take up her testimony against Sergeant Bothwell, than I – to speak my mind in this matter of the popish 'lecture pieuse.' However, I did manage somehow to curb and rein in; and though always, as soon as Rosine

came to light the lamps, I shot from the room quickly, yet also I did
it quietly; seizing that vantage moment given by the little bustle
before the dead silence, and vanishing whilst the boarders put their
books away.

(pp. 183–5)

This extract has its own humour, but unlike the extract from *Shirley*,
it is a bitter, self-destructive humour. Above all, our first impression
of this extract, as of much of *Villette*, is probably to do with its
authenticity: the details suggest actual lived experience; details, such
as the two lamps being lit at dusk or the sizes of the rooms, suggest
an autobiographical accuracy. Playing over the authenticity of the
situation, Lucy Snowe's jaundiced eye lights the whole with a bitterly
critical, satirical tone. The humour emerges from her illuminating
the silliness attached to the way the étude is practised at the Beck
pensionnat, and perhaps, too, from our sensing that hers may be an
overly violent reaction to it.

What Lucy describes is a convention of reading aloud from a
more or less religious text at a specific time of day; the custom has
persisted in schools and seminaries, in this country as in others, into
our own times. The 'lecture pieuse' is a religious reading. In *Villette*,
it consists of stories from the lives of the saints, and other material
which Lucy describes vaguely as 'priestly matters'; and it is a regular
evening study. As it is described here, it is clearly a stultifying convention. For Lucy, the 'lecture' is much worse: an outlandish practice, foreign to her experience, and inimical to her religious ideas.

At no point are we in doubt about Lucy's views. She wholeheart-
edly detests and despises the 'lecture', which for her reeks of popish
chicanery. As we move through the extract, we notice increasingly
outspoken criticism. At the beginning, she implies in saying that 'a
grave demeanour [was] assumed, general silence enforced', that the
pupils are almost as unimpressed as she is with their daily 'lecture'.
She is able to make what seems a valid criticism implicitly when she
states that the 'venerable . . . old . . . gray' book 'was never changed,
but when finished, recommenced'. Most of the criticism, however, is
anything but implicit. Lucy is not permitted to look at or hold the

book, but merely, as she ironically puts it, 'to drink in with my bewildered ears'. She speaks darkly of 'monkish extravagances', 'dread boasts of confessors, who had wickedly abused their office', leading towards the climax, at the end of the third paragraph of the extract, where Lucy refers to accounts of 'dreadful viciousness, sickening tyranny and black impiety: tales that were nightmares of oppression, privation, and agony'. Well, it has not taken us until this point in the novel to discover that Lucy is not objective.

It is, though, with the semblance of objectivity – the thinnest semblance – that Lucy suggests that the content of the book is false. Her bias is evident in her dismissal of all she sees as false or insincere. The pupils' serious demeanour is 'assumed' only for the sake of appearances. She refers to 'legends' of the saints who 'boasted' of their feats and 'invented' the miracles in the book. All these legends she describes as 'monkery' over which 'one laughed inwardly'; does that impersonal 'one' imply that Lucy laughed? Or, rather, that she would have liked to be able to laugh, but was too angry to do so? Her reference to Roman 'priestcraft' perhaps implies fear of the power of Roman deceit, as well as contempt for its dishonesty.

Lucy's deep suspicion of the Church of Rome is everywhere apparent in *Villette*: it is, in fact, a great deal more apparent than the detail of Lucy's own beliefs. She is even-handed to the extent that she refers also to the 'seasoning of excitation and fanaticism' that she has found in 'certain Wesleyan Methodist tracts' (Chapter 36, p. 508), but, reasonably enough in view of the importance Catholicism assumes in her life, she spends far more time criticising Rome. Given the plentiful evidence of Lucy's anti-Catholicism, it is not altogether a shock when, towards the end of the novel, Lucy casts herself in the figure of Christ resisting the temptations of the devil – represented in this case by the Church of Rome!

Though there is little said in the extract which clearly expresses Lucy's positive beliefs, we can see there the germs of her ideas in her use of personification and allusion. She describes the reading ironically as 'wholesome mortification of the Intellect, a useful humiliation of the Reason . . . a dose for Common Sense'. For her, reason is the source of religious conviction. On the other hand, the pages of the book from which the readings are taken are described, with heavy irony, as 'sacred': reverenced, indeed, to all appearances, by adherents of Rome; but a brew of falsehoods for Lucy. Here, as elsewhere in the novel, she describes herself, ironically again, as 'an unworthy heretic'. The irony is the effect of a bitter, impotent fury that she is condemned to sit through the reading with the appearance of patience; it is a fury which Brontë vividly dramatises in Lucy's breaking her scissors by stabbing them violently into 'the worm-eaten board of the table', which perhaps symbolises, in its decay and unresponsiveness, the Church of Rome in her perception. The understatement – she 'only once' buried the point of her scissors 'somewhat' deep – is not gratuitous: we are to imagine her repeatedly stabbing with the scissors in muted relief of barely contained rage. Her emotions produce physical effects of fever and sleeplessness. She is moved almost to the point of open defiance, and alludes to Mause Headrigg as the model of staunch Protestantism in Sir Walter Scott's novel, *Old Mortality*. Lucy, of course, does not dare to disturb her universe. Her standards, and very Protestant ones they are too, are Prudence, Reason and Common Sense. By their light she is able to 'curb and rein in' her rage, and though she learns to seize the right moment to shoot quickly from the room, she 'did it quietly', and preserves her sanity with discretion.

The extract is characteristic of the novel in that Lucy's own formal position is made clear only as a side-effect of the process of condemnation of others' beliefs. When she visits the priest in the confessional in Chapter 15, she states plainly, 'Mon père, je suis Protestante' (p. 233). At the end of their colloquy, he invites her return on the ground that 'Protestantism is altogether too dry, cold, prosaic for you' (p. 234), but she reassures us in tones of horror that she should 'As soon . . . have thought of walking into a Babylonish furnace' (p. 235). As far as Protestantism goes, Lucy's tolerance is broad enough: in Chapter 36 she says that she visits the Presbyterian, Lutheran and Episcopalian chapels in Villette in turn, wonders at their doctrinal differences, and sees no reason why they should not be 'one day fused into one grand Holy Alliance'; she declares that she 'respected them all' despite what she sees as 'faults of form' (all p. 513). Catholicism falls into a different category. A little later in the chapter, in response to M. Paul's giving her a proselytic pamphlet on

Catholicism, she asserts that she 'thought Romanism wrong' (p. 514). She shortly afterwards becomes more forceful and dismisses 'Popery' in favour of the 'severely pure' directness and simplicity of her own church; she cannot, she says, 'care for chanting priests or murmuring officials', while prayer in Latin, 'a language learned and dead' (all p. 516), is merely a 'hindrance' to the sincere heart.

Although Lucy's beliefs do not change, her attitude to Catholicism does. For a time she is placed under the spiritual direction of Père Silas so that she can discover the riches of Rome – its good works, its ritual, its promise of salvation. Instead, she discovers only 'ignorance, abasement, and bigotry' (p. 514). She apostrophises the Roman priesthood in a style which expresses her own faith:

> Oh, mitred aspirants for this world's kingdoms! an hour will come, even to you, when it will be well for your hearts – pausing faint at each broken beat – that there is a Mercy beyond human compassions, a Love stronger than this strong death which even you must face, and before it, fall; a Charity more potent than any sin, even yours; a Pity which redeems worlds – nay, absolves Priests.

> (Chapter 36, p. 515)

The parallelisms and personifications in this paragraph give an exalted tone to the ideas expressed. We have to accept them as sincere. One of the things which must strike us about Lucy's beliefs here is their generosity. There is no sense now, after the pains of the cul-de-sac of her life, of the prejudice and grudge which colours her outlook in much of the novel. All, in the end, will be forgiveness and reconciliation.

There is earlier evidence, too, of the schooling of Lucy's heart to charity. Her religious feeling is clearly presented, without the distortion of criticisms of Catholicism, in the conversation she holds with Paulina in Chapter 32. Sacrificing her own inclination towards Graham, she selflessly supports Polly in her more fortunate love for him. Here, speaking of Polly and Graham as singled out by Providence for serenity and success, she expresses the sense of a divine providence under which human happiness and misery are ultimately to be reconciled:

'Some lives *are* thus blessed: it is God's will: it is the attesting trace
and lingering evidence of Eden. Other lives run from the first another
course. Other travellers encounter weather fitful and gusty, wild and
variable – breast adverse winds, are belated and overtaken by the early
closing winter night. Neither can this happen without the sanction of
God; and I know that, amidst His boundless works, is somewhere
stored the secret of this last fate's justice: I know that His treasures
contain the proof as the promise of its mercy.'

(p. 468)

In this declaration, expressed, in a manner characteristic of Brontë,
largely by means of natural imagery, we find an attractive side of
Lucy Snowe. Here she shows a sincere belief in the Deity, without
expectation of special treatment for an elect group. What she
expresses is at a far remove from the day-to-day practice of Rome,
and we can see in it reasons for her objection to Roman ceremonial:
her beliefs are general and elemental, and she does not expect
favours from God. Divorced from the petty sneers at Rome
('popish', 'Romish', 'popery', 'monkery'), Lucy Snowe's outlook is
one that attracts our sympathy and respect. It remains to be seen, of
course, how her faith will endure the 'weather fitful and gusty, wild
and variable' which is yet to come.

The religious questions considered in the account of the 'lecture
pieuse' are central to the novel, for they are a source of conflict in
her relationship with Monsieur Paul. She sees him, with his unpre-
dictable and temperamental behaviour, as the expression of Romish
irrationality. It is not until she becomes by degrees convinced that
behind the appearance of shallowness there is a deeply religious and
sensible man, that she is able to see him as her future husband. In
Chapter 35, having been shown the innermost heart of Monsieur
Paul by Père Silas, she comes to think of him as her 'half-knightly,
half-saintly . . . Christian hero' (p. 491). Only after she can see him
as a religious partner can she imagine him as an emotional and
sexual partner. Beginning as a source of conflict, therefore, their religious difference becomes a source of their closer understanding.

It is easy to underestimate the real importance of the religious
theme in *Villette*. Lucy holds her religious beliefs, in general, in an

undemonstrative style; reason is their basis. Reason, however, fails to guide her judgement of the Church of Rome; her criticisms of Catholicism often appear wildly exaggerated, the result of ignorance instead of experience, and thus are more vivid in our minds than her positive values. Even after she comes to understand Monsieur Paul and respect his religious feelings, Romanism and bigotry remain almost synonymous to her mind. Lucy's positive convictions are none the less powerful, and the importance of religion in her relationship with Monsieur Paul shows that religious faith, together with a particular kind of religious practice, is a crucial part of the framework of her life.

Conclusions

1. Religion is an important theme in Charlotte Brontë's novels, and is an important part of her background and that of her characters.
2. Brontë shows little inclination for theological or doctrinal debate; her interest is in the impact of religious faith on human behaviour.
3. No specific religious message is purveyed in the novels; she shows knowledge of Protestantism, and perhaps favours it because she knows it well.
4. Brontë shows characters as having good or bad traits irrespective of their religious beliefs.
5. Religion receives both comic and serious treatment in the novels, and Brontë is often critical or satirical about religious behaviour.
6. Although her religious point of view is imprecise, Brontë's major characters are all conscientious; that is, they are concerned with right behaviour, and endeavour to guard their moral welfare.
7. Brontë does not question the existence of God, nor question the need for the support of religious ideas.
8. Brontë's major characters all spring from a background which is essentially Christian. There are no atheists among them; nor Hindus, Muslims, Buddhists, Confucians, Jews or Taoists. The old Jew broker of *Villette* is exceptional even among the minor characters.

9. Charlotte Brontë's own beliefs seem, from the evidence in the novels, to be general, and to have a foundation in Christian principle and her love of the natural world.

Methods of Analysis

1. We have not been unduly concerned to distinguish between concepts such as religion, theology, doctrine and morality. Literature is by its nature promiscuous about such matters, and the critic may allow himself a cautious latitude, too.
2. We may choose to treat the topic from a variety of perspectives. In this chapter we have considered both serious and comic uses of religion; we have looked at the ways in which different beliefs are presented; we have dealt with the way major characters are affected by religion. Other approaches are attractive: *Jane Eyre* and *Villette* could be treated as spiritual pilgrimages, with religion as their main focus.
3. Obviously, if the author makes direct statements about religion in the course of a novel, they demand discussion. Generally, and certainly in Brontë's work, the approach is more indirect, and requires that we analyse characters:
   • Look at what the characters think and say about religion, whether in the abstract, or as expressed in other characters. How does what they say express their own beliefs? Do their actions match their words?
   • What do the characters say about their own conflicts, their own sense of a deity or of a personal moral code? Are they sincere?
4. Keep in mind that in a novel, the author's aim is probably not to express religious convictions or to argue a particular philosophy, but rather to show the struggles his characters experience in dealing with the choices which religion imposes.
5. What practical use is made of religion by the author? – for example, to generate conflict within or between characters, to entertain, or to raise important moral questions.

Further Work

Jane Eyre: You might choose for further analysis from two passages: the conversation between Jane and Helen Burns
in Volume 1, Chapter 8 (beginning after about one page
with Helen's speech 'Mr Brocklehurst is not a god . . .'
and continuing for about a page to the end of the paragraph concluding '. . . death is so certain an entrance to
happiness – to glory?', p. 82); or, one of many interesting passages concerning St John Rivers, perhaps the
last page or so of Volume 3, Chapter 5 in which he talks
to Rosamond Oliver (from 'As she patted the dog's head
. . .' to the end of the chapter, pp. 407–8).

Shirley: Look more closely at one of the episodes referred to
briefly in the discussion in this chapter. Look at the
beginning of the second section of Chapter 9, from
'Spring evenings are often cold . . .' to the paragraph
following the hymns, 'The roof of the chapel did *not* fly
off; which speaks volumes in praise of its solid slating'
(pp. 162–5). Alternatively, analyse the scene in which
Martin Yorke visits the church in the hope of seeing
Caroline Helstone in Chapter 34 (from the paragraph
two or three pages from the beginning, 'He looked
round . . .' and continuing for a little over a page down
to 'The sermon found an end; the benediction was pronounced; the congregation dispersed: she had not been
near him', pp. 547–8).

Villette: Study Lucy's confession at the end of Chapter 15, from
'Few worshippers were assembled . . .' until Lucy rises and
thanks the priest about a page and half later (pp. 233–4);
or, if you prefer, from Lucy's leaving the church, until the
end of the chapter (pp. 235–6). Another possibility is
Lucy's confrontation with Père Silas in the final section of
Chapter 36, from 'My third temptation was held out in
the pomp of Rome . . .' to the end of the chapter (pp.
515–17).

6

Old Maids and Womenites

The title for this chapter draws on *Shirley*: Chapter 10 is entitled 'Old Maids'; 'womenites' is Martin Yorke's term for those who espouse the cause of equality for women. It refers to a topic close to Charlotte Brontë's heart, and much written about by her biographers and critics: the difficulties facing Victorian educated single gentle-women of small means. Though only *Shirley* confronts it at length, the issue is significant in all Brontë's novels. More than a theme, it is a node which focuses a range of different motifs. Personal development, education, freedom, even the conflict of reason and passion, which may all be considered important themes in Brontë's novels, can be traced back to it; there is an obvious and particularly important link with the theme of love. We shall be making no attempt to deal with the issue itself: instead we will explore, by analysis of short extracts, how it relates to the whole structure of the novels.

The importance of the theme derives from its affecting all the heroines: Jane, Shirley, Caroline and Lucy all strive, if in different ways and to different extents, for control over their lives. Though it was her readers rather than the author who saw her work as having a practical impact on society, her novels are thought to have helped to advance the movement towards equality of status for women. Brontë's interest in this subject and her obvious support for the cause of female equality – though she was never as ardent a feminist as her friend, Mary Taylor – is one of the elements in her work which led to her being branded subversive by the more conservative among her contemporary critics.

134

As we shall see, a more sociological title for this chapter would be inappropriate. Brontë's concern with the position of women is usually non-polemical, and is quite restricted in scope. The issue of the status of women is always related directly to the situations in which her characters find themselves. Brontë does not occupy the soap-box at the expense of authenticity.

The place of women in society is closely related to sexual relationships and marriage. We will spend some of our time considering how Brontë's heroines are treated by the men to whom they are close, and what they expect from men and marriage. This is another broad topic, which might well merit a chapter to itself, and we shall do no more than sketch in its broad outlines.

In this chapter, the extracts will be briefer; reference to the novels will be correspondingly broader since we shall need to examine different parts of each novel to try to see how the theme develops. Although we will be using a variety of approaches in this chapter, we will be building on some common ways of tackling questions of theme. Look first for direct statements about the subject, by either author or narrator; look for comments on it by the characters; and look at how it is dramatised in the action. This is not to rule out other ways of expressing theme – symbolism and imagery may be used, too, for instance – but to illustrate useful starting-points.

I: *Jane Eyre*

The general statement we shall look at in *Jane Eyre* is from Volume 1, Chapter 12, when Jane is at Thornfield. There, as she paces the upper storey of the house and looks out over the surrounding landscape, she describes her discontent with her lot, comparing her fate with that of other young women in restricted circumstances. Within her dull camouflage, Jane has an insatiable appetite for other worlds and fresh experience, and she makes this explicit when she tries to excuse her feelings of frustration:

> Who blames me? Many, no doubt; and I shall be called discontented. I could not help it: the restlessness was in my nature; it agi-

tated me to pain sometimes. Then my sole relief was to walk along
the corridor of the third story, backwards and forwards, safe in the
silence and solitude of the spot, and allow my mind's eye to dwell on
whatever bright visions rose before it – and, certainly, they were many
and glowing; to let my heart be heaved by the exultant movement,
which, while it swelled it in trouble, expanded it with life; and, best
of all, to open my inward ear to a tale that was never ended – a tale
my imagination created, and narrated continuously; quickened with
all of incident, life, fire, feeling, that I desired and had not in my
actual existence.

It is vain to say human beings ought to be satisfied with tranquillity: they must have action; and they will make it if they cannot find
it. Millions are condemned to a stiller doom than mine, and millions
are in silent revolt against their lot. Nobody knows how many rebellions besides political rebellions ferment in the masses of life which
people earth. Women are supposed to be very calm generally: but
women feel just as men feel; they need exercise for their faculties, and
a field for their efforts as much as their brothers do; they suffer from
too rigid a restraint, too absolute a stagnation, precisely as men would
suffer; and it is narrow-minded in their more privileged fellow-creatures to say that they ought to confine themselves to making pud-
dings and knitting stockings, to playing on the piano and
embroidering bags. It is thoughtless to condemn them, or laugh at
them, if they seek to do more or learn more than custom has pronounced necessary for their sex.

(p. 125)

This is a rare foray into general moralising in the novel, and is all the
more noteworthy for that. The first paragraph is the more personal,
contrasting the dullness of Jane's actual existence with the vivid and
adventurous life which her imagination conjures up. The corridors
of Thornfield provide sustenance enough for an exotic fantasy – 'life,
fire, feeling': all that she has not in her daily life, her imagination
supplies. Here is the girl who invented fantasies from Bewick's scenes
of the lives of birds. Here, as in her window-seat at Gateshead, she
can be 'safe in the silence and solitude of the spot'. The muscular
language which she uses ('heaved . . . swelled . . . expanded') and the
exciting imagery, 'glowing' and 'quickened' with light and fire, hint

at the intensity of the 'bright visions' of her imagination which contrast so violently with the drab actuality of her life. There is only one specific image here: that of Jane walking in the corridor. But the language used emphatically communicates the frustrations of her 'exultant' heart confined, like a tiger restless in its cage, to pacing ceaselessly 'backwards and forwards' in a lonely corridor high enough to offer sight of an unattainable horizon.

Jane is able to make a positive judgement about her state of mind. While she recognises that she might be called 'discontented', she insists that 'the restlessness was in my nature'. It is, she argues, natural to feel the need for opening horizons; the implication is that acceptance of a dreary lot is no more natural than the cutting off of Julia Severn's curls; what Jane seeks is the opportunity to do what is consistent with her human and female nature. She had said at Lowood that she could never be a Helen Burns, and here – if the evidence could not be found elsewhere – is the proof.

The second paragraph of the extract is more political in style, but though its tone is temperate, there is still in the language an intensity of feeling which brings the general ideas in the paragraph to life. The strength of feeling is apparent, for example, in the language which Jane uses in referring to those 'condemned to a stiller doom than mine', and those 'in silent revolt against their lot'. The knowledge of the French Revolution underlies these remarks. She asks us to think of 'rebellions' other than political which ferment in the hearts of women – though, of course, she is making a statement which is, in a broader sense, very dangerously political. Then she speaks, with a scorn born of experience, of the accomplishments acceptable for ladies – cooking and knitting, music and embroidery. The second half of the paragraph balances its sympathy for women in states of 'restraint' or 'stagnation' with haranguing of men. They should, she argues, be more willing to sympathise with the need of women for equality. She stresses the point by again referring to nature – this time the common humanity of men and women. She speaks of men as '[women's] more privileged fellow-creatures' and, with pointed irony, as 'their brothers'. She denies that it is natural for women to be less free; the expectation that they should do or learn less is merely a matter of tyrannical 'custom'. Political this is;

but what strikes us most forcibly here is the broad sympathy with people and the common sense with which we are now familiar as characteristic of Charlotte Brontë.

Let us look now at how the dilemma Jane expresses at this turning-point develops in the course of the novel. From the first page, the novel tells of Jane's evolution towards freedom, maturity and independence – a difficult evolution, something of a struggle, indeed, partly because of her circumstances, and partly because of her sex. The theme dominates the whole book, embracing other important motifs – the meaning of nature and duty, and the relationships between Jane and other characters, as well as the subject of this chapter.

How, then, has the earlier action of the novel prepared for the outburst in Chapter 12? When we look at Jane's early experiences, we can see that the extract is a logical outcome of the pressures which have been exerted upon her during her childhood with the Reeds, and during her schooling. As we have noticed, Brontë depicts Jane as an victim. From the earliest days, when she is branded wicked at Gateshead and held up to scorn as a liar at Lowood, Jane is required to subdue her nature and behave in a way acceptable to others whose standards are hard, for us as for her, to agree with. Mrs Reed is unsympathetic, John Reed tyrannises her, Mr Brocklehurst is an unyielding, menacing black pillar. She is the victim of almost everybody, but it is men by whom she is most humiliated, and the extract shows her consciousness of it. With some women – Helen Burns, Miss Temple, even, to some degree, Bessie – she is able to get on very well, and she shares with Helen and Miss Temple humiliation under the yoke of the principles of Lowood.

It appears superficially that the institution is effective in schooling Jane. By the standards of Lowood Jane's situation at Thornfield counts as success. Her achievement answers Brocklehurst's mission – 'to mortify in these girls the lusts of the flesh, to teach them to clothe themselves with shame-facedness and sobriety' (p. 76). But those standards and his mission are based on inequality and injustice, as the behaviour of Brocklehurst himself makes clear. His mission leads Brocklehurst to demand the cutting off of the top-knots of all the girls who have them, and the removal in particular of the luxuriant – natural and therefore evil – curls of Julia Severn. It is an irony which might seem to indicate hypocrisy in Brocklehurst, that his wife and daughters appear, immediately after his condemnation of aberrant hair, dressed in the latest fashion, and sporting not merely curls, but – in the case of the elder lady – 'a false front of French curls' (p. 76). Brocklehurst is not put off his stroke by this ironic coincidence. Clearly he does not see serpents peeping from the curls of his family. The reason for this is economic. His family are of a different economic status from the poor girls whom he is castigating. It is reasonable, therefore, for them to behave differently. He is not discountenanced because he sees no irony; there is no hypocrisy in his eyes – merely a different standard of judgement. Thus to excise ambition and discontent among the poor inmates is the right, the only course. It prepares them for the confines of their future. Governessing, indeed, is what a hard-working and capable girl might in the end reasonably aspire to. Bessie sees Jane when she visits Lowood as 'like a lady' (p. 106); but, as Bessie's addendum ('it is as much as I ever expected of you') suggests, Jane is in fact fit only to be the servant of a wealthy patron. In this respect, she has much in common with Charlotte Brontë herself.

At Lowood, then, Jane is schooled to be submissive, and to accept her lowly lot in life. The institution has an apposite name. But when Miss Temple leaves to marry, it becomes clear that Jane's submission is superficial:

> I had given in allegiance to duty and order; I was quiet; I believed I
> was content; to the eyes of others, usually even to my own, I appeared
> a disciplined and subdued character.

(p. 98)

The underlying implications of this statement of submission are all of revolt and defiance. Her appearance, she suggests, is deceptive, to the point of deceiving herself. Although, when Jane decides to seek her fortune in the outside world, she appears to be fit only to be a governess, it is apparent that she cannot be content with her domestic role. Jane wants liberty – 'for liberty I gasped' (p. 99), but determined to satisfy herself with merely a 'new servitude' (p. 99). When she takes responsibility for Adèle, she has all the outward demeanour appropriate to a governess and a successful product of the hard discipline of Lowood. Inwardly, however, she chafes at her confines, and it is not long before she speaks of her liking for climbing up to the roof of the house and looking along the horizon; she refers to more than her physical environment when she says that she 'longed for a power of vision which might overpass that limit' (p. 125).

When we consider the sequel of the extract, we see that the patterns of her childhood persist into her adulthood. Still, it is men who present her with dilemmas. Rochester teases her and hoodwinks her, while demanding her absolute sacrifice to himself; and St John Rivers, a black pillar of male domination like Brocklehurst, demands another impossibility of her. At every stage, however, she is seen as having an independent mind: Mrs Reed views her as wicked, Mr Brocklehurst thinks of her as unruly. Rochester is titillated as well as vexed by her refusal to accept his sway: indeed, it is her independent character which attracts him and binds him to her almost against his will. St John Rivers believes that she must learn to practise (and practise to learn) Christian humility in order to submit to the will of God – which happens, oddly enough, to coincide with the will of St John Rivers.

That Jane does not fall prey to any of these influences is the effect of the streak of stubborn independence, even revolt, that lies deep in her personality. Brontë shows us that her heroine may be small and weak, and yet retains at bottom a stern confidence that saves her. She keeps her pride in herself, and she keeps her independence. She does not allow herself to be swayed by authority or power, and she does not submit to the dictates of custom or tradition. She does not subscribe to others' notions of what she ought to do or be; she is not a prisoner to convention. She makes her own choices – hence part of her appeal for late-twentieth-century readers.

Jane's evasion of the limitations of custom does not mean that she wishes to do away with convention, still less that she holds conventional morality in contempt. On the contrary, she shows herself ready to accept convention in her relationship with Rochester, and is concerned to adhere to principle – and these are her reasons for abandoning Thornfield. The new world which Rochester opens to her is one in which she may expect to flourish as the wife of a man who understands and respects her. However, he is often shown to treat her more lightly than she would wish to believe: in his role as the gipsy fortune-teller, and in his deceitful Irish plan, to mention only the most obvious pointers, Rochester shows that he underestimates her both in his willingness to deceive her, and in his arrogant confidence that he can get away with it. Jane, still presented as the victim, fails to understand or chooses to ignore these clues, but cannot evade the very material person of Bertha in the attic. When she finally rejects Rochester and leaves Thornfield, it is because he has failed her morally as well as because of the fact of his marriage.

Here, as elsewhere, Jane is constantly torn between what is right and what is desirable: the conflict between passion and duty is a central concern of the novel. Although the extract with which we began expresses Jane's will, her powerful moral sense is implicit in the rhetorical question with which it begins: 'Who blames me?' Jane shows a strong desire to excuse what she fears may be seen by others as bad behaviour, and a deep fear of punishment; it is as if she expects Mrs Reed suddenly to materialise and lock her in another red-room. In the novel as a whole, Jane expends a great deal of energy in trying to convince herself that what she wants is right, and in trying to reconcile her own wishes with convention. It is entirely characteristic that her statement of will in the extract should be dominated by a sense of threat.

At Thornfield, punishment is, in the event, meted out – by Jane herself, when she abandons the house, and Rochester with it. Just before she leaves, she assesses herself again in the last three paragraphs of Chapter 26 in a passage which brings together poetically all the concerns we have been discussing. It begins thus:

> Jane Eyre, who had been an ardent, expectant woman – almost a bride – was a cold, solitary girl again: her life was pale; her prospects were desolate. A Christmas frost had come at midsummer; a white December storm had whirled over June . . .

(p. 330)

The contrast between girl and woman says much. As a wife, Jane would, she thinks, have felt complete; as a girl, she remains a mere cipher. The imagery shows the contrast between the sense of adventure (in 'ardent'), and the feeling of useless imprisonment with which the earlier Jane was so familiar. Her future, which was a bright far horizon, has become a cul-de-sac. Typically, she represents the change by reference to natural imagery, of which the quotation gives only a little. As she develops these images later in the paragraph, they mingle with religious ideas when she thinks of the 'subtle doom, such as . . . fell on all the first-born in the land of Egypt' (p. 330). Later, biblical echoes become stronger as she strives to understand her misjudgement of Rochester ('Oh, how blind had been my eyes!', p. 331), and to describe her desolate state of mind ('I seemed to have laid me down in the dried-up bed of a great river', p. 331); she finds expression in the language of the Psalms in parallelisms such as 'to rise I had no will, to flee I had no strength'; (p. 331) and concludes the chapter with biblical quotations. The biblical language is used to heighten the power of this emotional climax, but also ensures that the moral perspective of the situation is prominent.

It is not until much later in the novel, in Volume 3, Chapter 30, after she is offered the position of schoolmistress at Morton School, that Jane is able to judge her behaviour towards Rochester coolly. The position which she is offered reminds her of the kinds of servitude which she escaped from, and which she ran to, in leaving Lowood for Thornfield:

> In truth it was humble – but then it was sheltered, and I wanted a safe asylum: it was plodding – but then, compared with that of a governess in a rich house, it was independent; and the fear of servitude with strangers entered my soul like iron: it was not ignoble – not unworthy – not mentally degrading.

(p. 397)

St John, who understands what her reservations may be, puts his offer in a manner hasty, almost embarrassed, and invites her to consider how she will feel in a situation which will, inevitably, limit her use of her abilities. Jane's decision, however, is based on the necessity imposed on her by economic circumstances and by principle. In Volume 3, Chapter 5, she pictures to herself what her life would have been as Rochester's mistress in France, 'delirious with his love', and contrasts what her new life is to be:

> Whether is it better, I ask, to be a slave in a fool's paradise at Marseilles – fevered with delusive bliss one hour – suffocating with the bitterest tears of remorse and shame the next – or to be a village schoolmistress, free and honest, in a breezy mountain nook in the healthy heart of England?
>
> Yes; I feel now that I was right when I adhered to principle and law, and scorned and crushed the insane promptings of a frenzied moment. God directed me to a correct choice: I thank His providence for the guidance!

(p. 402)

It is possible that Jane's choice may look less clear-cut for students at the end of the twentieth century than it would have appeared to Brontë's contemporary readers. For Jane, the decision is simply right: that true freedom lies in submission to her small fate is expressed in the image of 'breezy' and 'healthy' England, in contrast with 'suffocating' in the superficially more attractive Marseilles. The familiar imagery of slavery and freedom, applied here to a new situation, shows that her decision is right emotionally as well as morally. Adherence to 'principle and law', despite looking on the surface a hard choice, is the way to a liberated conscience, and escapes 'the bitterest tears of remorse and shame'.

For Jane, then, the quest for independence is not simple. The decision she comes to is the result of a conscientious assessment of her choices: material wealth is worthless if it is achieved at the price of virtue; while the narrow life of a village schoolmistress retains the liberation of spirit which goes with integrity. Moreover, freedom is not attained by enslavement to passion.

The conflict between passion and duty which complicates Jane's quest for independence is resolved for the moment. Life in

Marseilles with Rochester is represented as 'a fool's paradise', in which she would be 'fevered with delusive bliss', in an 'insane' and 'frenzied' condition. The guidance of Providence is a clear, bracing alternative. Jane has given up her idol, who for a time blurred her vision, for God. Here natural imagery is linked with obedience to conscience, for Jane is being true to her own nature.

Later, however, the link between Jane's personality and the natural world recurs with a different significance when Jane, breaking away from the imprisoning toils of St John's mission, hears Rochester's voice calling her. At first she suspects that she may be suffering from a kind of possession, but is persuaded that what she has heard is natural:

> 'Down superstition!' I commented, as that spectre rose up black by the black yew at the gate. 'This is not thy deception, nor thy witch-craft: it is the work of nature.'

> (p. 467)

The repeated 'black' stresses the real fear of evil which has been awakened in Jane. It is resolved not by any outside force, but by her conviction that what she has heard is 'the work of nature'. No outside agency is required to persuade her: her faith is instinctive, and it is as much faith in herself as faith in Providence. When she breaks from St John, she emphasises the independence which she has found:

> It was *my* time to assume ascendancy. *My* powers were in play and in force.

> (p. 467)

There is a self-assertiveness in these italics which we have not met quite as blatantly before in Jane, though the germs of it were always present. It is not, however, an insolent or overweening power which she feels; her new confidence is in herself under God, and when she is left alone, she 'fell on [her] knees; and prayed. . . .', and tells us that she 'seemed to penetrate very near a Mighty Spirit' (p. 467).

We cannot easily associate Jane's sense of spirit with a specific religious denomination. It is general enough to be felt vague; it has more in common with pantheism than with Wesleyanism or Protestantism. In submitting to its demands, Jane is admitting also the demands of her own nature, even to the point of accepting her need for her idol, Rochester, while at the same time maintaining a temperate and self-critical, genuinely conscientious discipline in her life.

It is made clear that Jane's sense of herself includes her physical and sexual nature as well as her emotional, moral and spiritual dimensions. Her response to Rochester – even to the impression of his voice – is physical. When she senses that he is calling, she says that 'My heart beat fast and thick: I heard its throb. Suddenly it stood still to an inexpressible feeling that thrilled it through' (p. 466). It is not so with St John. Jane says that she 'stood motionless under [her] hierophant's touch' (p. 465); her response to his marble or ice kiss was 'not striking' (p. 444). Jane rejects him because he is not a sexual partner for her: Rochester, difficult as he may be, whether blind or maimed, is.

Ideally, for Jane, and we may perhaps presume for Brontë, nature and law are one. Jane rises in the end above the choice of mistress or old maid, to become simply human, and in control of her own destiny. She wins her independence only to give it up; but submission to Rochester is in her eyes no servitude.

II: *Shirley*

The extracts from *Shirley* will show how theme is developed in dialogue as well as in direct statement. In this section, instead of beginning with an extract and back-tracking, we will consider the thematic context first. Both approaches are allowable; in the case of *Shirley*, which has a more complex organisation than *Jane Eyre*, a chronological method will help to avoid confusion, particularly when the novel is so replete with material on our subject.

Both the female protagonists in *Shirley* – not to mention several more minor characters – are used to present the social condition of women. Both make direct statements about the subject. Their personalities are very different, and it is therefore very different aspects of the issue which are highlighted; both Shirley and Caroline, however, settle for a limited revolution.

The fate which awaits gentlewomen of small means who fail to marry is vividly set before us in Chapter 10, entitled 'Old Maids', in which Caroline describes, sympathetically and with apprehension for her own future, Miss Ainley and Miss Mann. She is moved to visit them when Helstone's prohibition of her seeing Robert Moore brings her sharply to face her future prospects – or rather, the lack of them:

> 'I have to live, perhaps, till seventy years. As far as I know, I have good health: half a century of existence may lie before me. How am I to occupy it? What am I to do to fill the interval of time which spreads between me and the grave?'

> (p. 190)

Caroline's expectations are gloomy, as the language of this soliloquy shows with its consciousness of the empty space which intervenes before death. A little later she asks, 'what was I created for. . . . Where is my place in the world?' (p. 190) and decides that she may find the answer by examining the lives of old maids such as she expects to become herself. She discovers that there is much with which to sympathise behind the Medusa eye of Miss Mann; none the less, it is Miss Ainley who, though poorer and plainer, commands Caroline's allegiance by generosity of spirit, and whom Caroline determines to assist in her good works. The outcome is unsuccessful, however, despite Caroline's conscientious efforts, and Chapter 10 closes on a melancholy note:

> Winter seemed conquering her spring: the mind's soil and its treasures were freezing gradually to barren stagnation.

> (p. 199)

This complex of metaphors makes a powerful conclusion. Human nature is once more linked with the natural world: 'spring' is happily ambiguous, referring to the season and to the sense of vitality in the mind; 'barren' refers to the frosty dormancy of winter, and also to Caroline's unmarried state. In the sequel, she begins to wither away, worn out not by her duties, but by the lack of hope. Thinking of a change of situation, she considers becoming a governess, but that option is peremptorily rejected as 'too feminine a fancy' (p. 205) by the uncomprehending Helstone (Shirley dismisses the idea too, in Chapter 13, in language which recalls *Jane Eyre*: 'Better be a slave at once', p. 245). Helstone tells her to 'put all crotchets out of your head, and amuse yourself'. Caroline's bitter response, 'What with? My doll?' (p. 205) is uttered only to herself after Helstone leaves the room. She has no words with which to confront him: she cannot tell him that his reference to 'crotchets' is a casual dismissal of her real anxieties as trivial, or that by 'amuse yourself' he means 'pass your time with nothing serious': even if she were to find tongue, he would not be likely to understand. Caroline needs occupation, and serious occupation; as it is, she feels treated, and expected to behave, as a child. Without prospect of marriage and children, she is reduced to playing with the doll, which symbolises the pointlessness, as she sees it, of any occupation which she is entitled to pursue. She senses pity in the eyes of visitors who consider her 'disappointed' (p. 206). Her desperation in this condition is the pattern of the desperation which, Brontë implies, is felt by maids, old and not so old, the length and breadth of England.

Caroline is in no position to deal with her problems as Shirley does. Captain Keeldar's response to them is more active and confrontational. More powerful economically and socially, she is better able to control the men she meets. We see her expelling Mr Donne from her house, standing up to Mr Sympson, and cleverly controlling the meeting with the senior clergy at the end of Chapter 14 (pp. 269–74) when, like Caroline, she 'seeks to be saved by works'. Caroline's struggle turns inwards, as we see in the comment on old maids which she makes in conversation with Shirley in Chapter 12:

> 'And what does it signify, whether unmarried and never-to-be-married women are unattractive and inelegant, or not? – provided

only they are decent, decorous, and neat, it is enough. The utmost which ought to be required of old maids, in the way of appearance, is that they should not absolutely offend men's eyes as they pass them in the street; for the rest, they should be allowed, without too much scorn, to be as absorbed, grave, plain-looking, and plain-dressed as they please.'

(p. 235)

She is not joking here. Shirley says that her friend speaks 'earnestly'; but what readers glean from Caroline's words is, I think, rather a latent bitterness than mere earnestness. The understatements in 'not absolutely offend' and 'without too much scorn' are the most obvious clues in this sardonic paragraph to an underlying feeling of near-violent vengefulness. At this stage, of course, Caroline is convinced that she will never marry.

The problems faced by women, whether married or not, are dramatised in Chapter 18 in the conversation between Shirley and Joe Scott, an unworthy but none the less determined supporter of St Paul, a well-known biblical misogynist:

'Joe, do you seriously think all the wisdom in the world is lodged in male skulls?'

'I think that women are a kittle and froward generation; and I've a great respect for the doctrines delivered in the second chapter of St Paul's first Epistle to Timothy.'

'What doctrines, Joe?'

'Let the woman learn in silence, with all subjection. I suffer not a woman to teach, nor to usurp authority over the man; but to be in silence. For Adam was first formed, then Eve.'

'What has that to do with the business?' interjected Shirley: 'that smacks of rights of primogeniture. I'll bring it up to Mr Yorke the first time he inveighs against those rights.'

'And,' continued Joe Scott, 'Adam was not deceived; but the woman, being deceived, was in the transgression.'

'More shame to Adam to sin with his eyes open!' cried Miss Keeldar. 'To confess the honest truth, Joe, I never was easy in my mind concerning that chapter: it puzzles me.'

'It is very plain, Miss: he that runs may read.'

'He may read it in his own fashion,' remarked Caroline, now joining in the dialogue for the first time. 'You allow the right of private judgment, I suppose, Joe?'

'My certy, that I do! I allow and claim it for every line of the holy Book.'

'Women may exercise it as well as men?'

'Nay: women is to take their husbands' opinions, both in politics and religion: it's wholesomest for them.'

'Oh! oh!' exclaimed both Shirley and Caroline.

(pp. 322–3)

This extract, though perhaps rather obvious by comparison with others we have studied, contains several points of interest; they are important points, too, for Joe Scott is not alone in his attitude towards women. First, his conviction of the superiority of men is unshakeable; he is evidently less well educated than the women, but that matters not. Secondly, religion supports him – or at least, his interpretation of one part of the Bible does; later Caroline gives a different view of the interpretation of St Paul, though she does not dare to question St Paul's authority. Thirdly, the only basis Joe has for his belief that women are not allowed to have views of their own, but must adopt their husbands' views in religion and politics, is tradition; he has no other authority beyond his instinctive conviction that 'it's wholesomest'. The implication is that an unmarried woman has no right to views at all. Joe certainly feels that Shirley has no call to interfere in farming or any other business which he would consider a male preserve. Although Shirley dismisses him in the end as a 'Man of prejudice' (p. 324), and although he appears unreasoning in his views, he is no fool: he has time for some shrewd cuts against his opponents, with some justice accusing Caroline of failure to understand money, and Shirley of not attending church, and of being inattentive when Moore talks of business matters.

Joe Scott's views are not exceptional: he voices attitudes both widespread and respected. Later in the novel, Mr Sympson, though of vastly different social and educational background, exhibits the same sort of arrogance when he scolds Shirley for rejecting the offer of marriage from Samuel Fawthrop Wynne. She discounts him because 'His views are narrow; his feelings are blunt; his tastes are coarse; his manners vulgar' (p. 444); Mr Sympson, shocked at her objections, counters, with striking obtuseness, that Mr Wynne is 'a respectable, wealthy man', and suggests that 'To refuse him is presumption on [her] part' (p. 444). Clearly, Shirley and her uncle differ in their interpretation of 'respectable', as well as of 'suitable' and 'proper'. More significantly, Mr Sympson's use of 'presumption' appears to ignore the possibility that a young lady of means and position should be other than gratified to receive the attentions of a man of any social rank, no matter how lacking in finer qualities. Caroline and Shirley are shown to inhabit a world which is confidently hostile to independence of thought and action in women. Their frustration is dramatised in the chapter following the conversation with Joe Scott, when the women watch the attack on the mill. Here Caroline is restrained by Shirley, with difficulty, from going down to help the wounded. Fighting is, of course, a male activity, and Caroline's sense of being 'curbed and kept down' (p. 339) reflects her feeling about her life as a woman in general.

It is in the voice of Caroline that the issue is given its clearest expression. At the end of Chapter 22, after having listened in Chapter 21 to Mrs Pryor speaking of her life as a governess and her disillusionment in her marriage, Caroline recalls how much more equably Miss Ainley bears her solitude. In a long meditation she considers the circumstances and causes of the subjection of women. Characteristically, Caroline seeks to blame no one, but analyses quietly; and reaches a powerful peroration:

> 'Men of England! look at your poor girls, many of them fading around you, dropping off in consumption or decline; or, what is worse, degenerating to sour old maids, – envious, backbiting, wretched, because life is a desert to them; or, what is worst of all, reduced to strive, by scarce modest coquetry and debasing artifice, to gain that position and consideration by marriage, which to celibacy is denied. Fathers! cannot you alter these things? Perhaps not all at once; but consider the matter well when it is brought before you, receive it as a theme worthy of thought: do not dismiss it with an idle jest or an unmanly insult. You would wish to be proud of your daughters and not to blush for them – then seek for them an interest

and an occupation which shall raise them above the flirt, the manœuvrer, the mischief-making tale-bearer. Keep your girls' minds narrow and fettered – they will still be a plague and a care, sometimes a disgrace to you: cultivate them – give them scope and work – they will be your gayest companions in health; your tenderest nurses in sickness; your most faithful prop in age.'

(pp. 378–9)

It is hard to see this address to the nation as anything other than a thinly-disguised plea from the author herself. The reference to 'consumption or decline' recalls not only Caroline's illness, but also the illnesses of Charlotte's sisters and brother – Anne's death particularly affected the writing of *Shirley*. The dark picture of celibate maturity as 'envious, backbiting, wretched' shows a very personal fear of that fate. Equally heartfelt is the scornful emphasis given to the undignified methods to which women are compelled to resort to win husbands: 'coquetry' and 'artifice'. All this is rather beyond the experience and character of Caroline.

The extract shows how limited is the demand made on behalf of women. The request for 'scope and work' is not merely for the advantage of women themselves: it is to be seen as enhancing their usefulness to men. That idea is very much in keeping with the pattern of the novel as a whole. Caroline is frustrated, furiously anxious for an outlet for her energies and abilities; but, ultimately, requires only that Robert Moore be her husband. It is, perhaps, what we have always expected. Shirley, however, is more surprising. Having dictated to everyone and refused proposals from all around her, she settles on the unlikely Louis Moore to be her husband. Not only that: she insists on his being her master in their relationship, as he once was as her teacher of French. She deliberately seeks to become subservient to him, and to encourage him to be more assertive towards her.

The novel is far from revolutionary, then, in its view of the social position of women. Brontë is not attempting to alter society radically. In so far as she has social purpose, she may be hoping to make society more fair, and more understanding towards women, and to make it easier for women to engage in serious work alongside men and on the basis of equality with men.

On the subject of personal relationships, however, *Shirley* is more forthright than *Jane Eyre*. The confrontation between Victorian convention and the emotional rights of women is most violently dramatised in the arguments between Mr Sympson and Shirley over Mr Wynne and Sir Philip Nunnely. It is not only Shirley's objections to Sam Wynne which awaken her uncle's ire: it is her assumption of the right to please herself in determining her emotional and sexual future. When she tells him that, before she will marry, she is 'resolved to esteem – to admire – to *love*', the italics show exactly what it is that Mr Sympson finds 'Preposterous stuff! – indecorous – unwomanly!' (p. 444). When she is driven by his obtuseness to be more direct, he condemns her for using 'Unladylike language' (p. 445), and wonders, with hands and eyes raised heavenwards as if to call on God to support the right, why she will not 'hear reason' (p. 445). Just as much as Joe Scott, Mr Sympson is shown to be a victim of the prejudices of his society.

Mr Sympson is painted with a broad brush, with more than a touch of Lady Catherine de Burgh about him. In the battle between him and Shirley over Sir Philip Nunnely in Chapter 31, Shirley, like Elizabeth in Jane Austen's novel, achieves victory by silence in the face of aggression, and firmness in the midst of fury. After a quietly ominous beginning in which Mr Sympson demands to know what has occurred between Shirley and Sir Philip, she disputes his right over her as her guardian, for, she argues, 'Having ceased to be a ward, I have no guardian' (p. 512). Then, appalled at the information that she has refused her suitor's proposal, he insists on knowing Shirley's matrimonial intentions, only to be told that she will do 'just as I please' (p. 512). He accuses her of 'acknowledg[ing] no rules – no limitations' and of being 'Regardless of decorum . . . prepared to fly in the face of propriety' (both p. 513). Alternately cajoling and threatening, addressing his niece variously as 'Madam' and 'girl', he froths and foams, describing her as 'mad' and 'cynical', as she defends herself by a near-hysterical teasing. Through it all, Shirley remains consistent. She rejects her uncle's assumptions of authority more strongly later in the scene, when she tells her soi-disant guardian, 'I disdain your dictatorship' (p. 517); at the same time, she rejects the assumption of the authority of men over women. She continues, too, to believe in her right to be true to her feelings. When Mr Sympson questions whether her direct language is appropriate for her rank and sex, thus also questioning her moral probity in general, her confidence is summed up in two lines of the dialogue:

> 'Are you a young lady?'
> 'I am a thousand times better: I am an honest woman, and as such I will be treated.'

(p. 517)

Mr Sympson is incapable of seeing Shirley as she is, and mirrors in this the general inability – as Shirley postulates – of men to understand women. If she cannot behave as a conventional 'young lady', she must in his eyes be morally reprehensible. When she is honest in response to his demands, he condemns her for 'too much freedom' (p. 515); when she confesses to being drawn to several men, he calls her 'cynical' (p. 515); he suggests that her mind is 'poisoned with French novels' (p. 513). What he expects of her is that she will behave with propriety; that is, in a manner properly submissive to male dominance. Her demand to be treated as an 'honest woman' shakes the foundations of his world.

Mr Sympson also fails to understand Shirley's desire for a husband who can 'hold [her] in check', and condemns her as 'vastly inconsistent' (p. 513). His error is instructive: he does not distinguish between submission out of respect, or out of love, and submission enforced by convention; in other words, he fails to make allowance for Shirley's feelings. In this he is at one with St John Rivers. But where St John's authority may claim divine origin, Mr Sympson's is entirely worldly. Our comparison with Lady Catherine de Burgh in *Pride and Prejudice* is illuminating, too: where she attempts to sway Elizabeth by the power of money, rank and name, Mr Sympson, once his attempt to wield the authority of his guardianship has failed, has only his personality and his masculinity. These are not enough: 'feeble' (p. 520) is the word Shirley uses to describe him, and so indeed he seems to us. Flailing ineffectually in his confrontation with Shirley, he is too stupid to understand her reference to atheism (she claims to be 'an atheist to *your* god', p. 518), and is in the end completely bewildered. The moment of his abject surrender, which comes shortly afterwards, is a cruel delight for readers – cruel because Mr Sympson is, after all, a frail dictator, doomed before he begins.

What Shirley wants is not freedom from all constraint, as her uncle fears, but the right to choose her own form of submission. Like Jane Eyre, she chooses devotion and service. The point in both novels is simply that it must be a free choice, not enforced by convention or propriety. When she chooses Louis Moore, it is out of respect and out of love. Brontë stresses the point by contrast. Louis Moore, once Shirley's tutor, could hardly be more different from her uncle. He is a most unwilling master, and has to be taught, by Shirley herself, whatever he will attain of tyranny. Indeed, if there is a weakness here, it is that Louis is perhaps too lacking in dynamism to be a convincing partner for the fiery Shirley. In this, however, Brontë is recognising the mystery of sexual attraction, and using romance to make a hard-headed point about her society.

III: *Villette*

Villette treats the social position of women from a much more exclusively personal point of view. There is no talk here of society, no attempt at rational discussion of the issues involved. Where *Jane Eyre* and *Shirley* deal with social injustices and personal relationships, *Villette* unites the two: Lucy's progress towards independence is dramatised through the medium of her relationship with Monsieur Paul. In several episodes, however, the question of equality is closely examined. Lucy Snowe is a victim of the servitude which is the lot of women in education. She is too poor and too alone to be anything else; the death of Miss Marchmont, to whom she is for a time companion, leaves her friendless; unlike Jane Eyre, she has no rich relatives overseas to drop an unexpected inheritance into her lap. Under the thumb of Madame Beck and the eagle eye of Monsieur Paul, she pursues her search for independence internally, until, towards the end, a modest gift from Monsieur Paul brings her all she tastes of freedom.

Two or three scenes will illustrate different aspects of the way the theme is developed in *Villette*. The problem, as with the other novels, is one of choice, and there will be plenty of room for you to look deeper into the subject.

We will begin with one of the most entertaining and pointed scenes in the book: the visit to the art gallery in Chapter 19, 'The Cleopatra', in which Lucy Snowe's jaundiced eye turns satirically to paintings. The paintings in question are carefully selected to give different pictures of the nature of women, and the way the characters respond to them reveals their personalities and their ideas about women. Brontë uses the method of character contrast, which we noted in Chapter 2, very effectively here.

The 'Cleopatra' from which the chapter takes its name comes first. The picture is of a heavily built woman – 'very much butcher's meat' (p. 275) is Lucy's opinion – who reclines on a couch managing to make 'inefficient raiment' out of 'seven-and-twenty yards, I should say' of material. Around her there is a mess of vases and goblets ('pots and pans') mingled with flowers. Lucy sums it up as 'very prettily painted' but 'on the whole, an enormous piece of clap-trap' (p. 276) – the word is chosen, presumably, for its amusing jingle with 'Cleopatra'. Lucy's attitude towards art is refreshingly unceremonious. The comedy is enhanced by Lucy's prim remarks, questioning why the woman should be reclining on a couch in broad daylight when she appears in perfect health; she should, declares the Victorian Miss Snowe, be 'standing, or at least sitting bolt upright' (p. 275); and she should be wearing 'decent garments'. But it is the absurdity of the whole piece of work which most forcefully strikes her. Soon she turns her attention to 'some exquisite little pictures of still life . . . hung modestly beneath that coarse and preposterous canvass' (p. 276).

It hardly surprises us that Lucy is out of sympathy with the bloated sensuality of the 'Cleopatra': it represents, in its imagery of flesh, plenty, untidiness and brazen abandon, the antipodes of Lucy's world. Monsieur Paul's views, as he comes upon her in the same room, in front of and, as he supposes, contemplating the same picture, are more ambivalent. His shock, as a man 'returned from Rome, and now a travelled man' – but, most evidently, hardly with enlarged mind – is comical. Did Lucy come accompanied? Did Dr Bretton tell her to look at '*that* picture' (p. 277)? It takes Lucy a moment or two to comprehend his drift, but finally she understands the nature of his horror:

> 'What is the matter, monsieur?'
> 'Matter! How dare you, a young person, sit coolly down, with the self-possession of a garçon and look at *that* picture?'
> 'It is a very ugly picture, but I cannot at all see why I should not look at it.'
> 'Bon! bon! Speak no more of it. But you ought not to be here alone.'
> 'If, however, I have no society – no *party*, as you say? And then, what does it signify whether I am alone, or unaccompanied? nobody meddles with me.'
> 'Taisez-vous, et asseyez-vous là – là!' Setting down a chair with emphasis in a particularly dull corner, before a series of most specially dreary 'cadres'.

(p. 277)

In several scenes in *Villette* Monsieur Paul is so dictatorial as to be comical. In this instance the nature of his outrage is also so irrational as to be difficult for us to take seriously. Brontë depicts it simply, by giving him a series of abrupt questions. There is no conversation worthy of the name; this is an interrogation, Lucy is guilty with no hope of being proven innocent and with scarcely a hearing, and that the nature of the crime is unclear is of no significance. First, it seems, Monsieur Paul is concerned that Lucy may be unaccompanied, then that Dr Bretton might have 'told' her to look at the 'Cleopatra', then that she has discovered it for herself – an 'Astounding insular audacity' as he, rather ironically, puts it. In the extract, these issues are referred to generally, and Monsieur Paul is unable or unwilling to give precise answers to Lucy's straightforward question about his objections. The emphatic echo, 'Matter!', shows that he regards the problem as so obvious as to require no discussion. His brief exclamations have a patronising air: he is explaining what she must know but has foolishly overlooked – that she is too 'young' to be looking at that picture, and she should not do so with 'the self-possession of a garçon'. On her further demurring, he resorts to excitable assertion: the repeated 'bon!' shows his irritation, 'Speak no more of it' means that he feels it inappropriate to discuss his reasons, and his objection to Lucy's presence before the picture is a retreat into a general paternalistic fear for the safety of women. Lucy's reasoned response is dismissed with an ill-tempered fury which would be intolerably rude were it not laughable.

Despite the comedy, there is a serious point here. We see Lucy treated in this scene as a creature not far removed from slavery. Monsieur Paul sets down the chair for her 'with emphasis', expecting her to do as he says, but his authority over her is based only on his mercurial temper and on his maleness. When we see Lucy meekly accept his authority, we recognise in her the characteristic tendency to take a defensive posture – no matter how independent her thoughts, she behaves in a way which will not threaten her stability; she makes it a policy to match the roles which others design for her. The scene in the 'particularly dull corner' where Monsieur Paul puts her is not quite, however, a parallel with the 'lecture pieuse' which we considered in the last chapter, for it is not only convention and self-protection which guide Lucy's behaviour in the gallery. We also recognise the beginnings of an unwilling affection for Monsieur Paul. She does not yet know that she is fond of him; but she does not want to disobey his wishes, however impolitely expressed. At the same time, there is also here, for the reader, the fear that being placed before 'a series of most specially dreary cadres' is what life may be like for her as the wife of Monsieur Paul: it can hardly be supposed at this point that such a man would prove an open-minded or liberal husband.

The tableaux which Lucy must now study show the antithesis of the 'Cleopatra'. The style of painting is 'flat, dead, pale and formal' (p. 277). One picture is of a 'Jeune Fille' emerging from church with missal in hand; other pictures show different stages in the life of a woman, concluding with a 'Veuve'. From youth to widowhood, they are 'grim and gray as burglars' in Lucy's eyes, 'cold and vapid as ghosts'. She sums up these 'Anges' as 'insincere, ill-humoured, blood-less, brainless nonentities! As bad in their way as the indolent gipsy-giantess, the Cleopatra' (p. 278). Though neither representation of womanhood matches Lucy's aspirations, it is no clearer what her aspirations are.

As Lucy's attention wanders to the rest of the room, Brontë shows through her eyes how other characters react to the 'Cleopatra'. There she sees Monsieur Paul studying the 'Cleopatra' 'quite at his ease' and at length. She notices also that nearly half the crowd at the 'Cleopatra' are ladies – but tells us that Monsieur Paul assured her that these were 'des dames' – married women – and that 'it was quite proper for them to contemplate what no "demoiselle" ought to glance at' (p. 278).

In contrast with Monsieur Paul, Colonel de Hamal seems to find a salacious delight in the 'Cleopatra'. Lucy sees him tittering and whispering to his friend. She sarcastically comments on his sense, refinement, taste and tact, as she notes that 'he was exceedingly taken with this dusk and portly Venus of the Nile' (p. 281). Here, once more, we are invited to see Lucy as a character superior in intellect and feeling, who is yet driven into subservience because of her sex.

The chapter concludes with yet another point of view, amusing for different reasons. After entertaining Dr John with the account of her meeting with Monsieur Paul, Lucy asks his opinion of the 'Cleopatra':

> 'Pooh!' said he, 'My mother is a better-looking woman. I heard some French fops, yonder, designating her as "le type du voluptueux;" if so, I can only say, "le voluptueux" is little to my liking. Compare that mulatto with Ginevra!'

(p. 282)

That Dr Bretton finds points of comparison between Ginevra and the portrait reveals much about him. For us, it is a great deal easier to compare chalk and cheese. Dr Bretton's infatuation with Ginevra is thus rendered comically silly.

In this chapter, we see Lucy maintaining her independence of thought, and reviewing the attitudes of men towards women, as expressed both in the paintings, and in the views of the men she knows at the gallery. As usual, Lucy is detached, cynical, amused and a great deal less tolerant than her dependent situation forces her to appear. It is hard to see at this stage that she can possibly bring herself to accept the love of Monsieur Paul: how could someone with a mind as independent as hers put up with his foolish despotism? At the same time, Dr Bretton seems altogether too light a character to match her.

Monsieur Paul's unattractive status as the caricature of Victorian conservatism about women is broadened later in the novel when his self-imposed office as Lucy's spiritual guardian expands from pictures to include novels, mathematics and languages as well. The novels he lends Lucy are carefully pruned with his pen-knife (Chapter 29); she mildly comments that 'I was a little provoked at the severity of his censorship' (p. 435). Later, in Chapter 30, discovering Lucy to be 'in a state of wretchedly imperfect mental development' (p. 439) in mathematics, he begins to instruct her. Yet, when at long last Lucy shows signs of grasping the science, Monsieur Paul becomes suddenly jealous of the secret knowledge which has been his male preserve:

> . . . then flowed out the bitterest innuendoes against the 'pride of intellect'. I was vaguely threatened with, I know not what doom, if I ever trespassed the limits proper to my sex, and conceived a contraband appetite for unfeminine knowledge.

> (p. 440)

Under this sway, Lucy only briefly experiences the 'godlike thirst after discovery' (p. 440), and eventually tells Monsieur Paul to take his books away, and cease to plague her. Monsieur Paul's contradictory attitude to Lucy is a caricature of the view that women shall be educated, but only to such an extent as to provide wifely support for men. Knowledge for its own sake – 'the noble hunger for science in the abstract' (p. 440) – is 'unfeminine'. The language used here –

'trespassed', 'proper', 'contraband' – expresses Monsieur Paul's sense
that the desire for knowledge is for women unnatural, illegal and
immoral.

Monsieur Paul is worried about more than mathematics. He also
harbours in his soul 'a chronic suspicion that [Lucy] knew both
Greek and Latin' (p. 442), and he sets all sorts of traps to discover
her crafty concealment of these accomplishments. Thwarted in his
efforts, he turns his attention to an attack on learning in women in a
passage which briefly summarises his attitudes:

> A 'woman of intellect', it appeared, was a sort of 'lusus naturæ,' a
> luckless accident, a thing for which there was neither place nor use in
> creation, wanted neither as wife nor worker. Beauty anticipated her in
> the first office. He believed in his soul that lovely, placid, and passive
> feminine mediocrity was the only pillow on which manly thought
> and sense could find rest for its aching temples; and as to work, male
> mind alone could work to any good practical result – hein?

> (p. 443)

The final 'hein?' has a double effect. It is intended by Monsieur Paul
to evoke a response – submissive, of course – from Lucy. It also, by
placing the argument in the accent of Monsieur Paul, suggests the
preposterousness of the argument in Lucy's eyes. It must seem ludicrous to us, too – if only because the large issue of work is thrown in
by the way, as an addendum to the issue of intellect.

Although the argument has Monsieur Paul's accent, not all the
words have. The precise 'lovely, placid, and passive feminine medioc-
rity' is Lucy's own: every ironic word counts; in every word we sense
her quiet fury of desperation. In the next part of the sentence, the
argument is Monsieur Paul's, but the expression is Lucy's: woman is
outrageously described as the 'pillow' for man's 'aching temples' –
the aching being the physical penalty for the extraordinary feats of
intellect which must be attempted within those temples. The paragraph is a good illustration of the virtuosity with which Brontë
makes Lucy move in and out of Monsieur Paul's voice at will, and to
speak with his voice while retaining her own tone. The effect is both
to express Lucy's understanding of, and, to that extent, sympathy

with Monsieur Paul, while retaining her own well-developed critical faculty.

The issue of the role of women in society is clearly central to the relationship of Lucy and Monsieur Paul. The outcome of their conflict is Monsieur Paul's decision to subject Lucy to a test. She will, he insists, sit in the class and write an impromptu essay with the pupils. She refuses; instead, confronted without warning in Chapter 35 by Messieurs Boissec and Rochemorte (well named dry-wood and dead-rock), she is made to write the threatened essay in more painful circumstances. Inspired as she did not expect by recognising her judges as two of the faces which had terrified her and chased her through the town on her first night in Villette, she produces an ironic sketch on 'Human Justice'. Lucy, then, is clearly aware of the wider implications of her situation. Her progress towards independence continues, nevertheless, to be acted out on the battleground of her relationship with Monsieur Paul.

Though very different from Louis Moore, Monsieur Paul shares with him an unlikely status as a romantic hero. Far from Byronic, he has nothing Shelleyan about him, either. Often Lucy thinks him despotic, but his harsh qualities are always tempered by his littleness – she sees him as comic, ludicrous, tragic (ironically – when he thinks she has no present for his birthday), irritable. Graham Bretton has far greater physical beauty, which Lucy is always aware of, and he has sensitivity. However, she recognises an innate weakness in Graham, whereas she becomes progressively more aware of Monsieur Paul's inner strength. She sees beyond his freakishness and volatility, and it is indeed at one of his silliest moments, when she catches him rifling her drawer, that she realises that she 'did not dislike' him (p. 431).

As the relationship develops, we are left in no doubt of the physical power of the attraction between them. Monsieur Paul has power in a word or a look over her happiness or misery. When he withdraws his good will during their mathematics lessons, she describes laying her head on her arms in disappointment, and refusing to speak to him. 'His affection,' she tells us, 'had been very sweet and dear' (p. 440), and once it is withdrawn, her interest in learning ceases. A little later, speaking of Monsieur Paul's insistence that she should sit an examination, she describes their tempestuous relationship:

> . . . M. Paul and I did battle more than once – strong battle, with
> confused noise of demand and rejection, exaction and repulse.

(p. 445)

The later pages of the novel resound with the clamour of these desultory battles. Yet there is also the softer sound, sensuous and narcotic, in Monsieur Paul's voice, 'harmonious with the silver whisper, the gush, the musical sigh, in which light breeze, fountain, and foliage intoned their lulling vesper' (p. 588). There is the softness of touching, too, when 'I first caressed the soft velvet on his cuff, and then I stroked the hand it surrounded' (p. 586). The sexual actuality of their relationship is intense.

Like Shirley, Lucy chooses devotion and service only after she has won the right to determine for herself. She must battle with Monsieur Paul, as Shirley, in different ways, battles with Mr Sympson and with Louis. The successful conclusion of her relationship with Monsieur Paul depends on their mutual recognition of separateness. This phase of their relationship is dramatised at the end of Chapter 36, after Monsieur Paul has ignored Lucy for a week, and then tried to win her to his own religious convictions by leaving a tract on Catholicism in her desk. Incensed, Lucy confronts him, and at last persuades him to acknowledge her separateness. She details all the features of his religion which she finds distasteful or inferior. Concluding her diatribe with the simplicity of prayer which she holds to, in the conviction that she has alienated him for ever, she finds in his response an unexpected softening and an unexpected echo:

> 'God be merciful to me, a sinner!'
> When I had so spoken, so declared my faith, and so widely severed
> myself from him I addressed – then, at last, came a tone accordant,
> an echo responsive, one sweet chord of harmony in two conflicting
> spirits.
> 'Whatever say priests or controversialists,' murmured M. Emanuel,

'God is good, and loves all the sincere. Believe, then, what you can; believe it as you can; one prayer, at least, we have in common; I also cry – "O Dieu, sois appaisé envers moi qui suis pécheur!"'

(p. 517)

The accord between them is strongly depicted. These paragraphs are full of sounds – English, French, speaking, crying, murmuring and music. Monsieur Paul's voice, so often strident, is soft, ruminative. Lucy often notes its musical quality, and here it is matched by an image of harmony in music, which is sustained through the final pages of the novel. The related idea of 'an echo responsive', sandwiched between a parallel musical phrase, the 'tone accordant', and 'one sweet chord of harmony', points to the meaningful shape of the passage: it concludes with the French version of the English with which it begins. Monsieur Paul thus concedes: it is not unexpected, for we are used to surprising changes of mood and opinion from him, and we are used to the generosity which his veneer of imperiousness and savagery often masks. The understanding he and Lucy reach is a rational one: to accept their differences – which, though superficial, are real – and to be aware of their underlying unanimity of sincere purpose.

Like *Shirley* and *Jane Eyre*, Lucy does not ask to be given the right to her freedom, for she knows she has it. Her effort is to make other people – and especially men – realise it. Once her freedom is recognised, she feels free to give it up, and in the end worships her beloved as a demi-god:

. . . he gently raised his hand to stroke my hair; it touched my lips in passing; I pressed it close, I paid it tribute. He was my king; royal for me had been that hand's bounty; to offer homage was both a joy and a duty.

(p. 587)

The language used here of tribute and bounty is ancient, savouring of primitive or feudal loyalties. Monsieur Paul has just given Lucy charge of the house in the Faubourg Clotilde, and she is expressing gratitude. But the house is more symbol than material object: it represents his trust in her, and his acceptance of her right to independence. Thus it is that Lucy can give expression to her sexual loyalty by kissing his hand – again, a feudal gesture, but here signifying much more than a formal relationship. This is not slavery – indeed, she is sensitive on this point and disdains Dr Bretton as slavish in his devotion to Ginevra (pp. 263–4) – but a freely given submission.

In romance Lucy is, of course, doomed. She loses Dr Bretton, and she loses Monsieur Paul. Seemingly 'born only to work for a piece of bread, to await the pains of death, and steadily through all life to despond' (pp. 307–8), Lucy achieves much more in the experience of love for Monsieur Paul, defeating fate and her own predictions. This is something of which even his death cannot wholly rob her.

In practical terms, a kind of justice is meted out to Lucy in the end. As directrice of her own pensionnat, and a successful one, she achieves a measure of control over her own life, a measure of responsibility, and a measure of fulfilment. She has challenges of both work and intellect to answer. She is well able to meet those challenges, and she describes the period when she runs her school at number 7, Faubourg Clotilde in Monsieur Paul's absence as 'the three happiest years of [her] life' (p. 593). The school is, of course, the gift of Monsieur Paul. But despite that, and despite the romantic fulfilments which the later parts of the novel bring to Lucy, it is largely the achievement of independent work and responsibility which brings Lucy 'that Freedom and Renovation which [she] won' (p. 578) at the conclusion of her period at the pensionnat of Madame Beck. Marriage is not essential to her sense of fulfilment; but perhaps the possibility of marriage is. What is crucial to her well-being is not to be required to match a pattern that men, or society, might wish to impose on her. Married, she will retain responsibility; unmarried, she will live a worthwhile and rewarding life. It is a greater success than Lucy Snowe could have expected in the social climate and personal circumstances from which she sprang.

Lucy's problems are resolved, like Jane Eyre's, only with outside help. Whereas Jane's legacy is a bolt from the blue, however, Lucy's is, to some degree at least, a rational outcome of her relationship with Monsieur Paul, and it allows her to fulfil her ambition. It is therefore something like a real solution to her difficulties. The same cannot be said of the 'unexpected chance' (p. 593) which throws £100 from Mr Marchmont in her path, but it is no *sine qua non*: the expansion from externat to pensionnat which it enables Lucy to expedite is a step which she might conceivably have been able to take at some time from her own resources. Nevertheless, the inability of Lucy, as of Jane, to become independent entirely from her own resources seems to indicate Brontë's conviction that for women in comparable situations, salvation is a practical impossibility. The positive elements in each novel point paradoxically to negative elements in real life.

Conclusions

1. The place of women in society is a central theme in Charlotte Brontë's novels. The subject was significant in the author's life as it is in the lives of her heroines. The position of the governess is given particular emphasis, because it forges a particularly cruel link between ability and subservience.
2. This theme is closely related to a range of other themes: freedom, marriage, education, nature, religion, the conflict of passion and duty, the conflict of private and public worlds. These are, indeed, different aspects of a single theme.
3. Major characters are shown to develop towards greater independence of outlook and towards greater power over their circumstances.
4. Brontë stresses the importance of work for women. She sees it as an opportunity for women to fulfil their potential, as a source of self-respect, and as a means of enhancing their worth both as wives and as members of society at large.
5. However, in both *Jane Eyre* and *Villette*, chance, in the form of inheritance or gift, plays a more important catalytic part than work in the changes which are brought about in the protagonists' circumstances.
6. Brontë is particularly concerned with the right of women to equality with men. Her heroines desire control over their own lives, and show individual ability to confront men on level terms.

7. Brontë is not a social revolutionary: despite her concern for the equality of women, the novels uphold traditional ideas of the conduct of women in society and of the relationship between men and women in marriage. Her heroines find their fulfilment in service.

8. The ideas which the novels present about the position of women, marriage and freedom are subtle, and open to various interpretation. There has been, and will continue to be, much discussion among critics about the extent to which, and the way in which, at different levels of analysis, Brontë does and/or does not uphold Victorian values.

Methods of Analysis

1. We have selected the role of woman in society as a clearly defined way into the themes of the novel. It would be possible to select other themes, such as marriage, and deal with it similarly – as suggested below.

2. It is important to keep in mind that no one theme is distinct from the others. Discussing a theme is simply to adopt one way of looking at the subject-matter of the whole novel. We must be aware always of the interrelationship between all the themes, and we should endeavour to show the light that one sheds on another.

3. Look for statements about the theme by narrator or author. Remember that such statements do not necessarily sum up the idea of the novel. They will, even so, form an important part of the discussion.

4. Consider how the theme relates to the characters. It grows naturally out of their concerns, and is often developed by oppositions between characters.
   - Look out for what characters say about the theme, and how other characters react. An important theme is likely to be a source of conflict between characters. That is how a novel 'discusses' a theme.
   - In dealing with the subject of this chapter in particular, it is crucial to look closely at relationships between characters. It is

hard, to say the least, to discuss the place of women in society without discussing love and marriage.

5. Look at the relationship between the theme and the setting. The setting, or some aspects of setting, are likely to reflect the theme or to express ideas about the theme.

6. Do not neglect imagery, symbolism and style in dealing with themes: they may be just as important as character and incident in the presentation of theme.

7. Important themes develop in the course of a novel. It is therefore essential to consider more than one location in discussing them. Look at what precedes and succeeds the extract you are dealing with, and consider how different aspects of the theme are presented from one stage to another in the action.

Further Work

Rather than looking at other locations which deal with the place of women in society, it is probably more useful to consider a different theme. Marriage, or perhaps love and marriage, is a distinct yet closely related theme well worth studying, and I suggest below some passages which deal with it. Many of them also deal with the sorts of issues we have been looking at in this chapter.

Jane Eyre: Consider Rochester's relationships with Bertha and Jane. Useful locations to consider would be Jane's feelings on arriving at church in Volume 2, Chapter 11 (two paragraphs beginning, 'And now I can recall the picture of the grey old house of God . . .' on p. 322), Rochester's remarks about his wife later in the same chapter (the long paragraph beginning, 'Mr Rochester continued, hardily and recklessly . . .' on pp. 326–7), and an extract from the penultimate chapter, perhaps about one page beginning on p. 487, 'I came down as soon as I thought there was a prospect of breakfast . . .'). Another possibility would be to look at St John's relationships with Jane and Rosamond Oliver. Consider his views about marrying Rosamond in

Volume 3, Chapter 6 (a page or two beginning on p. 416, 'By this time he had sat down . . .'), and the conversation between Jane and St John on their walk to Marsh Glen in Volume 3, Chapter 8 (about two pages beginning on p. 446, 'I took a seat: St John stood near me . . .').

Shirley: Look at the discussion of marriage between Shirley and Caroline at the end of the first section of Chapter 12 (from Caroline's speech beginning 'I often wonder, Shirley, whether most men resemble my uncle in their domestic relations . . .', p. 223) and select extracts for yourself; look through Chapter 30 in which Robert Moore and Mr Yorke discuss women, marriage and commerce; finally, consider in detail the episodes in which Shirley explains to Mr Sympson her rejection of Sir Philip and accepts Louis in Chapter 36 (these incidents are reported in Louis' diary entry, in a passage of about one page, beginning 'Apparently, Miss Keeldar, you are as little likely to marry as myself . . .' on p. 574, and in a dialogue between Louis and Shirley on pp. 577–80, beginning '"My pupil," I said . . .' and continuing to the end of the section).

Villette: Analyse the story of Monsieur Paul's constancy to Justine Marie, her memory, and her family as it is told in Chapter 34 (two or three pages beginning with 'The hero of his tale was some former pupil . . .' on p. 485). Then look over a page towards the end of Chapter 35, beginning 'Now, Mademoiselle Lucy, look at me . . .' and continuing down to '. . . if all melted like a dream, as once before had happened' (pp. 500–1). Finally, study the last section of Chapter 37, from 'Not long after, perhaps a fortnight . . .' to the conclusion of the chapter (pp. 531–3).

7

Conclusions

In this chapter we consider how the concluding pages of Charlotte Brontë's novels draw together some of the ideas we have been exploring, especially nature, religion, and the social position of women. The style of the extracts will require as much attention as their content, for it is just as important. As usual, however, we shall allow the novels to determine the direction of discussion.

First, a short recapitulation will be helpful. In the extracts we have considered, there is a central conflict between a major character and her circumstances. Since the protagonists are female, and share some of their author's concerns, their efforts to control their environment tend to involve relationships with men as lovers and possible husbands; avoiding the problems which beset single women is a major issue, too. There is a linked conflict between the spontaneous, or instinctive demands of these protagonists and the claims of society upon them: the opposition is often expressed in ideas associated with nature and with religion. Nature here means both the natural setting, which Brontë feels as animate, and human nature; religious ideas are dramatised in moral questions which characters face, in relationships between characters, and in the behaviour of clergymen. Brontë seems, on the whole, to allow her protagonists to lean towards belief in the essential goodness of human nature and its inspirations, rather than the more formal structures of conventional religious faith. However, as we shall see in this chapter, she is instinctively shy of hard-and-fast distinctions like this, and seems to bend her efforts to avoid over-simple resolution of the conflicts which she has set up.

In each section we shall need to review the context of the extracts. Practically speaking, this means considering how the final chapter in each novel prepares the ground for the few concluding paragraphs which we analyse in detail.

I: *Jane Eyre*

The final chapter of *Jane Eyre* begins with the well-known sentence, 'Reader, I married him' (p. 498) – so well-known as to be the sole entry for Charlotte Brontë in *The Concise Oxford Dictionary of Quotations*. Some readers have found bathos in the statement: it is too obvious, too blunt. Others point to the significance of its structure: its bold address to the audience, and the active form of the statement both suggest that Jane is at last in control of her life. Certainly the statement makes an apposite goal in this novel of the progress of a victim – deceived, ill-treated when regarded at all – towards independence. The sequel stresses the change. Jane's world is practical and domestic, and the language of the first paragraph matches it. In a homely inversion, Jane states that 'A quiet wedding we had' (p. 498); she returns home to find 'Mary . . . cooking the dinner, and John cleaning the knives' (p. 498). Then Jane tells them the news of the wedding, to their quiet and undemonstrative satisfaction. John pulls his forelock, and Jane gives him a five-pound note. As she goes out, she overhears Mary and John speaking of her doing 'better for him nor ony o' t' grand ladies' (p. 498) and of her being not one of the handsomest, but very good-natured. Thus Jane achieves, by being herself, her final victory over the Blanche Ingrams of her world. The use of dialect in the speech of her servants indicates the ordinariness of the scene; there is no hint of Gothic excitement here.

This, then, is the same Jane as before, but translated into a position of greater power. She has money thanks to her legacy, and position thanks to her marriage, and she can look forward to a stable future. From her narrative present Jane is able to speak of ten successful years of married life, 'supremely blest – blest beyond what language can express' (p. 500). Much of the final chapter is devoted to supporting this impression of stable happiness. Adèle's 'sound English education corrected in a great measure her French defects' (p. 499–500). Rochester's vision improves, and since, on the birth of their first child, a boy, he 'acknowledged that God had tempered judgment with mercy' (p. 501), so does his moral insight. Thus, it seems at first glance, is resolved one of the main conflicts in the novel: the claims of nature appear to be satisfied within the bounds of a proper reverence for God. In their different ways, Adèle and Rochester are both brought closer to the ideal. Passion and reason are in happy balance.

Closer examination tells a different story, particularly when we look at the conclusion. The final page is not a popular focus of study among students, who like to see the dénouement of the relationship between Rochester and Jane as the target of the novel. It is extraordinary how many readers fail to notice, or at least fail to give proper weight to, these final three paragraphs:

> As to St John Rivers, he left England: he went to India. He entered on the path he had marked for himself; he pursues it still. A more resolute, indefatigable pioneer never wrought amidst rocks and dangers. Firm, faithful, and devoted; full of energy, and zeal, and truth, he labours for his race: he clears their painful way to improvement; he hews down like a giant the prejudices of creed and caste that encumber it. He may be stern; he may be exacting; he may be ambitious yet; but his is the sternness of the warrior Greatheart, who guards his pilgrim-convoy from the onslaught of Apollyon. His is the exaction of the apostle, who speaks but for Christ, when he says – 'Whosoever will come after me, let him deny himself, and take up his cross and follow me.' His is the ambition of the high master-spirit, which aims to fill a place in the first rank of those who are redeemed from the earth – who stand without fault before the throne of God; who share the last mighty victories of the Lamb; who are called, and chosen, and faithful.
>
> St John is unmarried: he never will marry now. Himself has hitherto sufficed to the toil; and the toil draws near its close: his glorious sun hastens to its setting. The last letter I received from him drew from my eyes human tears, and yet filled my heart with Divine joy: he anticipated his sure reward, his incorruptible crown. I know that a stranger's hand will write to me next, to say that the good and faithful

servant has been called at length into the joy of his Lord. And why
weep for this? No fear of death will darken St John's last hour: his
mind will be unclouded; his heart will be undaunted; his hope will be
sure; his faith steadfast. His own words are a pledge of this: –
   'My Master,' he says, 'has forewarned me. Daily he announces
more distinctly, – "Surely I come quickly!" and hourly I more eagerly
respond, – "Amen; even so come, Lord Jesus!"'

                                                          (p. 501–2)

Quite simply, the question over the end of the novel is, why does it
end with St John Rivers? We might wish to argue that it is merely to
fall in with the Victorian convention of tying up loose ends in the
final chapter. The offhand phrase, 'As to St John Rivers', which
introduces the extract seems to support the idea, as if including his
fate simply for the sake of completeness, in the course of tidying up.
He should not, we may think, be important, for he has been
rejected, both as a lover and as a moral leader, by Jane. She saw him
as a fanatical, and to that extent blind man; his moral blindness is in
some lights greater than Rochester's. The opening of the extract
appears to dismiss him as one who simply took a different, and less
attractive, path. Yet the extract as a whole is a powerful peroration,
one of the most heightened passages in the novel. It cannot be irrelevant to the impact of the whole. The answer to the question, then,
must be that St John and his way remain important.
   It is not, surely, sufficient to see the conclusion simply as a reitera-
tion of the rejected pole of an antithesis, as, in the introduction to
the 1986 Penguin Classics edition of the novel, Q. D. Leavis does.
She argues that the ending shows Rochester as 'contrite and capable
of humility because he is capable of giving and accepting love', and
offers as a contrast the 'inflexible spiritual pride and ambition' of St
John Rivers:

> We are certainly meant to see the opposition here between dogmatic
> religion and instinctive goodness.

                                                          (p. 25)

I think the word I like best here is 'certainly'! Perhaps it is best interpreted by contraries. Surely we must question whether 'instinctive goodness' is a concept which sits any more happily on a deceitful would-be bigamist than the untidy badge on Helen Burns; but admittedly our perception of Rochester does change at the end of the novel. St John Rivers looks rather more like 'dogmatic religion': but it is not what the conclusion expresses. The error which leads to the Q. D. Leavis view is twofold: it pays too little attention to the text; and, in presuming that Jane can have only one view of St John Rivers, it fails to take sufficient account of the evolutionary theme of the novel.

If we look first at the judgement made on St John in the extract, we can come to only one, unambiguous conclusion: he is much admired, by Jane and by Brontë, for his zeal, his dedication, his self-lessness. Jane describes him as a moral 'giant', one who may ultimately become – unlikely though it may seem to us – 'without fault'. The praise becomes yet more extravagant when he is compared with a 'glorious sun'. The adjectives fall in cascades of honour: 'resolute, indefatigable . . . Firm, faithful, and devoted, full of energy and zeal, and truth . . . called, and chosen, and faithful . . . unclouded . . . undaunted . . . steadfast'; he has 'the ambition of the high master-spirit'. There is power in this; the extravagance appears to be simply and purely that; there is no hint of irony that I can see. Jane's feelings towards St John go beyond admiration and respect, for he gives a voice to the stirrings of her soul.

What, then, does the style of the extract suggest? If what Jane says of St John stresses the importance of religion in her life, her manner of expression signs and seals it. Jane alludes, in the comparison of St John to Greatheart defending his pilgrims against the onslaught of Apollyon, to *The Pilgrim's Progress*, a book dear to Brontë's heart. The extract quotes from the Bible; its language draws on the Bible in its vocabulary ('the last mighty victories of the Lamb', for example) and in its ideas ('stand without fault before the throne of God', 'the toil draws near its close', 'his incorruptible crown', 'the joy of his Lord'). There is a magniloquent virtuosity in the mingling of spiritual abstraction and emotional image in this passage. The best example is a sentence which gains power by piling up parallel phrases: 'No fear of death will darken St John's last hour: his mind will be unclouded; his heart will be undaunted; his hope will be sure; his faith steadfast'; the phrases contain rhythmic echoes; their pace increases as they become briefer; the transition from negative to positive grammatical forms ('No fear . . . unclouded . . . undaunted . . . sure . . . steadfast') strengthens the impression of emotional climax. The tone is triumphal: it suggests firm faith in the religious life.

The outcome – the final paragraph – is a magnificent affirmation of the heavenly reward which the righteous may look forward to beyond the grave. The final sentence expects, even actively seeks, the ultimate confrontation between God and Man. The reference to death and judgement – 'Surely I come quickly' and St John's response – which quotes the penultimate sentence of Revelation, might carry the mood of either promise or threat. St John, however, who 'eagerly' awaits the ending of his earthly existence, looks only to reward. 'Amen' means 'so be it', but here signifies much more than resignation: it expresses the will to participate and rejoice in dissolution and resurrection.

Although the final words belong to St John Rivers, it is hard not to feel that they express Jane's views, too. The powerful influence over her of Miss Temple and of Helen Burns, as well as that of St John Rivers, here finds its most powerful expression. We can conclude only that St John Rivers's strong declaration of faith is also, to some degree, Jane's.

How does this interpretation match the novel as a whole? Clearly, the feeling expressed is not what we would expect. As the content of the conclusion seems a diversion from the plot, so the feeling appears in conflict with the tendency of the novel as a whole. We have watched Jane rejecting the way of Helen Burns as too saintly for her own rebellious disposition (she states flatly in Volume 1, Chapter 7, p. 77, that 'I was no Helen Burns'); we have watched her turning away from Rochester when his bigamous intention is revealed; and we have seen her reject St John Rivers in favour of returning to Rochester – before she is aware of any changes in his circumstances. We have noticed already how Jane came to view her feeling for Rochester as a form of idolatry, and their relationship as an obstacle in the path to God for both of them. In the last chapter, it seemed, she had chosen her fleshly idol instead of the claims of God – at least in so far as those claims were represented by St John. Now, at the end, she appears to wish to change direction again.

The effect is to remove certainties; instead of a conventional tying up of loose ends, this conclusion weakens the knots which have appeared secure – it is only too literally a 'dénouement'. It denies an ending, and seeks continuing. It takes the story of Jane out of history and places it instead in the realm of what is yet to be determined. That simple and, superficially, definitive opening statement of the chapter – 'Reader, I married him' – is contradicted; the traditional culmination of a novel is turned into a staging-post in Jane's life. At the end it is evident that Jane's relationship with Rochester has continued to change during ten years in response to his changing health and ideas; but that is little in comparison with how Jane is presented: as still incomplete, still a developing being, and without knowledge of the outcome of her development. She has outgrown the influences which acted upon her. Economically, the dependant has become her own mistress. With her legacy and her marriage and her child (or perhaps more than one), she seems secure. 'Edward and I are happy', she tells us. But there is a denial of moral stability in this ending, and a stressing of transience and of evolution. Concluding with St John's certainty has, ironically, the effect of stressing the lack of it in Jane: at the end of the novel she remains unended, undefined, and still to be.

The implications of the conclusion touch on all the themes we have been considering. Jane's reaction to St John's letter which 'drew from my eyes human tears and yet filled my heart with Divine joy' reflects, in its contrast of human and divine, central antitheses on which the novel is built: the clash between nature and religion, and the parallel opposition between passion and reason. At the end, the balance of passion and reason remains in tension; the conflicting claims of religion and nature remain unresolved. Jane's nature embraces both human and divine elements. What we are left with is the sense of continuing struggle. Jane's victory over her circumstances is, perhaps, complete; but she is still required to stand guard over her moral welfare. That is a struggle which, like St John's, will end only with death.

But the conclusion does more than revise Jane's ambitions: it involves a dislocation of our perception of the whole novel. It shifts the balance from romance to spiritual pilgrimage. Clearly, *Jane Eyre* is both of these things; but whereas the romance strand has reached a successful conclusion, the spiritual strand is yet to be resolved and thus appears, in retrospect, more significant.

II: *Shirley*

The final chapter of *Shirley* begins in sound business style with an urbane warning to the reader that 'we must settle accounts now' (p. 587), and offers to shake hands on the deal. What follows is indeed a rounding of the complex content of the novel, but it is hardly conclusive. The main focus of this final chapter is the relationship of Robert and Caroline, but there is a great deal else in it. Brontë tries to encapsulate here all the materials with which she has been working, devoting a section of the chapter to each, and attempts to link the private and public aspects of the novel. We need to review its structure very briefly before going on to analyse the conclusion.

The first two sections of the chapter deal with the background action of the novel. The lives of the curates with whom the novel began are summarised – and then a new one, Macarthey, is introduced, a successor to the mysteriously disappeared Malone: Brontë refuses to offer any explanation. She moves on to deal with the aftermath of the attack on Robert Moore. No prosecution is brought for the shooting of Robert Moore, but it is known that the perpetrator of the deed was Michael Hartley, 'the half-crazed weaver once before alluded to, a frantic Antinomian in religion, and a mad leveller in politics' (p. 589), who dies of delirium tremens a year after the attack. In an effort, perhaps, to generate a mood of reconciliation, Brontë writes that Robert Moore gave the widow a guinea for the burial; it is hardly an over-generous gift, however, and is perhaps better seen as a sign of Moore's business acumen!

The second section of the chapter widens the panorama. It begins with the turning of seasons from winter, through spring, to the summer. Having located the 'burning weather' (p. 590) in June 1812, and described it as fitting the period – it also recalls the aridity of the opening chapter and thus helps to round the structure of the novel – Brontë reviews the progress of Wellington and Bonaparte, refers to the Anti-Corn Law League which criticised Wellington, and comments on economic changes in England following the repeal of the Orders in Council, when 'many a solid fortune was realized' (p. 591).

The backdrop thus briefly sketched, Brontë turns at last in the third section to her major characters. As the nuptials of Shirley and Louis approach, Louis is left in charge of the arrangements while Shirley mopes and dreams. Her excuse is a direct and concise expression of the changes which we have witnessed in her:

> 'Louis,' she said, 'would never have learned to rule, if she had not ceased to govern: the incapacity of the sovereign had developed the powers of the premier.'

(p. 592)

It may be possible to see here an effort, in the use of the political metaphor, to relate the private and the more public worlds with which the novel deals. However, a somewhat similar metaphor is used, as we saw in Chapter 6, of the relationship of Monsieur Paul and Lucy in *Villette*. Here, as there, Brontë's language stresses the reciprocity of a marital relationship characterised by service, and not domination.

At once, using as a fulcrum Caroline's ruling herself by marriage out of the role of bridesmaid, Brontë turns to the happy outcome of her relationship with Robert. He declares his love for her as she stands with the pot she has used to water her plants still in her hand, looking up to see Venus, the silver, twinkling Star of Love. There is a link here with Chapter 1: unlike the shower of curates there, the 'refreshing shower' (p. 592) which Caroline gives her plants appears a fertile and bountiful moistening. It forges a further link, too, in the association between water and fertility which forms a sustained motif in the novel – we noted this in Chapter 4. Furthermore, the star recalls a scene in Chapter 12 of the novel in which Caroline sees the constellations while watching for her own star of love – the beacon of light at Moore's home (p. 238). It is evident that Brontë is anxious to present the climax of their relationship as having thematic meaning.

The relationship of Caroline and Robert associates the private and public themes in action as well as image. Caroline's world is the personal world of feeling; Robert's the tougher world of trade. Of course, each reaches into the other world, or tries to. But their relationship can develop only because the repeal of the Orders in Council has saved his business, and he is now in an economic position to marry.

Robert's new material security also brings him closer to fulfilling his vision of the future of his mill and of the advantages which it will bring to the community:

> 'The copse shall be firewood ere five years elapse: the beautiful
> wild ravine shall be a smooth descent; the green natural terrace shall
> be a paved street: there shall be cottages in the dark ravine, and cot-
> tages on the lonely slopes: the rough pebbled track shall be an even,
> firm, broad, black, sooty road, bedded with the cinders from my mill:
> and my mill, Caroline – my mill shall fill its present yard.'

(p. 597)

We hardly require Caroline's response, 'Horrible!' (p. 598), to sense an element of irony in Moore's vision. The repeated 'my mill' suggests a pride rather too great to go unquestioned. The replacement of 'beautiful' and 'natural' by 'broad, black, sooty' shows Brontë's divided view of his utilitarian plans. The ambiguity of view is maintained a little later when we hear of Moore's intention of enclosing Nunnely Commons, and of his ambition that 'the houseless, the starving, the unemployed, shall come to Hollow's mill from far and near'. There is no resolution of the issue raised – a many-faceted antithesis of utilitarian and rural – beyond a kiss which prefaces the flight indoors of Robert and Caroline to escape the dew. Since they are associated respectively with business and feeling, their kiss may be felt as a kind of union of opposites; but it can hardly bear the weight of the complex of oppositions – imperial, industrial and social against emotional, moral and local – which the novel touches on.

The short final section of the chapter, which takes us to August of the narrative, changes focus more wildly than did the opening of the first chapter, switching rapidly into the narrator's present, then into a dimly remembered past. The mood of the section changes likewise. It begins triumphally enough in both private and public spheres, with the winning of Salamanca and the marriages of the protagonists at Briarfield. Soon, however, the tone modulates to something a little nostalgic as the reverie of the narrator takes precedence:

> I suppose Robert Moore's prophecies were, partially, at least, fulfilled. The other day I passed up the Hollow, which tradition says was once green, and lone, and wild; and there I saw the manufacturer's day-dreams embodied in substantial stone and brick and ashes – the cinder-black highway, the cottages, and the cottage-gardens; there I saw a mighty mill, and a chimney, ambitious as the tower of Babel. I told my old housekeeper when I came home where I had been.
> 'Ay!' said she; 'this world has queer changes. I can remember the old mill being built – the very first it was in all the district; and then, I can remember it being pulled down, and going with my lake-lasses (companions) to see the foundation-stone of the new one laid: the two Mr Moores made a great stir about it; they were there, and a deal of fine folk beside, and both their ladies; very bonnie and grand they looked; but Mrs Louis was the grandest, she always wore such handsome dresses: Mrs Robert was quieter-like. Mrs Louis smiled when she talked: she had a real happy, glad, good-natured look; but she had een that pierced a body through: there is no such ladies now-a-days.'
> 'What was the Hollow like then, Martha?'
> 'Different to what it is now; but I can tell of it clean different again: when there was neither mill, nor cot, nor hall, except Fieldhead, within two miles of it. I can tell, one summer-evening, fifty years syne, my mother coming running in just at the edge of dark, almost fleyed out of her wits, saying, she had seen a fairish (fairy) in Fieldhead Hollow; and that was the last fairish that ever was seen on this country side (though they've been heard within these forty years). A lonesome spot it was – a bonnie spot – full of oak trees and nut trees. It is altered now.'

The story is told. I think I now see the judicious reader putting on his spectacles to look for the moral. It would be an insult to his sagacity to offer directions. I only say, God speed him in the quest!

(p. 599)

This conclusion is a drastic withdrawal from the action. The characters have already receded; now they are consigned to the past. Here, at the end of the novel, our attention is turned to the narrator, with whom we come more nearly face-to-face than before, only to be introduced to another, Martha, the narrator's 'old housekeeper'.

The process of withdrawal from the narrative begins with the first narrator: the opening 'I suppose' emphasises the withdrawal. The phrase introduces a casual note which is developed in the familiarity with the location of 'The other day I passed up the Hollow'. Then the figures in the novel become a subject of unheated discussion between narrator and housekeeper. Martha helps to round off the novel with her thumb-nail sketch of the main characters, which has the effect of a curtain-call; Shirley and Caroline take a bow in a style typical of the impressions we have received of them, Mrs Louis smiling and sharp-eyed and 'the grandest', Mrs Robert 'quieter-like'; Shirley's being styled conventionally 'Mrs Louis' reflects her progress through the novel, for it stresses Shirley's subordinate status in marriage, while clearly her personality makes her shine more brightly than the others, Louis included. There is grandeur and happiness in the scene, and success with the fruition of Robert's ambitions.

The effect of the introduction of this new narrator is to modify the perspective from which we review not just this moment, but the whole of the action. Martha is old, and has seen much. The main characters are set back in time, and diminished in importance; we zoom out to see the protagonists in a broader framework. The effect is accentuated by the stylistic contrast between the major part of the narrative and the housekeeper's dialect. Her Yorkshire vocabulary ('lake-lasses', two instances of 'bonnie', 'syne', 'fleyed', 'een' and two instances of 'fairish') and grammar ('quieter-like', 'a deal of fine folk' and 'there is no such ladies') are more extreme than in the speech of the 'low persons' whom Brontë introduced into the novel. The frequency of her local forms in a short space implies a deliberate effort to make the story of Shirley and Caroline recede into a foreign region. The housekeeper sees the 'fine folk' as a different species – very 'bonnie and grand' with 'handsome dresses', but no longer of significance. They are of a time long past – 'There is no such ladies now-a-days' – and thus they attain the enchantment of distance, taking on something of the glamour of the knights and damsels of Arthurian legend. The comparisons which we have noted between Shirley and a fairy, and between Caroline and a wood-nymph, are given a new twist here: they are late resonances of the world of the vanished 'fairishes', and share its insubstantial poetry. There is nostalgia for a romantic world long gone, as well as practicality, in Martha's refrain of alteration and loss.

How does this affect our view of the novel and its themes?

First, let us remember that Martha's view is not the only view, and in particular it is not Robert Moore's view. The nature of the changes which he has wrought is in the direction of utility. The Hollow, once 'green, and lone, and wild' is now 'substantial stone and brick and ashes'. His aim in building 'lines of cottages' (p. 597), ugly though they may be, is to bring to 'the houseless, the starving, the unemployed' (p. 598) the advantages of shelter and a wage.

Then let us remember that Robert's motives are not unmixed: this is the man of whom it is said in the course of the attack on the mill at the beginning of the novel that 'he did not sufficiently care when the new inventions threw the old work-people out of employ' (p. 61); here, at the end, he is at least as anxious to 'double the value' (p. 597) of his property as to bring advantage to the community. The biblical reference to the tower of Babel shows that the narrator questions the value of the improvements which have been made in accordance with Robert Moore's vision: it recalls the pride of ownership and achievement implicit in his repeated 'my mill', which we noticed earlier; and the confusion of tongues with which God answered the building of the tower points to the disorganisation of the environment which development of the mill brings with it. The impact of Moore's ambition is therefore mixed.

Martha in turn reflects this ambiguity about the development of the Hollow from a point of view seasoned by time and experience:

she may believe in fairies, but she knows that people do not behave like them. Her healthy scepticism is implied in her saying that 'the two Mr Moores made a great stir' about the laying of the foundation stone of the new mill. She is neither cynical nor naïve about the real importance of the affairs of the great personages who are so exercised about their plans and achievements. Though she admires the people, she is unenchanted with the changes they have brought about. Martha's sense of loss is evident in the contrast between her final reference to Fieldhead Hollow as 'a bonnie spot – full of oak trees and nut trees', and her flat conclusion that 'It is altered now'; but the change is evidently one she accepts.

Martha's resignation is the fruit of her length of vision. She knows not only the Moores and the mill. She can look back into her childhood to a time when 'there was neither mill, nor cot, nor hall', when Fieldhead occupied a comparatively vast area, lonesome, full of oak and nut trees, and her mother ran home in fear and excitement to tell her of having sighted the last fairy to have been found in the region. The setting is magical: a summer evening, 'just at the edge of dark' – at the dark borders of Martha's consciousness, too. Thus Martha knows – just – from experience what the narrator knows only from what 'tradition says': the imaginative power of the setting as it used to be, 'green, and lone, and wild'. In her reference to the world of fairies, Martha strikes a note which recalls whole chords in the novel. The implication of the hidden, of imagination and enchantment, recalls those reverberations throughout the novel of the turbulence and torture of powerful feeling: Martin's feeling towards Caroline and the strange behaviour it generates; Mr Sympson's and Louis's contrasting attitudes towards Shirley; the passion for Robert Moore underlying Caroline's illness; Shirley's feelings for Louis, and the instincts latent in her escapade with the iron. All those features of romance of which the first chapter promised only modest helpings now take the foreground – the balance has altered, as the opening chapter also promised.

To that extent, the novel has a satisfying ending. But it is not the whole story, for the keynote of the conclusion is transience. Change is the theme common to both speakers: the narrator describes how Robert Moore's ambitions have changed the Hollow; the housekeeper's comments take up the theme, opening with 'queer changes' and concluding with 'It is altered now'.

Both narrator and housekeeper refer to the same aspect of the theme of change: the pragmatic present of brick and stone is contrasted with an earlier period of romance. Though neither refers to the social and economic advantages which Robert Moore perhaps hoped to win for the ordinary people of his neighbourhood, his agenda is implicit in their discussion. We might, then, be tempted to think of the conclusion as offering for the theme of the novel something to do with the opposition between imagination and pragmatism. After all, the opening paragraphs, as we saw in Chapter 1, offer a contrast between romance and the workaday world . The novel concludes, fittingly we might say, with the marriage of Robert Moore, the hard-headed businessman, and Caroline Helstone, the wood-nymph. Thus it seeks to show the final reconciliation of the terms of the central opposition: imagination is married to practicality; feeling is married to business. We might indeed think along these lines, were it not for the final paragraph. There Brontë invites the 'judicious' reader to seek out the 'moral' for himself. She calls for the blessing of God to help him in his quest – for she certainly will not!

Brontë's refusal in the conclusion to offer a moral perhaps throws some light on the way she handles themes. The problem is not lack of one, but that there are too many. The novel is full of antitheses: not just romance and pragmatism, not only love and business; religion and war is there too, nature and religion, independence and marriage, nature and society – any of these might be viewed as a major theme. The novel also deals with several social and political subjects: the effect of the corn laws, the exploits of Wellington and Bonaparte, the Orders in Council, the social role of the clergy, the rights of women. The result is a panorama – without much in the way of balance, and without much in the way of integration, as our review of the final chapter has indicated. There is much in *Shirley* to interest us, but it is hard to see the novel as a whole as an expression of the kind of response to experience for which Charlotte Brontë is famed. Here, Brontë's refusal to offer a definitive conclusion has different sources, and a different effect from, her refusal at the end of *Jane Eyre*.

III: *Villette*

The conclusion of *Villette* is much more focused than that of *Shirley*, but it is no more definitive than the ending of either of the earlier novels. On the contrary, Brontë goes to greater lengths to deny her readers certainty.

The final chapter contains two sections, the first of which recounts Lucy's progress in the three years of Monsieur Paul's absence. She describes them, paradoxically, as the happiest years of her life. She works hard at her externat, and expands it into a pensionnat with the aid of a legacy of £100 from Mrs Marchmont. She does not congratulate herself: her success was due, she argues, to change in circumstances: to the gift of the house at 7, Faubourg Clotilde by Monsieur Paul, and to the stimulus of his existence 'far away beyond seas' (p. 594) and the promise of his return. She paints a glowing portrait of the Monsieur Paul of her imagination, as a man 'honest, and not false – artless, and not cunning – a free man, and not a slave' (p. 595); he is happy that she remain a Protestant, for 'All Rome could not put him into bigotry' (p. 595). Her life seems a preparation for his return. Like Penelope, she toils at her spindle against the coming of her heroic voyager.

Even at this stage, it is hard for us to imagine his return. His separation by sea is, after all, symbolic of their relationship, and perhaps essential to it. Divided by nationality, by language, by religion, they are hardly of similar temperament. They are at one, it seems, only in acknowledging their differences: spiritually and emotionally, he seems as far distant from Lucy as India from Belgium. Thus the first section begins with a portrait of Lucy happy in her independent life and with the promise of Monsieur Paul's return, and concludes with a restatement of their religious disparity.

The second and final section, the whole of which is our extract, begins by looking forward to Monsieur Paul's imminent return:

> And now the three years are past: M. Emanuel's return is fixed. It is Autumn; he is to be with me ere the mists of November come. My school flourishes, my house is ready: I have made him a little library, filled its shelves with the books he left in my care: I have cultivated

out of love for him (I was naturally no florist) the plants he preferred, and some of them are yet in bloom. I thought I loved him when he went away; I love him now in another degree; he is more my own.

The sun passes the equinox; the days shorten, the leaves grow sere; but – he is coming.

Frosts appear at night; November has sent his fogs in advance; the wind takes its autumn moan; but – he is coming.

The skies hang full and dark – a rack sails from the west; the clouds cast themselves into strange forms – arches and broad radiations; there rise resplendent mornings – glorious, royal, purple as monarch in his state; the heavens are one flame; so wild are they, they rival battle at its thickest – so bloody, they shame Victory in her pride. I know some signs of the sky; I have noted them ever since childhood. God, watch that sail! Oh! guard it!

The wind shifts to the west. Peace, peace, Banshee – 'keening' at every window! It will rise – it will swell – it shrieks out long: wander as I may through the house this night, I cannot lull the blast. The advancing hours make it strong: by midnight, all sleepless watchers hear and fear a wild south-west storm.

That storm roared frenzied for seven days. It did not cease till the Atlantic was strewn with wrecks: it did not lull till the deeps had gorged their full sustenance. Not till the destroying angel of tempest had achieved his perfect work, would he fold the wings whose waft was thunder – the tremor of whose plumes was storm.

Peace, be still! Oh! a thousand weepers, praying in agony on waiting shores, listened for that voice, but it was not uttered – not uttered till, when the hush came, some could not feel it: till, when the sun returned, his light was night to some!

Here pause: pause at once. There is enough said. Trouble no quiet, kind heart; leave sunny imaginations hope. Let it be theirs to conceive the delight of joy born again fresh out of great terror, the rapture of rescue from peril, the wondrous reprieve from dread, the fruition of return. Let them picture union and a happy succeeding life.

Madame Beck prospered all the days of her life; so did Père Silas; Madame Walravens fulfilled her ninetieth year before she died. Farewell.

(pp. 595–6)

Charlotte Brontë brings her love of inconclusiveness to a new level in these final paragraphs of *Villette*. Where *Jane Eyre* concluded with the possibility of new directions, and *Shirley* faded with the recollected clamour of conflicting interests, *Villette* actually proposes two mutually exclusive endings: Monsieur Paul perishes at sea, or he returns safely. To some degree she thus steals the thunder of John Fowles; however, where *The French Lieutenant's Woman* offers two possible endings, *Villette* offers, so to speak, a 'real' ending and an 'imaginary' alternative. And this is only the most obvious of the ambiguities of the conclusion.

The ambiguity is partly of accidental origin. Objections were raised by, among others, Patrick Brontë, to the ruthless killing off of Monsieur Paul, and Charlotte, unwilling to change what she had done, tried to appease her critics by rendering the ending sufficiently mysterious to allow of various interpretation. Another reason perhaps lies in the simple painfulness of the tragic version. None the less, the tragic version is the more convincing.

The tragic ending is presented first, poetically – in image and rhyme – in the extinguishing of light by night; thus, Lucy Snowe suggests, are her hopes dashed, with Monsieur Emanuel's ship, by the storm. Characteristically for Brontë, the horror of the event is rendered by description of setting. The seasons reflect Lucy's mood: like the light and dark imagery here, this is something of a cliché, used in a thousand other works; yet how individual and potent the metaphor becomes in the context of Lucy's life and expectations! From the flowers which drop their blossoms, to the gathering fogs and steelier frosts, to the longer and darker nights, everything points to a closing in of the claw of impending disaster. Everything suggests that Lucy's life is about to return to its dark cul-de-sac. Then, at the last moment, she retreats from open statement. Instead, sustaining the nature imagery, she offers those with 'sunny imaginations' the option of the ending they prefer.

The happy ending does not convince. The language used to describe it contains the markers to its unlikelihood. To say that optimists may 'conceive' or 'picture' a happy outcome is as much as to state that they are deluded. The transports of 'the delight of joy born again . . . the rapture of rescue from peril, the wondrous reprieve from dread' do not match the sour vision which we have come to expect from Lucy Snowe. Her second-hand experience of love and marriage – through Paulina and Ginevra – suggests that it is unlikely to lead to 'union and a happy succeeding life'. The happy version of the ending, that is, does not match the mood of the novel.

Unhappiness, frustration, confinement and denial, however, do, and those are the ideas which the tragic ending drives home. The darker ending is the more convincing because it is the more fully felt. The extract takes us, quite deliberately, into a fluid present of the narrator's experience, with the narration hovering uneasily between tenses: compare 'I have cultivated . . . plants' with 'I was . . . no florist', or 'watchers hear and fear' with 'The storm roared'. She speaks of Autumn, moving from the beginning of November, when her hero is due to return, to beyond all hope that he can do so. Lucy's eagerness is stressed by the preparations which she makes: the little library of his books, the flowers she has cultivated. She notes the closing season – the shorter days, the fading leaves, which contrast with her hope – nay, her conviction – that 'he is coming'. The phrase is repeated against the backdrop of fog and moaning wind. We feel with Lucy as she paces through her lonely house in the night, waiting and hoping against hope, one among a host of 'sleepless watchers'. The decision over Monsieur Emanuel's fate is made into an apocalyptic vision of natural disorder, prepared by the kind of animation of nature which we have noticed before in Brontë's writing. Every aspect of nature is active. The sun 'passes' the equinox, days 'shorten', leaves 'grow sere', clouds 'hang' or 'sail from the west' or 'cast themselves' into strange shapes, fine mornings 'rise', the wind 'shifts' and moans like a living being. The climax is reached with flaming skies and a storm so frenzied as to prefigure the day of judgement – though the vision has a Celtic as well as a Christian aspect, with the reference to the Banshee 'keening' (an Irish/Scottish word) its message of death. Sound is used with particular intensity: the wind moves from 'keening' to shrieking; the storm 'roared', there is thunder; Lucy hears 'a thousand weepers, praying'; rhyme stresses that to hear is to fear. Finally comes the image of the storm as a 'destroying angel', with thunder in the beating of his wings, and tempest in his proud plumes, who rests only when his work of waste is 'perfect'. The 'tremor' of his crest appositely conjures up the quaking waters and the shaking terror of those whose lives are sundered. With dramatic suddenness, all is hushed, while Lucy listens for a voice that remains silent. For all those destroyed in the storm, the hush has become eternal. Throughout this passage, the external violence mirrors the storm in Lucy's feelings; the silence is the sound of Lucy's final years.

There is little comfort in this ending. The angel is no Ariel; there is no Prospero to allay the wild array of the waters and bring all to a peaceful reconciliation. We are left with the desolate image of 'a thousand weepers, praying in agony on waiting shores'. The sea suggests the vastness of eternity, and it remains empty in the aftermath of the storm. There is little religious hope here. Against the power of these images of destruction and pain, the plea to God, 'God, watch that sail! Oh! guard it', seems feeble indeed. Those weeping on the shore seem to be praying to propitiate a God of vengeance.

In such a context, the offer of a 'sunny' ending is intended only for those who prefer fantasy. The claustrophobic existence of Lucy Snowe is ruled now, as before, by frustration and loss. We may perhaps see in this Brontë's own profound sense of loss after being deprived by disease of her brother and four sisters. Whatever the source, however, Lucy's vision presents vengeance and destruction as the normal state of the world. The selection of the word 'perfect' for the end of the devastation wrought by the angel of the storm is interesting. Does it express ironic bitterness? Or rather resignation? The word means, of course, not 'ideal', but 'finished'. But there is in it, inevitably, a feeling that destruction is right: it is the rule.

Is there any glimpse of hope in this ending? Perhaps, from the point of view of a reader, Lucy's stoicism in the face of adversity may appear noble. If there is a hint of comfort for Lucy, it must reside in the image she retains of her hero. He is, for her, hope and light in an existence largely dark and hopeless. Now, as before, despite her new-found security and independence, Lucy is a gloomy figure. Winter is her time. Snow caps her. Here, she meets her fate at a time when 'Frosts appear at night'. She achieves the fate that she expects, for she is, as she has told us earlier, not one of fortune's darlings. The best she attains is to be 'inoffensive as a shadow' (Chapter 27, p. 403), 'a shadow in Life's sunshine' (Chapter 28, p. 421). Darkness and gloom are her native element. In this half-light of Lucy's jaded imagination, Monsieur Emanuel remains a beacon. He is not now as he was – cantankerous, querulous, over-sensitive, tyrannical. Now he is the Christian hero that his noble behaviour towards the family of his beloved Justine Marie made him seem. Perhaps, indeed, he is more than flesh and blood could ever be, for Lucy says that she 'thought [she] loved him when he went away', but that now she loves him in 'another degree'. He has been away for three years – three years during which her memory of his actuality has had time to dim – and now, she insists, 'he is more my own'. The implication of this statement is that the image she has of him is better than the reality. Lucy, in short, is better off with her dreams of what might have been, than she could ever have been with Monsieur Emanuel in the flesh. He has left her a greater legacy in her imagination, where he burns with preternatural brightness, than the house in Faubourg Clotilde.

The power of Paul Carl David Emanuel in Lucy's mind is registered in the significant change in his nomenclature. He began as Monsieur Paul – named for the misogynist and writer of epistles – and is known as such for most of the novel. Only towards the end does he turn into Monsieur Emanuel – named now with double irony for Christ the Saviour who will come again.

However, it is not with hope that the novel ends. Setting aside the spurious offer of the 'delight of joy born again', the bleak final paragraph bitterly reviews the lives of the characters whom, we know, Lucy more or less despises for their machinations: the manipulative, eavesdropping Madame Beck; the witch-like Madame Walravens; the scheming-friendly Père Silas – together, the unholy trinity whom Lucy sees as having contrived Monsieur Paul's ruin. They have prospered well enough, we may assume, though the summit of their achievement is to have lived until they died: Lucy's only victory in the end is to have survived them. She dismisses them in three laconic statements like blows, one for each. And with the final 'Farewell' – short as a stab – Lucy retreats, outraged by unjust fate, into an embittered silence.

This is, of course, not the only way to interpret the conclusion. The very flatness of the final statements denies specific interpretation. Like the ending of *Jane Eyre*, they seem to take the novel beyond the parameters of romance into a more comprehensive realm in keeping with the apocalyptic vision of the storm. As with the earlier novel, we are encouraged to review the whole, and give stronger emphasis to the spiritual development in Lucy's story than to its romantic aspect; the return of Monsieur Paul would, as a matter of practicality, get in the way.

Another idea is to focus on the curious mixture of tenses which we have noticed. It may be seen as harshly apposite: present and past have become one because Lucy's life inhabits for ever the twilight of the days following the storm, when it became clear that Monsieur Paul was not to return to her. The ending, then, is very far from arbitrary. Lucy bids 'Farewell' to a life which has remained ended since her loss: she is in stasis, waiting for the physical fact of death to perfect her psychological annihilation.

The openness of the ending shows Brontë inviting us, almost compelling us, to participate actively in her work. Our feelings about the ending may well lead us to review the whole novel, perhaps to see earlier scenes in a new way from this retrospective vantage point. However we wish to interpret the meaning of this conclusion, it is not a comfortable one. Lucy has her independence: she has it at the cost of isolation – but that is, perhaps, what she always wanted.

Conclusions

1. Brontë avoids clear-cut endings. In all three novels, she shows a desire to strike out in a new direction, to suggest that she has told only part of a story.
2. Otherwise the three novels end very differently. *Jane Eyre* suggests a new turn in Jane's moral development. Martha, the narrator's housekeeper concludes *Shirley* in a style which reduces its plethora of themes to the status of folk tale. *Villette* offers a disputed ending, while nevertheless allowing only one interpretation for those who read with any attention.
3. Whereas *Shirley* ends in the down-to-earth style of Yorkshire dialect, the other novels conclude in a heightened, poetic manner, triumphal in *Jane Eyre* and tragic in *Villette*.

4. *Jane Eyre* and *Villette* both conclude with the narrator's mind on distant places, with St John and with Monsieur Paul, seemingly in distraction from the actual world.
5. All Brontë's heroines achieve some measure of independence or maturity, and get who or what they want – even Lucy Snowe.
6. Only *Jane Eyre* ends on a note of religious fervour, though religion plays an important part in all the novels.
7. In all three conclusions, a significant element is the natural setting (*Shirley* and *Villette*), or the idea of nature (*Jane Eyre*).

Methods of Analysis

1. The conclusion of each novel is considered both as a conclusion to the final chapter, and as a conclusion to the novel.
2. It is useful to look at the immediate context – that is to say, the content of the whole chapter – by means of selective summary.
3. The conclusion may be considered from the point of view of any or all of the elements which we have covered. In particular:
   - Does our perception of the characters match our earlier ideas?
   - Is the conclusion stylistically consistent with the rest of the novel?
   - What is said in the conclusion about the themes of the novel?
   - How does the mood of the conclusion affect our interpretation of the novel as a whole?
4. Thinking over these points should help to develop some ideas about the final impact of the novel as a whole.

Further Work

There are, obviously, no other concluding pages to analyse in these novels, and there are already suggestions for thematic study appended to Chapters 5 and 6. Instead, you could try a different novel. You might like to look at *The Professor*, or perhaps at one of Anne Brontë's novels, *Agnes Grey* or *The Tenant of Wildfell Hall*. All of these are worth reading. If you feel confident enough, you could tackle Emily's masterpiece, *Wuthering Heights*. Select promising passages for analysis along the lines we have used: see what you can dig out of the extracts about narrative method, characterisation and setting. You should then be in a position to invent your own thematic topics. Finally, look at the conclusions. You will find the whole exercise both enjoyable and illuminating.

PART 2

THE CONTEXT
AND THE CRITICS

8

Charlotte Brontë's Life and Works

Charlotte Brontë's work is inseparable from her life. More often than not, critics acknowledge the fact by making frequent cross-references between them. *The Professor* and *Villette* draw heavily on her experience in Belgium, and particularly on the relationship which developed between her and Monsieur Héger while she was at the pensionnat run by him and Madame Héger. The Lowood section of *Jane Eyre* is based closely on the experiences of Charlotte and her sisters at The Clergy Daughters' School at Cowan Bridge. Her experiences as a governess, and her familiarity with the manners and character of clergymen are everywhere apparent in her work. The natural scenery of the West Riding is a constant backdrop in her novels, and characters often appear speaking in the rhythms and dialect of the locality.

This is to mention only the most obvious of the links between Brontë's life and her work. Critics and biographers have established much more detailed – and, sometimes, more questionable – influences in her novels. They have endeavoured, for example, to show exactly which characters in her life moulded which characters in her novels. While such efforts can be valuable, they are not always enlightening for those whose main interest is in the novels and their impact. There is, for instance, general agreement that Helen Burns in *Jane Eyre* is a portrait of Charlotte's sister, Maria, who died in a typhoid outbreak at Cowan Bridge. The link is interesting, but it hardly alters our perception of the novel to know it.

The facts of Charlotte Brontë's life may be told briefly – for it was not varied or broad – or at length – for it was intricate. For those who desire detail, there are excellent biographies available, some mentioned in the suggestions for further reading. Here there is room only for the minimum.

Charlotte was born on 21 April 1816 at Thornton, the third daughter of Patrick Brontë, a clergyman of Irish origin, and his wife, Maria Branwell, a saintly woman who came from a Wesleyan family in Penzance. The first child, Maria, had been born in 1814, and the second, Elizabeth, in 1815. Branwell, the only boy, and therefore something of a favourite, was born the year after Charlotte, followed by Emily in 1818 and, lastly, in 1820, by Anne. Soon afterwards the family moved to Haworth, where Patrick became rector. The parsonage at Haworth was the centre of the world of the Brontës henceforth. The Brontë children spent most of their lives immersed in the restricted society of the same house and in the neighbouring raw Yorkshire countryside. Their lives were measured in loss. Less than two years after the family moved to Haworth, Patrick's wife, Maria, died, and her sister, Elizabeth, known to the children as Aunt Branwell, took up residence in her place. One by one, over the years, the children died, Charlotte last, leaving Patrick alone and childless. Elizabeth Branwell, too, predeceased him. The impact on the novels of the Celtic strain in the family, of the wild natural world around Haworth, of the religious intensity of the lives of the sisters, of their circumscribed social life, and of their being constantly touched by death, has been often traced.

Charlotte's earliest writing was not hers alone, but was constructed in company with her siblings; together, in their childhood, they invented the fantasy realms of Angria and Gondal, peopled them, and developed their histories. At first, these stories were told orally; later they took written form. For these children, rather neglected emotionally by their reclusive father and surrogate mother, brought up in partial isolation, rather like – as Charlotte's friend, Mary Taylor, memorably put it – potatoes left to sprout in a cellar (alluded to in F. B. Pinion, *A Brontë Companion*, Macmillan 1975, p. 168), the stories of their inner world began to become almost equally important with the real world outside. Indeed, the children inhabited their fictitious realms in imagination more richly than their bodies inhabited Haworth. What has been preserved of these chronicles, which were developed intermittently over a period of many years, has been collated and published.

The writing of the chronicles took shape in an intermission in the children's schooling. Charlotte and Emily were withdrawn from the school for the daughters of poor clergy at Cowan Bridge when a typhoid outbreak there claimed the lives of their elder sisters, Elizabeth and Maria. They returned home and remained there for five years before Patrick, encouraged by a bout of illness to consider seriously his responsibility for his daughters' future, determined that they must return to school. Only then did he send first Charlotte, and later Emily and Anne, to Miss Wooler's School at Roe Head.

Beginning as something of a savage at Roe Head, Charlotte made rapid progress, showing special talent in literature, scripture, art and French. She made firm friends there in Ellen Nussey and Mary Taylor, both of whom had considerable influence upon her.

After a period of retreat at Haworth – and in Angria and Gondal – Charlotte, rather like Jane Eyre, became a teacher at Roe Head, and remained so until 1838. The following year, again like Jane, she sampled the life of a governess in two large houses; she did not last long in either. During this period, Charlotte maintained an influential friendship with Mary Taylor, an ardent and outspoken feminist whose ideas surely coloured Charlotte's thinking. Mary Taylor's influence is most evident in *Shirley*.

Charlotte's visit to Brussels, initially in company with Emily, between 1842 and 1844 was another significant phase. Her life at the pensionnat Héger is mirrored, in both setting and events, in *The Professor*, and in Lucy Snowe's experiences in *Villette*; Charlotte's abortive passion for Monsieur Héger is reflected in the relationship of Crimsworth and Frances, and in Lucy's love for Monsieur Paul. By the end of her time in Brussels, the raw experience on which Charlotte drew for her work was largely complete. The processes of assimilation, however, were still in progress.

It was not until the end of 1845, when Charlotte chanced upon some poems by Emily, that the literary efforts of the sisters took a formal turn. Charlotte showed a certain dominance at this time, persuading Emily and Anne to join her in submitting for publication a volume entitled *Poems by Currer, Ellis, and Acton Bell*, which appeared in 1846. There is general agreement that Emily's poems have an intensity and a directness which place them well beyond the worthy quality attained by her sisters.

In July 1846, the Bell brothers submitted three novels for publication: *The Professor* by Charlotte, *Wuthering Heights* by Emily, and *Agnes Grey* by Anne. In *The Professor*, which is distinguished by being narrated by a male character, Charlotte drew heavily on her experiences in Brussels. The novel recounts the experiences of William Crimsworth who, after an unsatisfactory period working for his brother, a tyrannical mill owner, goes to Brussels. There he works for a time as a teacher in a boys' school. Later, he takes a post in a girls' school, where he gives English lessons to Frances Evans Henri, a Swiss girl, with whom he develops a relationship which is the subject of the second half of the novel. Charlotte says in the Preface which she wrote for *The Professor*, shortly after the publication of *Shirley*, that it was far from an immature work, and that she had torn up many an earlier effort. Her intention, she claims, was to write in a 'plain and homely' manner, and that the subject likewise should be plain – that 'no sudden turns should lift [Crimsworth] in a moment to wealth and high station'. Crimsworth, who is both narrator and hero, confides at the end of Chapter 1 that his narrative 'is not exciting, and above all, not marvellous' (p. 47). *The Professor* shares common themes with her later novels – notably in focusing on Crimsworth's search for independence from a way of life he sees as enslavement, and in dealing with a passionate relationship between unequal partners – but it is very different from them in style and effect.

Although *The Professor* was rejected, it was with such generous comments as to encourage Charlotte to submit *Jane Eyre* for publication in 1847. Written in a more sensational style than her earlier novel – it contains more than its fair share of 'sudden turns' and 'marvellous' events – it met with a better reception, was published that year, and was rewarded with immediate success. It awakened controversy, too, for although there were many, very many, who loved the novel, there were others who objected to its encouragement to social unrest. Its honesty in discussing passionate, and sexual, feeling, and its sincerity in considering the status of women – precisely those qualities which readers today find most interesting – were condemned by some of Charlotte's contemporaries. Yet, *Jane Eyre* has stood the test of time, and is now a part of the international canon of literature in English.

This success was followed by domestic tribulation. Charlotte was speedily bereft of her brother and sisters. Branwell and Emily died within months of each other at the end of 1848. In the new year, Anne, too, was discovered to be suffering from tuberculosis, and died in July 1849: the only member of the family not buried at Haworth, she found her resting place at Scarborough. Charlotte wrote of her feelings in words which can hardly fail to move:

> I felt that the house was all silent – the rooms were all empty. I remembered where the three were laid – in what narrow dark dwellings – never were they to reappear on earth. So the sense of bitterness and desolation took possession of me – the agony that *was to be undergone* and *was not* to be avoided came on.

> (From a letter to her editor, William Smith Williams, quoted in Winifred Gérin: *Charlotte Brontë*, OUP, 1967, p. 388)

The writing of *Shirley* straddled the family tragedy. The novel, to which Charlotte returned with renewed energy after her loss, and which was published in 1849, clearly shows the marks of her agony. Intended as a panoramic novel, a contrast with, or even corrective to, its predecessor, it aims at objectivity, and has no first-person actor-narrator. It allowed Brontë to express the comic invention which was muted in *Jane Eyre*. Instead of a single narrative thread, there are several intertwined. Ironically, despite the effort at breadth and detachment, the novel is touched repeatedly by a tone of personal sadness which we can sense in its frequent insistence on death, especially early death, and on illness. Chapter 24, entitled 'The Valley of the Shadow of Death', rots with the black melancholy which followed the death of Anne, and Chapter 25 is harrowingly bleak; the novel concludes on an elegiac note. The impact of the domestic tragedy seems to have strengthened the intensity of parts of the novel, but not to have helped it structurally. *Shirley* is an uneven and uncertain novel, unbalanced and sprawling – yet with scenes of remarkable vividness and large themes.

After an interlude in which Charlotte visited London, toured in Scotland, and made the acquaintance of Mrs Gaskell, who became her friend and biographer, she began on *Villette* in 1851. It was published two years later in 1853. Brontë abandoned the style she had adopted in *Shirley*, and returned to an evolution of that of *Jane Eyre*, which seemed more natural to her. She introduced again elements of the Gothic style which added entertainment to the earlier novel. Regarded by many critics as Charlotte's finest work, *Villette* was acclaimed on its appearance and has remained a favourite; even so, it has not seized the popular imagination quite as strongly *Jane Eyre*. Part of the reason for this is the comparatively unsavoury personality of the actor-narrator herself: Lucy Snowe, a grudging, deceitful, priggish and critical character (perhaps this is to exaggerate a little), is harder to feel sympathetic towards than the more open and generous Jane; her toughness is, correspondingly, more difficult to respect. However, *Villette* is utterly convincing in its use of authentic detail, and we never for a moment doubt the consistency of Lucy Snowe. The novel is based very largely on Brontë's experiences in Belgium, with characters who are thinly masked versions of the real people whom Brontë lived among; parts of it are a reworking of scenes from *The Professor*. The novel remains a powerful imaginative achievement. Again, there are vivid and dramatic scenes and passages of haunted melancholy, mingled seamlessly with more comic episodes, all dominated by the unattractive yet oddly absorbing narrator. The ending, however, is black melancholy, and it is hard not to see in it an expression of the feelings of Charlotte after Anne's death.

It is, of course, impossible to guess how Brontë's literary talent might have developed. *Villette* is a conclusion to her literary career merely because, having finished it, she at last omitted to reject a proposal of marriage from a curate, Mr Nicholls – who was much disapproved of by her father – and, after experiencing a brief period of marital happiness, died in 1855.

The Professor, Charlotte's earlier Belgian novel, was published posthumously at the instigation of Mrs Gaskell to coincide with the appearance of her biography, *The Life of Charlotte Brontë*, in 1857.

9

The Context of Charlotte Brontë's Work

Despite the evidence everywhere in her work that Charlotte Brontë's mind was steeped in the literary culture of her country, there remains something individual, even a little odd about her writing. F. R. Leavis excluded her from the mainstream of English fiction in *The Great Tradition*. The tradition, as he saw it, stretched from Jane Austen, through George Eliot and Joseph Conrad, to D. H. Lawrence. Charlotte was not part of it, and – by the way – Emily was most emphatically not. 'Charlotte,' he asserts with crushing moderation, 'though claiming no part in the great line of English fiction (it is significant that she couldn't see why any value should be attached to Jane Austen), has a permanent interest of a minor kind' (F. R. Leavis: *The Great Tradition*, 1948; Penguin, 1993, p. 39). Whether Leavis was entirely justified in his opinions is, fortunately, not a subject which we need to pursue. I have no desire to claim for Brontë a major niche in the tradition of English fiction – or even to argue that there is such a tradition. That her work grew out of her literary experience is, however, hard to deny; and although her literary experience extended to Europe, and included, for example, Rousseau, Schiller and Cervantes, it was as a whole overwhelmingly English.

Charlotte's absorption in literature, and her individuality, appear to spring from a single source. Thanks to the nature of the spiritual and moral environment of her early life, she grew up, with her brother and sisters, to know a great deal more of books than of the world. Later, when she left the parsonage at Haworth, it was to go to other closed environments – schools and great houses – which did not serve much to broaden her experience of men and manners; of men in the more restricted sense, her knowledge was largely circumscribed, as firmly as a neck in a clerical collar, by the little flocks of curates with whom she came into contact. No matter how far she roamed, Haworth, like an inescapable magnet, kept drawing her back within its confines. Equally, the ideas which she assimilated there dominated her thinking throughout her life.

She felt her lack of experience as a disadvantage for her writing. There was, she thought, a lack of social breadth, and a lack of social concern, in her novels; in *Shirley* she set out to amend this flaw, to change and broaden her perspective. As we have seen, her efforts met with limited success; for the aspects of *Shirley* which are most interesting are those in which Brontë more or less ignores the web of social, political and economic dimensions with which her narrative toys.

It is not hard to see why Brontë should have felt her inexperience as a disadvantage: her world was dominated by literary giants who wrote in a manner quite different from hers. When *Jane Eyre* was published, Jane Austen had been dead thirty years; the novel was no longer the suspect medium that it had been, but widely popular and respected as a serious form; Thackeray was in the middle of writing *Vanity Fair*, and Dickens, then writing *Dombey and Son*, was at his peak. These were the figures who defined the novel for their time; it was natural to want to emulate them. But, despite her hankerings, it would have been a plain impossibility for Brontë to transmute her experience into anything as sweeping as her most illustrious literary contemporaries could create. Brontë's novels grew from more private and intimate sources, and succeeded, by taking a different route, in winning just as much acclaim. *Jane Eyre* appealed particularly strongly to the reading public, and the year after its appearance was regarded as equal in popularity with *Vanity Fair*. Thackeray much admired it, as later did George Eliot. The diaries of Queen Victoria record her growing absorption in the novel as she read it with her beloved Albert. *Jane Eyre*, more than the other novels, has retained a perennial popularity. There are several film adaptations, and it has sprouted a number of literary offshoots, the best-known being Jean Rhys's *Wide Sargasso Sea*, which recounts the story of Rochester's first wife.

Although not part of the 'great tradition', Brontë's novels are very much a part of her cultural tradition, not only because they echo the minds and feelings of her countrymen, but also because they rely heavily on her experience as a reader, and thus on the literary culture of her country. We have noted in earlier chapters occasions when Brontë appeared to be using techniques and ideas similar to those in the novels of Fielding or Austen, if not necessarily because of direct influence. But those are not the most powerful influences upon her; indeed, when she wrote *Jane Eyre*, she had not read any of Austen's novels – and when later she did sample *Pride and Prejudice*, failed to be impressed. By far the most important influence on her is the Bible, which is quoted and alluded to throughout her work. The Bible, and her father's sermons drawn from it, did much to form her style: it is the source of her love of parallelism and incrementation; and it showed her how to dramatise abstraction. *The Pilgrim's Progress* was another major influence, with lessons in allegory to add to those in the Bible; she refers to its characters, and in her facility in the use of personification we can discern talents which Bunyan's prose must have helped to nurture. Brontë shows familiarity, too, with Shakespeare. She seems to have been particularly fond of *Othello*, but refers to many plays, including *Hamlet*, *Macbeth*, *King Lear*, *Antony and Cleopatra* and *Julius Caesar*; and she makes extended use of *Coriolanus* in *Shirley*. Brontë also had more than a passing acquaintance with the work of Milton – as we have seen, elements of *Paradise Lost* are discussed in *Shirley*. Her novels are, of course, quite unlike the works of the earlier writers; yet she has the ability to bring the grandeur of Shakespeare to the restricted lives with which she deals; and she shows how her ordinary characters and their situations can echo Milton.

There is another, very important strand in Brontë's reading which did much to form the nature of her novels. We may call it, in round terms, 'romance'. In particular, this means the poetry of Wordsworth and Coleridge and their successors, and the novels of Sir Walter

Scott; we noticed in Chapter 4, for example, a reference to *Old Mortality* in *Villette*. Brontë's novels reflect the prominence of the natural world in these writers; her feeling for nature owes something to Wordsworth; she surely learned much from Scott about the use of natural description in novels and, like him, she gives her characters local dialect to speak. Byron, too, was a powerful influence on her as on her contemporaries, and when Rochester excites mockery, it is because of his Byronic-heroic qualities – though Rochester has his more subtle aspects, too. Another frequent source of allusion is the stories of *The Arabian Nights*. These influences point to, as they helped to form, Brontë's complex fascination with the subterranean, magical, psychological elements in human personality and experience.

In the Gothic writing of Ann Radcliffe, among others, there is a less sophisticated, but not therefore less important, influence on Brontë's writing. Mrs Radcliffe received praise from Sir Walter Scott, and a compliment of the satirical variety from Jane Austen in *Northanger Abbey*. The Gothic influence is obvious in *Jane Eyre* in the mysterious corridors of Thornfield, in the madwoman in the attic, in the use of apparitions, and in the telepathic communication between Rochester and Jane; it appears in *Villette* in the nun scenes. It affects the language and imagery of both novels in many minor ways. The Gothic influence is largely banished from *Shirley*: but we can still detect traces of it in the 'fairish' strand in the novel.

We have noticed a note of parody and of self-parody about Brontë's use of these Gothic motifs. However, the Gothic influence is deeper and more subtle than first appears, as we shall see in the next chapter, in dealing with Robert B. Heilman's essay on the subject.

The importance of Gothic for Charlotte Brontë was not so much its sensational incident as its language. It provided her with a means of speaking about emotion and feeling in a way that had not been done previously. Brontë uses Gothic to explore areas of consciousness which were closed to those literary giants, Dickens and Thackeray. In the course of her exploration she also touches on sensual and sexual veins in human experience which were sensitive particularly for the later Victorians, and which those same giants assiduously avoided.

The rich – and, at first glance, rather unlikely – mix of biblical and Gothic in Brontë's background is a potent brew which enables her to write about personality and feeling in a richer way than had been done before. Her criticism of Jane Austen is famous, and much quoted (in, for example, the discussion by Leavis quoted at the beginning of this chapter):

> The Passions are perfectly unknown to her; she rejects even a speaking acquaintance with that stormy sisterhood. Even to the feelings she vouchsafes no more than an occasional graceful but distant recognition – too frequent converse with them would ruffle the smooth elegance of her progress. Her business is not half so much with the human heart as with the human eyes, mouth, hands, and feet. What sees keenly, speaks aptly, moves flexibly, it suits her to study; but what throbs fast and full, though hidden, what the blood rushes through, what is the unseen seat of life and the sentient target of death – this Miss Austen ignores.
>
> (from a letter to W.S.Williams, 1850, quoted in David Lodge (ed.): *Jane Austen: 'Emma'*, Macmillan, (Casebook Series) 1969, p. 50)

This great literary gaffe, based on Charlotte's reading of *Pride and Prejudice*, is more useful as a statement about Charlotte Brontë than about Jane Austen, for it expresses her own interests and purposes very vividly. Clearly, she did not approve of Austen because Austen did not write about anything interesting. Brontë saw interest only in individual passion, feeling and emotion: she was a romantic, while Austen wrote about sense and society. The blindness that failed to notice in Austen the clash of reason and passion which runs through Brontë's own work is interesting: Austen treated the theme from the wrong angle to communicate with Brontë; Brontë begins with individual feeling and considers society later – if at all.

In fact, as we have seen, Brontë's writing does address several contemporary social issues. Many facets of religious life – sectarianism, the hypocrisy of some of the clergy, the superfluity of the curacy, the human cruelty into which too formal religiosity can fall – appear in Brontë's writing. Education is treated too, just as powerfully at

Lowood as in Dickens. The social injustices suffered by women are evident in all her work. To speak of 'addressing' issues, however, is to suggest something rather too formal. Brontë's intention is not to discuss or analyse these issues as such. Rather, she shows how these issues impinge on the lives of the characters. In, for example, depicting the religious lives of characters like Brocklehurst, Eliza Reed, Helen Burns, St John Rivers, old Helstone, Mr Hall, Monsieur Paul and Père Silas, Brontë encompasses a wide and varied spectrum of emotion and conviction, ranging among the utterly obtuse, the tortured, and the utterly sincere; but only in *Shirley* is there much in the way of rational discussion. The world of education is treated with a fine brush, too, in *Jane Eyre* and *Villette*: how different is Jane's experience under Miss Scatcherd, and under Miss Temple! Again, however, the emphasis is on individual experience, not on the issue as such.

Wider issues are dealt with in *Shirley* than in the other novels, to the extent that it includes political comment, depends for its resolution on the repeal of the Orders in Council, and that its action illustrates the effects of industrialisation. The attack on Robert Moore's mill is based on an actual event, the storming of Rawfolds Mill in 1812. Brontë ducks discussion of the questions raised by the Luddite riots, however: Robert Moore's mill is typical of the mills which dotted Yorkshire, his vision is typical of the purposes which sprinkled Yorkshire with rows of millworkers' cottages, and he is typical of his kind in his failure to recognise the effect on working people of the introduction of mechanised methods of production. Instead of confronting the problem this raises – how to deal with a very imperfect (and not in the least Byronic) hero – Brontë simply excuses him as a foreigner, so that she can treat him as a hero and ignore his deficiencies in social responsibility. Clearly, again, it is the characters and their story which are most prominent in her mind, and not the social issues which impinge on them.

One social issue which, however, does appear to form part of the texture of Brontë's mind is slavery. Slavery was abolished in Great Britain and its dominions in 1807, and the emancipation of slaves in the British Empire took place in 1834 – that is to say, well before Charlotte Brontë wrote her novels. However, the subject was far from dead: mistreatment of negroes remained commonplace for a period in the West Indies; and, regardless of the historical facts, slavery was a part of Brontë's consciousness. This is not to say that the practice and details of slavery were subjects on which Brontë exercised her mind; but the concept itself was part of the Victorian mind. Brontë's interest in – it is tempting to say obsession with – the polarity of slavery and freedom is a thread in all her novels. William Crimsworth, Jane Eyre, Caroline Helstone and Lucy Snowe all see their lives as a journey towards liberation from a psychological and physical prison. Specifically, the work of the governess is considered a form of slavery.

The most prominent issue in Brontë's writing is the social situation of women. Shirley and Caroline discuss the role of women in society: their economic status and their career expectations – or rather, lack of them. Caroline feels these matters deeply. The portraits of Miss Mann and Miss Ainley, and the arguments of Joe Scott, show the author's awareness of the issue. The lives of Jane Eyre and Lucy Snowe exemplify it. But Brontë, try though she did in *Shirley*, was rarely able to treat the issue squarely. The potency of Brontë's portrayal of these characters stems from the unconscious generation of wider, social resonances by the experience of heroines whose only concern is not to address issues at all, but to deal with the intractable problems by which they are hemmed in. Social questions are addressed indirectly, through the medium of feeling. The heart is always Brontë's touchstone.

It is in her treatment of the heart that Brontë most squarely confronts her society. Her portrayal of personal, and particularly of sexual, relationships, was out of step with Victorian conventions. Thus *The Spectator* of 6 November 1847 discovered *Jane Eyre* to be 'somewhat sordid' (quoted in the Macmillan Casebook edited by Miriam Allott, p. 49). More violently, if rather damply, the *Christian Remembrancer* of April 1948 (loc.cit., p. 60) ungenerously and perhaps dishonestly argues that 'To say that *Jane Eyre* is positively immoral or antichristian would be to do the writer an injustice'! Matthew Arnold, in a letter to Mrs Forster dated 14 April 1853 (loc.cit. p. 93) accuses Brontë of being possessed of a mind which 'contains nothing but hunger, rebellion, and rage'. Some students nowadays find it hard to know what the fuss was about. In truth, it is not so hard to see. Low-key though it may be by our contemporary standards – and low-key is not intended here to mean insipid, but rather, subtle in its portrayal – Brontë's treatment of relationships is very frank. The relationships between Jane and first Rochester, whose mistress she is on the point of becoming, then St John Rivers, whom she rejects because he demands a platonic relationship with her, presume a demand – and a reasonable and natural demand – for sexual fulfilment. There is in this a will to see people as they are that many of her contemporary critics, and even her friends, could not share: she is at odds in this with the Victorian mind, and is thus variously seen as coarse or subversive. Equally, she represents marriage very critically, especially in *Shirley*, in the experience of Mrs Pryor, Mrs Yorke, Mrs Sympson and the deceased Mrs Helstone. Despite the importance of love for her heroines, marriage is not considered in Brontë's works to be the goal of women's lives. Jane, Caroline and Lucy have in common that they spend time assessing themselves, their potential, and their needs, with the consciousness that their lives are their own to do with as they see fit; marriage may form a part of that assessment, but it is not the whole. Lucy follows Madame Beck in carving for herself an independent place in the workaday world. Brontë's understanding of the way in which she had offended is clear in the 'Cleopatra' chapter in *Villette*: here Lucy observes the prejudices and weaknesses of men with amused detachment, even while, outwardly, she appears to behave as a perfectly submissive Victorian lady. Brontë's fault, then, lies in her recognition – it is implicit, she feels no need to argue it, and that perhaps enlarges the fault – that right behaviour is what is consistent with nature and with the human heart, and not what convention stipulates. Finally, that other cornerstone of social convention, religion, is criticised in a variety of ways: few indeed are the truly saintly characters – and even Helen Burns, though admired for her goodness, is not held up as a model to be emulated. In this context, as in the context of love and marriage, Brontë shows a marked belief in the ability and right of individuals to think for themselves, and this was not an idea with which the Victorians had much sympathy. Subversive by Victorian standards is hardly so by ours; readers in our own time are more likely to see in Brontë's work the virtue of honesty. It is a judgement of Victorian values that she was in effect criticised for being true to the heart; and of our own, perhaps, that it may be hard to perceive how her work might offend.

Brontë's absorption in individual feeling influenced her contemporaries and immediate successors: it is possible to see Dickens and George Eliot moving closer to Brontë's perception of the novel. More markedly, her work looks forward to writers beyond her own time – writers for whom psychological analysis was much more a matter of exploring established ideas than it was for Charlotte Brontë. She knew nothing of Sigmund Freud; yet, when we consider the psychological depth of characters such as St John Rivers or Madame Beck, and remember the confidence with which Brontë's heroines assume the right to choose their paths in life, it is, I think, rather to Lawrence than to George Eliot or Hardy that her work points. Of course, it was not entirely for his interest in psychological analysis that Lawrence was awarded a place in Leavis's great tradition. Still, there is satisfaction in feeling that Charlotte Brontë contributed something to its later expression.

There is also something very modern about Brontë's structural techniques. Often accused of structuring her novels poorly – all of them, not just *Shirley* – she may perhaps have been ill-served by some among her critics. In both *Jane Eyre* and *Shirley*, she shows a strong desire to avoid the neatness of a conventional ending. Instead, she tries to give the feeling of a life still to be lived after the novel – a few snapshots of that life – has ended. None of the novels begins *in medias res*; *Villette*, particularly, seems to begin at an almost arbitrary point. Yes, it may be that Charlotte Brontë, who took particular care over phrasing, was lacking in concern or ability to achieve structural neatness. It is equally possible that she was concerned with that difficulty of persuading art to mirror life which has led to the more adventurous experiments of much more recent novelists. Brontë's use of unreliability in narrators – especially Lucy Snowe – is beyond her time, too: we may see it as looking forward to the more iconoclastic kinds of writing which have mirrored the disintegration of imperialist confidence in the early years of the twentieth century.

10

Three Critical Approaches

The novels of Charlotte Brontë have attracted enormous attention from the critics. The balance of criticism, however, is heavily weighted towards *Jane Eyre*, while at the other extreme, *Shirley* is rather neglected. This is a little odd, since many critics claim to respect the qualities of *Villette* most highly among the three novels.

From the first, Brontë's work divided readers into fiercely opposed camps. Some develop a personal love for not only the works, but for the author whom they feel they have got to know through them; the perennial popularity of the literary shrine at Haworth bears testimony to the strength of interest which her works – and, of course, her sister Emily's – inspire. Her detractors – especially her earlier commentators – criticised her for coarseness or social divisiveness or, paradoxically, for failure to focus on the real world in her pursuit of sensation and emotion. More recent critics, happily, have made it their business to take a more reasoned approach to her work.

The variety of criticism to which Brontë has been subjected mirrors every critical fad or school. She has been a particular target of psychoanalytical criticism, and has been favoured by feminist critics. It is not hard to see why. Given the range, selecting a few critics for discussion is bound to be somewhat arbitrary. There can be no leak-proof justification of the three we are to consider, but all of them are well worth reading for different reasons.

ROBERT B. HEILMAN

The earliest criticism we deal with is an essay by Robert B. Heilman, 'Charlotte Brontë's "New" Gothic'. This essay did much to focus Brontë criticism and is readily available. It appeared in *From Jane Austen to Joseph Conrad* (University of Minnesota Press, 1958) edited by Robert C. Rathburn and Martin Steinmann, Jr., and later in two Macmillan Casebooks on Charlotte Brontë. Page numbers are taken from the essay as it appears in *Victorian Literature* (edited by Austin Wright, OUP, 1961, pp. 71–104). The version in the Casebook Series is slightly cut down.

Heilman deals with all four novels in a short space, in which he manages to say a great deal. He organises his argument indirectly, beginning with a discussion of the contrary impulses in *The Professor* towards Puritanism and its antithesis, which he variously terms 'vitality', or 'Liberty', or 'barbarous and sensual' (all p. 72). Only then does he announce the major theme of his essay:

> Charlotte's story is conventional; formally she is for 'reason' and 'real life'; but her characters keep escaping to glorify 'feeling' and 'Imagination.' Feeling is there in the story – evading repression, in author or in character – ranging from nervous excitement to emotional absorption; often tense and peremptory; sexuality, hate, irrational impulse, grasped, given life, not merely named and pigeon-holed. This is Charlotte's version of Gothic: in her later novels an extraordinary thing.

> (p. 72)

For Brontë, he argues, Gothic goes far beyond the convention: it means a venture into 'psychic darkness'. The difference lies in the purpose; Brontë's intention is not to frighten or provide a temporary thrill; rather, she uses the Gothic convention to explore the bases of feeling, and especially sexual feeling, in a manner acceptable to Victorian sensibility. Heilman points to her 'integrity of feeling that greatly deepens the convention' (p. 73).

In the course of his argument, Heilman distinguishes three versions of Gothic, using *Jane Eyre* to support his ideas. One is 'old

Gothic': the convention of sensationalism – the cheap thrill which exists for its own sake. He finds the bones of this convention in Brontë's novels, but notes that it is almost always modified. One of the ways in which Brontë adapts it is by undercutting it. This is the second version of Gothic, which Heilman calls 'Anti-Gothic': he cites the visit of the Blanche Ingram party to Thornfield as one instance of Brontë's tendency to treat Gothic in a comic manner; she adopts a style rather like Jane Austen's. Brontë likes, also, to treat Gothic incident in a manner of 'dry factuality' which debunks the sensational element. The third version of Gothic is more complex. Heilman sees in Brontë's use of Gothic a symbolic element which 'demands of the reader a more mature and complicated response than the relatively simple thrill of feeling sought by primitive Gothic'; he cites as examples the apparition, and the gutting of Thornfield. This symbolic use of Gothic allows Brontë to explore deep feelings, subterranean passions, illicit responses: thus she moves into the realm of Heilman's 'new Gothic' (all pp. 73–6).

The remainder of Heilman's essay is devoted to exploring the expression of 'new Gothic' in the major novels. He discusses the way in which Brontë denies superficial attractiveness to the protagonists of *Jane Eyre* in order to draw attention to their powerful inner attraction, in which love is mixed with hostility and violence, and with deep need which verges on the blasphemous. He shows, too, how use of the Gothic convention allowed Brontë to explore the innermost conflicts of St John Rivers and develop this most complex character as a strange and original mix of saintly and devilish.

Turning to *Shirley*, Heilman finds in it, despite its ostensibly public concerns, a constant flight from public into private worlds. He vividly describes how 'the story of industrial crisis is repeatedly swarmed over by the love stories' (p. 77). He contrasts the 'conventional, open, predictable tale' with the 'highly charged private sentiency' of the character portrayal. Heilman refers to the Gothic tendency in a number of major and less important characters: the 'tigress' (p. 77) quality in Shirley herself, the warrior in Helstone, the *amour propre* of Hiram Yorke, the strange insistence of Mr Sympson's paternal interest in Shirley, the adolescent game which Martin Yorke plays with Caroline, and the implicit sexual power of

Robert Moore. Using terms drawn from the novel, Heilman characterises these elements in the novel as expressing 'unpatterned feeling'
as opposed to 'patterned', or conventional, behaviour. '*Shirley*', he
argues, 'is probing psychic disturbance' (p. 79), and he cites the frequency with which illness occurs in the novel to support his contention: Caroline's decline under Robert's neglect, Shirley's fear of
contracting rabies, Robert's long convalescence from his gunshot
wound – all express the emergence of hidden feeling from depths far
beneath an acceptable social behaviour.

Villette is in Heilman's view 'most heavily saturated with Gothic'.
He finds in the novel the characteristic use of anti-Gothic and new
Gothic – 'an original, intense exploration of feeling that increases
the range and depth of fiction' (both p. 80). The trappings of Gothic
are evident enough – the nun, the haunting of the pensionnat by
Madame Beck. However, there are deeper Gothic elements. In
common with *Shirley*, *Villette* deals with states of heightened sensibility brought about by illness (Lucy's attack of hypochondria during
the vacation) or by drugs (the trance-like fête scene). Heilman
sees this surrealistic episode as 'the apex of Charlotte Brontë's
Gothic'.

Heilman's essay concludes with a review of the meanings which
critics have assigned to the term 'Gothic', and with a summary of its
meaning in Brontë's work:

> [Gothic] became then a great liberator of feeling. It acknowledged the
> nonrational – in the world of things and events, occasionally in the
> realm of the transcendental, ultimately and most persistently in the
> depths of the human being.

> (p. 84)

One of the notable features of Heilman's essay is the manner in
which he links his ideas about Gothic with his assessment of
Charlotte Brontë as essentially a reworker. She is good at
'remoulding of stock feeling', for example, in describing Rochester's
wooing of Jane. He sees Brontë as using the conventions established
by Jane Austen, or by conventional Gothic writers. But this is not to

belittle her, for she uses them in order to create something new and strikingly original. His essay is no dry academic exercise:

> To note the emergence of this 'new Gothic' in Charlotte Brontë is not, I think, to pursue an old mode into dusty corners but rather to identify historically the distinguishing, and distinguished, element in her work.

(p. 85)

Of course, it is hardly unknown for critics to claim that their analysis is central. Heilman's contention, however, is supported by the respectful notice which has been taken of his ideas by later critics.

DAVID LODGE

David Lodge's chapter on Charlotte Brontë in *Language of Fiction* (Routledge and Kegan Paul, 1966; second edition, 1984) is narrower in range than Heilman's essay. Although Lodge's subject is much broader than Charlotte Brontë, and in his discussion of her he confines himself to *Jane Eyre*, this is a worthwhile book, very readable and often witty or vivid, as well as influential. Lodge takes a straightforward and notably open approach. In the second edition, he explains how his ideas have changed, for example, and adds an appendix on his more recent ideas. He is especially enlightening when he discusses critics who have influenced him, and shows clearly how he has gained from them. He has, too, salutary things to say about the business of criticism. He points out that criticism cannot hope to be comprehensive; instead, he suggests, it is the task of the critic to choose one or some of many paths which it would be possible to tread through his subject.

Lodge's premiss – crystallised in the title of his book – is that 'all critical questions about a novel are reducible to questions about its language' (p. 272). Be it noted, however, that Lodge makes it his mission to incorporate life, the universe and everything in his concept of 'language'.

The discussion of *Jane Eyre,* entitled 'Fire and Eyre: Charlotte Brontë's War of Earthly Elements', opens with the proposal that Charlotte Brontë was, in essence, a romantic writer. Lodge contends that her romanticism extends far beyond the Gothic elements often noted in her work, to 'the struggle of an individual consciousness towards self-fulfilment' (p. 114), and to the settings she prefers – 'the romantic imagery of landscape, seascape, sun, moon, and the elements, through which this theme is expressed' (p. 114). However, he adds, her romanticism is not pure; there is another side to her, a Christian ethical side, which holds the romanticism in check. Thus he sees in her work a central tension between romantic sympathies and the restraint of Christian precept; he quotes Chapter 17 of *Jane Eyre,* in which 'conscience, turned tyrant, held passion by the throat'.

This basic opposition leads Lodge to a coherent interpretation of *Jane Eyre.* Leaving Thornfield is a passive renunciation of Rochester and, with him, the life of passion. Conversely, Jane later rejects the world of duty represented by St John Rivers. These questions of moral choice have been enunciated more than once; what is peculiar to Lodge's view is that he is able to relate them to matters of language. He notes in *Jane Eyre* two contrasting kinds of language: a firmly practical, realistic and literal mode, which stresses basic animal comfort, and is keenly aware of emotional states; and a visionary and poetic mode. Lodge tries to show that the powerful unity of tone in the novel, on which critics agree, is an effect of the reconciling of these two linguistic registers.

From this point, Lodge moves to more specific criticism. Drawing on E. M. W. Tillyard's *The Elizabethan World Picture,* he discusses Brontë's use of the elements – in particular, the element of fire. He enumerates a broad range of literal and figurative references to fire in the novel. Fire fits in well with Lodge's contention about the two registers, for it has its practical aspect – the hearth which warms the cockles of the heart – and its symbolic aspect, as an objective correlative (Lodge specifically quotes T. S. Eliot's phrase) of passion. He develops his idea by detailed discussion of references to fire in *Jane Eyre,* distinguishing different kinds of references and different meanings in the concept of fire, and showing how Brontë's language uses the complexity of fire to move easily from literal to figurative levels of language. He makes links between the central fire imagery and related imagery of hell, and of exotic place names and the hot climates they often suggest. He shows, too, how fire is particularly appropriate to Jane's character and its development. Lodge proceeds to consider fire as one term of a polarity: it is balanced, at the other end of the scale, by cold and damp. In general, fire is associated with life and passion, cold and damp with death. There is a range of images associated with cold as there is with fire: snow and ice prominent among them. The polarity of fire and ice allows Lodge to offer a consistent interpretation of all the major elements in the novel, though it is clear that the imagery is far from simple; fire means very different things at different points in the novel.

Lodge draws in a range of other imagery and symbolism. Fire is linked with sun, and thus with daylight. The sun suggests by contrast the moon and night. Thus another polarity is generated, and Lodge largely supports the suggestion of Robert B. Heilman, which he quotes, that the alternation of day and night is one of the basic rhythms of the book. The moon, however, he sees as having 'a multiple and ambivalent function' (p. 140) in the novel, relating both to inner states of being, and to non-rational events. Here he refers, with approbation, to both Heilman and to Robert Graves's *The White Goddess*.

At the conclusion of his chapter, Lodge tries to show that fire and its associated symbolism are used by Brontë to match the pattern of the conflicts through which Jane passes. His summary is that what is achieved is not resolution, but tension. The elements are balanced in everlasting conflict:

> In the war of earthly elements, in preserving a precarious equilibrium between opposing forces, Jane Eyre finds the meaning of life. Day is welcomed because it follows night, calm because it follows storm. Fire is a source of warmth and light, but it is most keenly enjoyed when snow and rain beat on the windows.

(p. 143)

This final statement shows the clever structuring of Lodge's discussion, and it illustrates his lucid, direct style. It is also, perhaps, rather neater than the preceding discussion has warranted: but there is no doubt that Lodge's ideas are persuasive. No doubt, either, but that the student has much to gain from reading this essay (and preferably the whole book), which says rational things in plain English.

Let us conclude with more cursory reference to Lodge's second thoughts, as expressed in the Afterword to the second edition of his book (pp. 268 ff.). There he focuses on two major points. The first, and simpler, is that he feels he has understressed the originality of *Jane Eyre*, and he points out that no earlier novel had used the natural world so fully and effectively. The second major point he makes – and it perhaps seems somewhat in conflict with the first – is that he has given too much emphasis to the romantic and poetic elements in the novel; those are certainly important, but he now feels that the dramatic and narrative elements perhaps deserved greater attention. There are other, more specific differences of interpretation, too.

The practical point which emerges is that Lodge does not pretend, nor does he intend, to be definitive. His Afterword expresses the current state of his understanding, just as his original chapter expressed an earlier understanding, of the pattern of the novel; but it is not final. The message is one from which students, sometimes daunted at the demands of the tasks with which they are confronted, may take comfort: what they write does not constitute an eternal contract!

SHIRLEY FOSTER

Our third, and final essay is another contrast. Shirley Foster's aim in *Victorian Women's Fiction: Marriage, Freedom, and the Individual* (Croom Helm Ltd, 1985) is to develop her own theme; Charlotte Brontë is merely one of the authors on whom she bases her argument. The title of the chapter in question, 'Charlotte Brontë: A Vision of Duality', is a precise indicator of the nature of Foster's argument. Everything is based on duality of vision, ambivalence of attitude, ambiguity of approach.

After a little initial demarcation of her ground, in which she talks of Brontë's ambivalences about Haworth, about marriage, about women's rights, and about independence, Foster argues that Bronte 'Like so many mid-Victorian women . . . experienced the sense of a divided self' (p. 71), and suggests that her selves are represented by the different identities of Charlotte Brontë, woman, and of Currer Bell, novelist. In the question of female independence, fulfilment and marriage, Brontë's conflicts are especially evident. Foster then develops her theme in an exploration of Brontë's life.

Turning to the examination of sex, love and marriage in the novels, Foster notes an inevitable tendency towards conformity in Brontë. In *Shirley*, Shirley Keeldar and Caroline Helstone both think critically about marriage, yet both succumb to suitors. Foster notes – and it is not yet clear what her own view is – that feminist critics have taken the view that Brontë was obliged by the context within which she was writing, to adopt covert or devious strategies for writing about the feelings and views of women. Thus there is in the novels a conventional level of discourse, and a covert or subversive one in parallel, preaching a rather different message; her novels work within a conventional social framework of love and marriage, while obliquely criticising and dissenting from that framework.

Foster offers a neat summary of the methods which Brontë adopts:

1. Brontë's heroines question their own needs and desires;
2. They measure themselves against contrasting images of woman-hood;
3. They evaluate their own position in differing sexual relationships.

The effect on the structure of the novels is that Brontë gradually grows more confident in evading closed endings in favour of debating dualities. Brontë's development is not to resolve her doubts; rather she becomes more assured in presenting the ambiguities of female experience.

Foster doubts, however, that Brontë justifies the view of some of her contemporaries that she was socially subversive. Foster argues that in *Jane Eyre* Brontë shows a strong belief in love, and a consistent faith in marriage as a route to emotional fulfilment for women, which are modified only slightly in *Shirley* and *Villette*.

There is not the space to delve into the detail of the interpretation which Foster offers of *Jane Eyre*. She concludes with the view that the use of structural and thematic contrasts allows the novel to be read in either of two ways: either as a capitulation to orthodoxy; or as a vindication of female assertiveness. The truth, Foster suggests, is somewhere between the two extremes: Rochester and Jane end by serving and supporting each other; Jane adopts a conventional role by her own will, and not in obedience to external pressures.

Shirley is obviously more overtly propagandist, and Foster notes that it directly questions the view that woman's highest fulfilment lies in marriage. Many different characters in the novel discuss the social role of women. This leads Foster to declare that 'The nature of sexual relationships is indeed the most widely and thoroughly articulated theme in the novel, showing how the author's anguished loneliness at this time, when she was left the sole survivor of the Brontë children, was driving her to take stock of her own future' (p. 93). To support her claim, Foster offers a brief analysis of the way many of the characters contribute to the debate – not just the protagonists, but a vast range, from Hortense to Mrs Yorke and Mrs Pryor among others. Shirley's masculinity is used in the debate, as is the contrast between Caroline (conventional woman) and Shirley (emancipated woman). After all, however, the novel finishes on the side of convention: Shirley sees men at their best as Lords of Creation, and marries a man who complements her.

Villette Foster sees as Brontë's most interesting study of the single woman. According to Foster, the action of the novel offers Lucy Snowe a series of versions of the single woman, ranging from Miss Marchmont, through Madame Beck, to the younger, and contrasting, Paulina and Ginevra, against any or all of whom she may measure herself and her future. Foster sees these distorted images as the heart of the novel:

> These alternative modes of female self-definition give Lucy the means of assessing and establishing her own selfhood; and it is in Brontë's presentation of her heroine's self-exploration that her sense of dichotomies is most readily expressed.

(p. 103)

Foster sees Lucy as combining in one person the dualities of *Shirley*, and quotes Lucy's statement that she lives two lives, 'the life of thought, and that of reality' – a dichotomy symbolised in the frequent use of mirror scenes as evidence of the continuing process of self-assessment by Lucy. Thus a central dichotomy may be variously interpreted as a clash between feeling and reason, or between escapism and stoicism, or between image and reality.

The ending of *Villette* avoids reaching a definitive conclusion, in Foster's view. Lucy is aware of the deficiencies of both Dr Bretton and Monsieur Paul, but sees virtues in both; Brontë refuses to determine Monsieur Paul's fate; Lucy makes no decision about the desirability or otherwise of matrimony. What remains is questioning and honest confrontation of the complexity of existence.

Shirley Foster thus sees Brontë's work as illustrating a development of her ideas about the social and sexual role of women, but not as coming to any firm conclusion. The development moves not towards resolution, but towards intensification; towards complication, and not towards simplicity.

Foster's work is a good example of a thematic approach to Charlotte Brontë. She explores the novels from the point of view of a subject which is partly external to their content. In the exercise she is able to place Brontë in a social and ethical context, and to show her subtlety of response to her world.

All three of the critics we have considered are very persuasive. All are, as it were, right. What the enormous differences in their approach illustrate is the richness of the novels with which they are dealing. Charlotte Brontë's novels are remarkably intense, remarkably diverse in their implication, and above all have the quality of authenticity. Brontë matches the complexity and mystery of actuality; she rejects simplistic formulas; and thus, by confronting the unknowable, the paradoxical, and the unquantifiable in our experience, she wins the interest of readers, and provides critics with a seemingly inexhaustible source of debate.

Further Reading

The obvious place to begin is probably the best. Read and reread the novels of Charlotte Brontë, including *The Professor*, and including the introductions. Collections of the early writings and fragments written by Charlotte are probably worth dipping into, too: these are available in *Charlotte Brontë: Juvenilia 1829–1835*, edited by Juliet Barker (Penguin, 1996).

It is difficult to know where to stop with background reading, but beginning is easy. You should certainly be familiar with the work of Emily – *Wuthering Heights* – and Anne – *Agnes Grey* and *The Tenant of Wildfell Hall*. If you have not already done so, you should read Dickens – perhaps *David Copperfield*, since comparisons have been drawn between it and *Jane Eyre* – and Thackeray – *Vanity Fair*, of course. Then, if you are not already familiar with them, you should read Austen's novels: *Pride and Prejudice* and *Emma* awakened strong responses of a negative kind in Charlotte, as we have noted. The Gothic literature on which Charlotte drew comes into consideration, too: Mrs Radcliffe's *Mysteries of Udolpho* (1794) is widely available, and so are many other examples.

An enormous amount has been written about Charlotte Brontë and her work. Any modestly sized public library will have some biographical and critical works, and academic libraries will have shelves of them. There is, in the end, no substitute for browsing and sampling for yourself. Reading one book is likely to lead on to reading others referred to or recommended in it. My suggestions are a beginning, and no more.

Biographical material is easy to find. Two books stand out from the heap. One is the biography by Mrs Gaskell, *The Life of Charlotte Brontë* (1857; Penguin, 1975), valuable because she was herself a novelist and therefore had a good understanding of her subject, and because she knew Charlotte, if only towards the end of her life, as a friend. At the other extreme, there is the most authoritative among the recent heavyweight biographies, Juliet Barker's *The Brontës* (Weidenfeld & Nicolson, 1994). This obviously does not restrict itself to Charlotte, but is quite massive enough to offer mines of information and insight about her. I have also used another notable biography, Winifred Gérin's *Charlotte Brontë* (OUP, 1967).

Coffee-table books are not to be despised. They contain pictures and photographs which can help to bring Charlotte's environment to life, and are likely to contain social and political snippets which provide useful background. One such is Jane O'Neill's *The World of the Brontës* (Sevenoaks, 1997). Juliet Gardiner's *The World Within: The Brontës at Haworth* (Collins & Brown, 1992) focuses on the Brontës' letters.

Moving on towards the vast mass of criticism, you could look initially at some very general books. Two which outline the Brontës' lives, world and works are *Everyman's Companion to the Brontës* by Barbara and Gareth Lloyd Evans (J. M. Dent & Sons Limited, 1982), and F. B. Pinion's *A Brontë Companion: Literary Assessment, Background and Reference* (Macmillan Press Ltd, 1975). For the critical background, there is a very valuable book which gives early reviews and criticism, as well as some more recent essays: *The Brontës: The Critical Heritage* (Routledge & Kegan Paul, 1974) edited by Miriam Allott.

Modern criticism is a wide-ranging and confusing tract. There are useful routes into its variety in two Macmillan Casebooks on Charlotte Brontë, one dealing with *Jane Eyre* (edited by Heather Glen, Macmillan New Casebooks, 1997), and the other on *Jane Eyre* and *Villette* (*Charlotte Brontë: 'Jane Eyre' and 'Villette': A Casebook*, edited by Miriam Allott, Macmillan, 1973).

Of specific critical works, three are discussed in Chapter 9. First is Robert B. Heilman's 'Charlotte Brontë's "New" Gothic', which was originally published in *From Jane Austen to Joseph Conrad: Essays in*

Memory of James T. Hillhouse, edited by Robert C. Rathburn and Martin Steinmann, Jr. (Minneapolis: University of Minnesota Press, 1958), but is easier to find in the earlier of the Macmillan Casebooks mentioned above, or in *Victorian Literature: Modern Essays in Criticism* (edited by Austin Wright, OUP, 1961). Next is the chapter entitled 'Fire and Eyre: Charlotte Brontë's War of Earthly Elements' in David Lodge's *Language of Fiction* (Routledge & Kegan Paul, 1966; second edition, 1984). The third criticism is the chapter on 'Charlotte Brontë: A Vision of Duality' in Shirley Foster's *Victorian Women's Fiction: Marriage, Freedom and the Individual* (Croom Helm, 1985).

Among other mainstream criticism which is likely to be useful, you might look at Robert Bernard Martin: *The Accents of Persuasion: Charlotte Brontë's Novels* (Faber & Faber, 1966), or Valerie Grosvenor-Myers: *Charlotte Brontë: Truculent Spirit* (Vision and Barnes & Noble, 1987).

For those who wish to explore more widely, Terry Eagleton's *Myths of Power: A Marxist Study of the Brontës* (Macmillan, 1975) takes an interesting constructivist approach. A major feminist work on the Brontës, Sandra M. Gilbert and Susan Gubar: *The Madwoman in the Attic: The Woman Writer and the Nineteenth-Century Literary Imagination* (Yale University Press, 1979), has a chapter on each of the novels. A very idiosyncratic discussion of *Jane Eyre*, among other things, is Elizabeth Imlay's *Charlotte Brontë and the Mysteries of Love: Myth and Allegory in 'Jane Eyre'* (Imlay Publications, 1989). This begins as a kind of extension of Lodge's ideas, expanded with a wealth of scholarship in an effort, in the words of the author, to 'appreciate [Brontë's] craft, to demonstrate a further dimension of Charlotte's intelligence and achievement, and to explore the psychology and metaphysics of *Jane Eyre*, in terms of the culture from which it sprang'. The book is full of persuasive evidence and guesswork; it ranges over folk tales, classical philosophy, religion and earth myths; it is original, witty and entertaining.

An interesting discussion of the Gothic background to Charlotte Brontë's work is Carol Ann Howells's *Love, Mystery and Misery: Feeling in Gothic Fiction* (University of London: Athlone Press, 1978).

Finally, as an illustration of the tendency of criticism to refine its focus, there is a chapter entitled 'The Heroine as Reader: *Jane Eyre*' in Michael Wheeler's *The Art of Allusion in Victorian Fiction* (Macmillan, 1979).

None of these criticical works is definitive. Remember that critical opinion, no matter how expert the author, is no more than opinion; most criticism is more profitably read as sport than as truth, and exists to be disputed.

Index